Second Edition

Current Perspectives
in Radical/Critical
Criminology and
Criminal Justice

CUTTING
the EDGE

Jeffrey Ian Ross

Revised, with a new introduction by the editor

Transaction Publishers
New Brunswick (U.S.A.) and London (U.K.)

Library of Congress Catalog Number: 2008042532
ISBN: 978-1-4128-0755-5
Printed in the United States of America

Library of Congress Cataloging-in-Publication Data

Cutting the edge : current perspectives in radical/critical criminology and
    criminal justice / [edited by] Jeffrey Ian Ross. -- 2nd ed.
        p. cm.
    Includes bibliographical references and index.
    ISBN 978-1-4128-0755-5 (alk. paper)
        1. Criminology. 2. Radicalism. 3. Justice, Administration of. I. Ross,
Jeffrey Ian.

HV6025.C87 2009
364--dc22

                                                                2008042532

CUTTING the EDGE

Contents

Preface to the First Edition

In the fall of 1995, I was invited to organize a series of panels for the Radical and Critical Criminology section of the Academy of Criminal Justice Sciences annual conference. I believe not only that this was an excellent opportunity to showcase a considerable amount of new scholarship in this area of theory and praxis, but that this work should be made available more widely, thus in print. With these goals in mind, I invited individuals simultaneously to present papers at the meeting and to deliver their papers to this edited book. Although not all the manuscripts submitted were selected, nor all the papers included presented at the conference. I chose the set of papers included in this volume because the quality of scholarship and the authors' creativity pushes the field forward. I think the reader will find that these papers are thought provoking and stimulating.

A concerted effort was made to include the views of well-respected scholars, experts, and activists who work in the area of radical and critical criminology who represent a diversity of genders, nationalities, races, religions, and ethnic groups. Similarly almost every conceivable subtopic was considered for coverage. Most of these authors are familiar names in the radical and critical criminology field. They are both active in the scholarly journals and at conferences. Unfortunately, it was not possible to secure the contribution of more women, visible minorities, and international writers was not possible. This state of affairs is reflective of a larger set of issues underlying the field of radical criminology/criminal justice.

There's little utility in preaching to the converted. Thus this book is aimed at readers who most likely have a firm grounding in conservative, liberal, and radical/critical thought, research and praxis. Freshman undergraduate and graduate students should be able to use *Cutting the Edge* as a core text in a course on radical or critical criminology, or as a complementary or suggested reading book for introduction to criminology, introduction to criminal justice, or criminological theory courses. For those more advanced students of criminology/criminal justice, this book offers a review of radical/critical justice and a guide to where we are going.

Nothing important is accomplished by one person alone. I have to thank my contributors for patience, scholarship, diligence and wise council. I also thank Nik Street, Maryln Brownstein and Heather Ruland at Greenwood and John Donahue at Rainsford Type who shepherded this project with committment and understanding. Many thanks to my wife Natasha Cabrera who tolerated my divided attention.

This book is dedicated to my children, Keanu Gabriel and Dakota Zoe, whom I took care of during the time I organized this project. They made this work all the more pleasant for me.

Foreword to the First Edition

"Not another book proving that women, minorities and the poor are treated badly by the criminal justice system!"

The Eminent and Respected Conservative Criminologist (ERCC) appeared to be in pain. We were having our semi-annual cup of coffee and sharing the news. He was not pleased to hear that I was writing an introduction to a book of critical criminology.

"Well, if people still believe that the law is blind to issues of gender, color, and class, maybe the data in this book will help convince them otherwise."

The ERCC winced. "Nobody with a grain of sense believes that," he stated firmly. "We knew better decades ago when I was a Big City Cop. It doesn't take a genius to see that folks with money and power fare better than those without. We don't need more studies from your radical friends to prove that."

"How about the consensus theory of law?" I offered. "Don't lots of people think that the criminal law embodies those values shared most broadly by members of society and that only morally defective types break that law?"

The ERCC looked at me with pity. "You've got to be pretty naive to think that those people with law-making power don't make laws to protect and expand that power; do you think you are the only person to notice that penalties for the types of crime usually committed by the poor are heavier than those usually committed by the rich?"

"What about the economy?" I was getting desperate now. "Surely we still need to convince people that there is a relationship between crime and unemployment and between incarceration and unemployment. I am constantly hearing how law-abiding everyone was during the Depression, when society was permeated with strong family values."

The ERCC's pity was rapidly changing to contempt. "Unemployment at the macro level may not tell us much about crime. But unemployment is rarely distributed evenly among social classes. In the lower classes—which are disproportionately minority—unemployment is directly related both to crime rates and to probability of incarceration."

I took a mental step backwards. Usually, the ERCC and I spent our coffee breaks in happy argument. Our sudden spate of agreement was taking me by surprise. Why were my radical assertions being received as common knowledge? It took a moment for me to realize what had happened—that critical criminology had won, that it was setting the terms for any debate the ERCC and I might have. Thanks to decades of rigorous research and persistent publication, the injustice of the criminal justice system is no longer in doubt; the criminological discussion now begins at the place where it once left off.

The subject of that debate concerns the implications of that injustice. Conservatives consider injustice an inevitable byproduct of a desirable economic system, while liberals see the injustices as remediable within that system. But what these two schools of thought often have in common is a belief in positivism, in the idea that criminology progresses through objective and dispassionate observation and analysis of social data. The results of such studies may support either functional or amelioristic programs, but they dictate neither. Research and social action remain carefully separated.

The studies comprising this volume demonstrate vividly the difference between critical criminology and other schools. These articles bristle with indignation and anger. The authors' rage over injustices based on class, race and gender is palpable. They do not approach the inequalities of the criminal justice system as phenomena that should be studied, but as wrongs that must be righted. Their scholarship is informed by their deeply held beliefs that disparities in the definitions of crime and in the processes of arrest, conviction, sentencing, and correctional treatment are immoral and the product of an immoral economic and social system. They reject any pretense to scientific objectivity, often telling us of personal experiences of discrimination and dehumanization. Their demands for change in the system do not follow from their research, they drive it.

Anger by itself may be invigorating, but it does not necessarily provide intellectual tools. Cutting edge critical criminology makes its contribution by combining the anger and its traditional intellectual tool of class analysis with the insights of feminism, post-modernism, ethnography, and literary criticism and the authors represented here wield these newer tools with elegance and enthusiasm. These are articles that engage the mind as fully as they engage the emotions. This is a volume that will provoke thought as fully as it provokes action.

Dorothy H. Bracey
John Jay College of Criminal Justice and the Graduate School,
The City University of New York

Preface to the Second Edition

This book owes a deep sense of gratitude to many people. I would like to thank my contributors who worked diligently on their chapters in a relative short period off time. Many thanks also the staff at Transaction Publishers, especially Mary Curtis, Irving Louis Horowitz, Laurence Mintz, and Angel L. Soto, for not only for taking this project on, but also for their incredible patience and support thought-out this process.

Thanks again to my wife, Natasha J. Cabrera and children Keanu Gabriel and Dakota Zoe who respectively tolerated their husband and father's divided attention

1

Introduction to the Second Edition: *Cutting the Edge*: What a Difference a Decade Makes?[1]

Jeffrey Ian Ross

The First Edition of *Cutting the Edge*

In the first edition of *Cutting the Edge* (1998) twelve scholars examined different subtopics in the field of radical and critical criminology. Their chapters included stock takings and discussions on a diverse range of subjects including the contemporary relevance of well-known social theorists (e.g., Marx, Weber, Simmel, and Lacan) to critical criminology, the role of the economy in politics and crime in countries that have market economies, the evolution of an integrative criminology, and the application of postmodernist theories to the study of critical criminology.

Other chapters in the first edition examined traditional concerns in the field of criminology and criminal justice (e.g., white collar crime, municipal policing, corrections, community corrections, juvenile justice, and sentencing) from a radical and/or critical criminological point of view. The contributors reviewed the history and current status of radical/critical criminology, and provided a lens through which to conceptualize future scholarship in the area of critical criminology. The first edition was generally well received by the scholarly community with the bulk of the reviews praising the overall quality of the work, the range of contributions, and the book's suitability for undergraduate and graduate students.

Ten years later, the first edition remains an important contribution to our understanding of radical and critical criminology. Nevertheless, critical criminology is a multidimensional and continually evolving concept as well as a scholarly field of inquiry. In the meantime, social, political, and historical events as well as

1

research and policy developments of the last decade have respectively produced new scholarship and insights and have had an effect on criminal justice policies and practice.

What Has Changed Since the Publication of the First Edition?

Over the past decade, social, economic, and political events at both the national and international levels have had a profound impact on American society and beyond. These effects have been felt not only in the practitioner field of criminal justice, they have also had a noticeable impact on the nature and process of scholarship that approaches crime from a radical and critical point of view.

Over the past ten years these events and processes include but are not limited to:

- the changing dynamics in the war on drugs;
- the increased number of people who are incarcerated in the United States;
- predatory lending policies and practices of financial institutions;
- increasing globalization; and, most importantly,
- the terrorist attacks of September 11, 2001.

Each of these events have had important ripple and interconnected effects most noticeably felt by the poor, powerless, and marginalized sectors of our society. For example, the war on drugs that began during the Reagan administration has resulted in correctional facilities that are disproportionately full of first-time, nonviolent drug offenders. The burgeoning prison population translates into overcrowded jails and prisons, institutions that cannot achieve their stated goal of rehabilitation. Increasing globalization has led to noticeable shifts in what gets produced in our factories, sold at our box stores, and on the web, and by whom.

The 9/11 attacks, in particular, were the catalyst for the expanded war on terrorism. A significant policy consequence is the PATRIOT Act, which includes, among other developments, a general erosion of our civil liberties. This legislation appeared coterminous with the wars in Afghanistan and Iraq (ostensibly to root out terrorist threats against Americans) which are not only putting Americans in harm's way, but bankrupting our nation. The invasion of Afghanistan and Iraq also prompted the reliance on Guantanamo to hold "enemy combatants," the use of torture to extract information, rendition of suspected terrorists to other states, and the abuse of prisoners in Abu Ghraib just outside of Baghdad. These events have been the subject of papers at our scholarly conferences, have been represented in the pages of our academic journals, and occasionally been the subject matter of books published by critical criminologists.

There are some who suggest that two of these events, such as the wars on drugs and terrorism, have more recently had some positive impact at least in the United States. For example, had it not been for the excesses of Abu Ghraib and Guantanamo, then it might not have led to the development of the National Commission on Safety and Abuse in Prisoner Abuse (2005-2006) that examined the state of correctional facilities in our country and the passage of key legislation like the *Prisoner Rape Elimination Act* (2003) and the *Prisoner Reentry Act* (2008).

Others see these developments as lip service, mere drops in the bucket, and that we are missing the bigger picture where the modern state is all powerful, one that works and operates with little compassion, and exists to further the interests of a powerful elite.

What Sorts of Publishing Developments Have Occurred Over the Last Decade in the Field of Critical Criminology?

For the past two decades the Division of Critical Criminology, which is part of the American Society of Criminology has been responsible for publishing the journal *Critical Criminology: An International Journal*. This venue is an important vehicle for promoting important scholarship in the field. But as with any scholarly journal, balance among the different themes in every issue is not easily achieved, nor should this necessarily be its mission or function.

Scholars and instructors wishing for an easily accessible comprehensive overview of the contemporary status of field of critical criminology have at their disposal a number of books. Since the first edition of *Cutting the Edge* was published, three somewhat similar books have been produced that have added to our understanding of radical/critical criminology. First, Kerry Carrington and Russell Hogg's *Critical Criminology: Issues, Debates, Challenges* (2002) is a collection of eleven essays focusing on among other interesting subjects the history of critical criminology, feminism, social control, and international influences. This book provides an analysis of major theoretical approaches and illustrates various issues drawing primarily from historical events and situations that have occurred in Britain and Australia.

Second, Schwartz and Hatty (2003) *Controversies in Critical Criminology* is also an excellent introduction to the field. Consisting of twelve chapters, and the shortest of the three, it is well balanced in terms of subjects of inquiry and experts in the field. The editors have included chapters on state crime, the relationship between crime and the body, the relationship between masculinity and male violence, and hate crime.

Third is Lynch and Michalowski's *Primer in Radical Criminology: Critical Perspectives on Crime, Power and Identity* (2006), which is now in its fourth edition and the longest of the three books described thus far. It is divided into eleven chapters, provides a masterful history of radical criminology, taking into account the environment, policing, the courts, state crime and terrorism, policing, the courts, and corrections.

Collectively, these books provide slightly different approaches to the field of critical criminology. And each has a different emphasis. Some topics and points of view are stressed more than others, while others are totally neglected. More importantly perhaps, as time marches on, these books are now becoming out of date.

The Second Edition of *Cutting the Edge*

The second edition of *Cutting the Edge* builds on and extends the writing and analysis presented in the first edition in several significant ways. Among the twelve chapters in the new edition, few of them are mainly reviews of literature. On the other hand, while the new edition includes three of the original eleven chapters, another three of the chapters are completely revised (e.g., Friedrichs, Richards, and Elrod), and the balance are either written by new authors or are on old subjects but written by new writers bringing a freshness of approach. In sum, these new chapters cover new and cutting-edge scholarship and include topics such as supranational criminology, cultural criminology, corporate crime, and restorative justice.

Meanwhile, in any enterprise of this size there will always be omissions. Had I more time I would have had a chapter specifically devoted to feminist criminology and one that focuses almost exclusively on race and ethnicity. I recognize this as a shortcoming. But with all collective projects and publishers deadlines there comes a point in time when one must deliver, and that time has gone and past.

The book is divided into two sections: the first looks at perspectives in criminology and the second examines different branches or processes in criminal justice. Following this chapter, the new edition starts out with an abridged version of the original introductory chapter, "Introduction to the First Edition. *Cutting the Edge*: Where Have We been and Where are We Going?" It outlines the original reasons why the book was developed and the goals as they then existed.

The next chapter is "Insurgent Possibilities: The Politics of Cultural Criminology," written by Jeff Ferrell and Keith Hayward. The piece attempts to "offer a brief introduction to the politics of cultural criminology, and to provide some examples of how cultural criminology seeks to critically account for the complex relationships that exist between crime, culture and contemporary political economy." In so doing, the authors confront capitalism as the only progressive explanation for crime and look into the politics of resistance.

Chapter 4, "White Collar Crime and Critical Criminology: Convergence and Divergence," is written by David O. Friedrichs. He looks at how the field of white collar crime has matured and how it has been adopted and integrated into the mainstream of critical criminology research. Friedrichs looks at white collar crime research through the backdrop of "four prominent strains of critical criminology in the contemporary era:" radical/critical criminology: peacemaking criminology, postmodernist criminology, feminist criminology, and left realism. He concludes his analysis of white collar crime through a review of four recent criminological trends: newsmaking criminology, cultural criminology, green criminology, and social harm and crime, state-corporate crime, and state crime.

In "Corporate Crime: A Panacea for Critical Criminology," Vincenzo Ruggiero argues that efforts to resume the use of critical tools in the analysis of crime and control have been made in different quarters. Most obviously, a critical criminological perspective has proven well equipped to address recent international violence, be it institutional or anti-institutional. This chapter suggests that, in the current situation, the area of study pertaining to corporate crime is the ideal area, within criminology, that lends itself to a radical approach. The chapter reviews a number of conceptualizations of corporate crime, then identifies a specific form of criminality that the author terms "power crime." Ruggiero then discusses causation and prevention, an exercise that he conducts with the tools offered by classical sociology as well as those made available by more contemporary analysis. The point is made that conceptualizations, causations, and prevention of corporate crime cannot be dealt with if a conventional criminological paradigm is adopted. In brief, the author argues that corporate crime is a panacea for critical criminology.

Christopher Mullins and Dawn L. Rothe, in their chapter "Toward a Supranational Criminology," investigate the phenomena of "violations of international criminal law that cause large amounts of human suffering and misery (i.e., genocide, crimes against humanity, war crimes, crimes of aggression and other gross human rights violations) by government actors acting in the name of or on behalf of state, paramilitaries, or militias." This definition has its origins in the phenomenon of state crime. Their chapter reviews the component parts of supranational criminology, the methodological issues for social scientists examining these phenomena., and the social context in which they operate (i.e., global economies, political instability, economic collapse, and ethnic tensions).

Chapter 7, "Radical and Critical Criminology's' Treatment of Municipal Policing" is written by Jeffrey Ian Ross. Ross reviews the conservative, liberal, and radical/critical criminological literature on municipal policing. In particular, he examines each of these types of research in terms of methodological approaches focus, and theoretical frameworks. In the final part of the chapter, Ross classifies radical/critical research into categories (e.g., overarching reviews, studies on the coercive capacity of police, police violence and homicides, working conditions of police, and the history of police) and offers a critique of each category.

In "A House Divided: Corrections in Conflict," (chapter 8) Angela West Crews updates and extends Michael Welch's original chapter "Critical Criminology, Social Control, and an Alternative View of Corrections," and integrates a decades worth of research and current affairs that have affected jails, prisons, and prisoners. She reviews the growth of corrections and the staggering numbers and rates related to incarceration in the United States. West Crews also examines the consequences of the race to incarcerate, and suggests lessons from the Abu

Ghraib and Guantanamo incarceration experiences. Therapeutic jurisprudence, problem-solving justice, and restorative justice are explored for their potential to provide alternatives to incarceration, and the latest preoccupation with release and reentry among some policymakers is critiqued.

Stephen C. Richards' "A Convict Criminology Perspective on Community Punishment: Further Lessons from the Darkness of Prison," (chapter 9) is a revision of his original essay "Critical and Radical Perspectives on Community Punishment: Lessons from the Darkness." It provides a critical critique of the traditional/utilitarian, and liberal studies on community corrections and argues for the adoption of a broader critical approach to the subject matter. Richards documents how the critical criminology literature has improved with the inclusion of feminist and peacemaking perspectives. By adding the convict criminology perspective, the research is finally incorporating the voices of prisoners in the community.

Chapter 10, "The Potential for Fundamental Change in Juvenile Justice: Implementing an Alternative Approach to Problem Youth," is authored by Preston Flood. Flood updates his original chapter from the first edition of this book by providing a historical overview of the juvenile justice research, looking at the failure of conservative and liberal juvenile justice policy, and puts forward not only "the key ingredients of humane and effective juvenile justice intervention," but also the politics involved in implementing successful strategies in this policy sphere.

Chapter 11, "Razing the Wall: A Feminist Critique of Sentencing Theory, Research, and Policy," is written by Jeanne Flavin. Since the sixties and seventies, much concern has been voiced over the possibility of gender and racial discrimination in sentencing. Although the topic has been widely studied, the findings from scores of sentencing studies are inconclusive, in part because the line between disparity (or justifiable difference) and discrimination is blurry. In this chapter, Flavin provides a critical examination of mainstream approaches to sentencing which have been based on androcentric assumptions and similarly flawed methodology. She also argues that attempts at legislating "neutrality" through guidelines or similar sentencing policies are destined to fail given that our society is neither gender-neutral nor race-neutral. She makes a case for adopting a feminist approach to sentencing; that is, one which considers the social locations attendant to race and gender (as well as their intersections) that shape an offender's sentencing experience.

Chapter 12, "A Geometry of Its Own: Restorative Justice, Relationships and Community in Democracy," is written by Liz Elliot. In this piece, Elliot examines not only the scholarly and practitioner literature on restorative justice, but also her personal experience trying to implement a restorative justice program in a medium-sized community located outside of Vancouver, British Columbia. She relates how, despite the good intentions of the advisory committee, the project was frustrated and soon co-opted by official municipal committee.

Understanding crime, criminals, and criminal justice from a radical/critical perspective provides an alternative discourse to mainstream criminology and criminal justice provided in most of our text books and by superficial news coverage. This approach is essential if students, practitioners, instructors, and scholars want to understand our society at a deeper level than what is all so conveniently handed to them on a daily basis.

Acknowledgements. Thanks to Natasha J. Cabrera for comments on this chapter.

Note

1. Subtitle inspired by Esther Phillips' song, "What a Difference a Day Makes."

2

Cutting the Edge: Where have We been and Where are We Going?

Jeffrey Ian Ross

Over the past three decades, since the early articulation of its theories during the 1960s, radical and critical criminology has matured into a diverse body of work. Today a variety of interesting perspectives can be subsumed under this domain including but not limited to postmodernism, left realism, feminism, and peacemaking.

This material has been communicated through a variety of channels including conference papers, articles, chapters in scholarly books, and monographs devoted to the critical/radical criminology enterprise. In particular, a handful of books have been published that fall under this general format, including but not limited to, Taylor, Walton, and Young's *The New Criminology: For a Social Theory of Deviance* (1973); Inciardi's *Radical Criminology: The Coming Crisis* (1980); Lynch and Groves' *A Primer in Radical Criminology* (1986); Pepinsky and Quinney's *Criminology as Peacemaking* (1991); and MacLean and Milovanovic's *New Directions in Critical Criminology* (1991).

Although building blocks in the historical treatment of radical and critical criminology, and worthwhile reading for those attempting to better understand recent trends in this area, some of these edited collections suffer from a number of shortcomings.

First, most of these works are outdated, or mainly consist of reprints of previously published material. In fact, since the early 1980s, the earlier radical and critical tradition has borrowed concepts and research and actually benefited from European thinkers like Bordeau, Christie, and Giddens. Second, some of the pieces are overwritten and their literature reviews make a questionable contribution to the advancement of radical and critical criminology. Third, an abundance of emotionally and ideologically loaded words that detract from the authors' ability to present a clear message to those in the policy community and in applied settings. Fourth, in an attempt to find cultural anchors, some authors make a number of minor errors. Fifth, with few exceptions, these works are heavily American oriented. Most of the contributors are Americans and so are their examples.

Sixth, unfortunately the relevance of many assertions are not clearly explored. Seventh, some contributions are primarily typology-building exercises, the utility of which are never explored by the authors. Eighth, other pieces are inaccessible, have questionable relevance, undecipherable policy and applied applications, and suffer from unnecessary hyperbole. Ninth, some authors seem content to summarize other radical and critical scholars' works without reflecting on this literature's shortcomings.

Tenth, authors can be criticized on a series of assumptions and overgeneralizations. In particular, faulty or unquestioned assumptions are made that border on philosophical rambling. Eleventh, the reasons for case selection in case study comparisons are often not justified. Twelfth, many of the authors can too easily be charged with bias, since most are activists in the programs that they are evaluating. None review why, for example, did any of their "radical" or "innovative" programs fail to work.

Finally, some writers are prone to present redundant or repetitive and unoriginal laundry lists of problems within the criminal justice system. Many of the pieces review the all-too-familiar problems with the criminal justice system but offer untested, if not utopian and vague, methods to change the process. While the practical applications are the most useful, it is doubtful that all are successful.

In sum, progressive scholarship and commitment to radical change should not be devoid of clear thinking and sound methods of social scientific research practices and must acknowledge their shortcomings and potential pitfalls.

Clearly there is a need for an up-to-date book on radical and critical criminology and criminal justice, one that not only deals with theoretical and policy issues, but also analyzes the various traditional branches of the criminal justice system from a radical or critical perspective.

The purpose of this chapter, then, is not to review the past three decades research on radical and critical criminology. Competent overviews are abundant (e.g., Michalowski, 1996). Rather, it is simply intended to introduce each of the forthcoming chapters of this book. Additionally, having a single definition of radical or critical criminology is impossible and not advisable.

Contributors to the present work synthesize the existing literature and then articulate new interpretations based on new data and new ways of looking at old things. The book introduces the reader to the critical issues, important trends, theories, and various sub-disciplines/approaches in the current manifestation of radical and critical criminology. It covers the most important themes in this discourse.

The book can be divided into two parts. Part I looks at theoretical issues, and Part II applies them to traditional concerns in criminal justice. In Part I, each chapter examines either a dominant or an emerging issue in the theory of radical or critical criminology (e.g., the importance of the classics in radical theory, the market economy, the introduction of anarchist theory). In Part II, each cintribution analyzes a brunch of the criminal justice system (e.g., white collar crime, police, prisons, community corrections, courts/sentencing, juvenile justice) but from a critical perspective. All contributors review the traditional literature, the extant radical and critical research and then postulate new directions that literature and praxis should take. In essence, contributors are performing a sort of edge work (Lyng 1990), pushing the boundaries of a mode of expression, inquiry, and research. The following is an overview of each chapter.

Understanding crime, criminals, and criminal justice from a radical/critical perspective is indispensible in today's academic, applied, and policy sectors. Neglect of this approach leads to narrow mindedness and the probability of repeating past mistakes and reinventing the wheel. Reading the contributions to *Cutting the Edge* will encourage individuals and organizations to think "outside the box" and experiment with new policy iniatives designed to improve not only criminal justice, but social and human justice as well.

Part 1

Perspectives in Criminology

3

Insurgent Possibilities: The Politics of Cultural Criminology

Jeff Ferrell and Keith Hayward

Cultural criminology explores the many ways in which cultural forces interweave with the practice of crime and crime control in contemporary society. It emphasizes the centrality of meaning, representation, and power in the contested construction of crime—whether crime is constructed as an everyday event or subcultural subversion, as social danger or state-sanctioned violence. From the perspective of cultural criminology, then, the subject matter of any useful and critical criminology must necessarily move beyond narrow notions of crime and criminal justice to incorporate symbolic displays of transgression and control, feelings and emotions that emerge within criminal events, and the ideological foundations of public and political campaigns designed to define (and delimit) both crime and its consequences. This wider focus allows for a new sort of criminology—a *cultural* criminology—better attuned to prevailing social conditions, and so more capable of conceptualizing and confronting contemporary crime and crime control. This cultural criminology seeks both to understand crime as an expressive human activity, and to critique the perceived wisdom surrounding the contemporary politics of crime and criminal justice.

Cultural criminologists understand "culture" to constitute the connecting tissue of collective meaning and collective identity; within it and by way of it, the government claims authority, the consumer considers brands of bread—and "the criminal," as both person and perception, comes alive. Culture suggests the search for meaning, and the meaning of the search itself; it reveals the capacity of people, acting together over time, to animate even the lowliest of objects—the pauper's shopping cart, the police officer's truncheon, the gang member's bandana—with importance and implication.

For us, this human culture—this symbolic environment created and occupied by individuals and groups—cannot be reduced to a by-product of social class or ethnicity, or a residue of social structure. Of course, culture doesn't take shape without these structures, either; both the cultural hegemony of those in power, and the subcultures of acquiescence and resistance of those marginalized, are scarcely independent of social class and other forms of engrained inequality. But cultural forces are those threads of symbolic discourse and collective meaning that wind in and around social class and inequality, animating the everyday troubles of social actors and the situations in which their troubles play out. For all the parties to crime and criminal justice—perpetrators, police officers, victims, parole violators, news reporters—*the negotiation of cultural meaning intertwines with the immediacy of criminal experience.*

Over the last decade or so, this cultural criminological approach has emerged as a distinct and vibrant perspective amidst the established forms of critical criminology—and on occasion even posing a critique of more conventional forms of critical criminology, as in the debate between Ferrell (2007) and Hall and Winlow (2007). Detailed introductions to the many themes and theoretical constellations that constitute cultural criminology exist elsewhere (see especially see Ferrell and Sanders, 1995; Ferrell, 1999; Ferrell et al., 2004, 2008; Hayward and Young, 2004, 2007). In this chapter, our goal is a more circumspect but nonetheless important one: to offer a brief introduction to *the politics of cultural criminology*, and to provide some examples of how cultural criminology seeks to critically account for the complex relationships that exist between crime, culture, and contemporary political economy.

Capitalism and Culture

As cultural criminologists have stated elsewhere (see e.g., Morrison, 1995; Ferrell, 2004a, Young, 2004), we can no longer afford the fiction of an "objective" criminology – a criminology devoid of moral passion and political meaning. The day-to-day inequalities of criminal justice, the sour drift toward institutionalized meanness and legal retribution, the ongoing abrogation of human rights in the name of "counter-terrorism" and "free trade"—all carry criminology with them, willingly or not. Building upon existing inequalities of ethnicity, gender, age, and social class, such injustices reinforce these inequalities and harden the hopelessness they produce. Increasingly crafted as media spectacles, consistently masked as information or entertainment, the inequitable dynamics of law and social control remain essential to the maintenance of political power, and so operate to prop up the system that produces them.

For us, that system is global capitalism. Tracing a particularly expansionist trajectory these days, late modern capitalism continues to contaminate one community after another, shaping social life into a series of predatory encounters and saturating everyday existence with criminogenic expectations of material convenience. All along this global trajectory, collectivities are converted into markets, people into consumers, and experiences and emotions into products. So steady is this seepage of consumer capitalism into social life, so pervasive are its crimes—both corporate and interpersonal—that they now seem to pervade most every situation.

That said, it's certainly not our contention that capitalism forms the essential bedrock of all social life, or of all crime. Other wellsprings of crime and inequality run deep as well; late capitalism is but a shifting part of the sour quagmire of patriarchy, racism, militarism, and institutionalized inhumanity in which we're currently caught. To reify "capitalism," to assign it a sort of foundational timelessness, is to grant it a status it doesn't deserve. Whatever its contemporary power, capitalism constitutes a trajectory, not an accomplishment, and there are other trajectories at play today as well, some moving with consumer capitalism, others moving against and beyond it. Still, as the currently ascendant form of economic exploitation, capitalism certainly merits the critical attention of cultural criminology.

And yet, even as we focus on this particular form of contemporary domination and inequality, we are drawn away from a simple materialist framework, and toward a cultural analysis of capitalism and its crimes. For capitalism is essentially a *cultural* enterprise these days; its economics are decisively cultural in nature. Perhaps more to the point for criminology, contemporary capitalism is a system of domination whose economic and political viability, its crimes and its controls, rest precisely on its cultural accomplishments. Late capitalism markets lifestyles, employing an advertising machinery that sells need, affect, and affiliation far more than material products themselves. It runs on service economies, economies that package privilege and manufacture experiences of imagined indulgence. Even the material fodder for all this—the cheap appliances and seasonal fashions–emerges from a global gulag of factories kept well hidden behind ideologies of free trade and economic opportunity. This is a capitalism founded not on Fordism, but on the manipulation of meaning and the seduction of the image; it is a cultural capitalism. Saturating destabilized working-class neighborhoods, swirling along with mobile populations cut loose from career or community, it is particularly contagious; it offers the seductions of the market where not much else remains.

As much as the Malaysian factory floor, then, *this* is the stuff of late capitalism, and so the contested turf of late modernity. If we're to do our jobs as criminologists—if we're to understand crime, crime control, and political conflict in this context—it seems we must conceptualize late capitalism in these terms. To describe the fluid, expansive, and culturally charged dynamics of contemporary capitalism is not to deny its power but to define it; it is to consider current conditions in such a way that they can be critically confronted. From the Frankfurt School to Fredric Jameson (1991) and beyond, the notion of "late capitalism" references many meanings, including for some a fondly anticipated demise—but among these meanings is surely this sense of a capitalism quite thoroughly transformed into a cultural operation, a capitalism unexplainable outside its own representational dynamics (Harvey, 1990; Hayward, 2004).

The social classes of capitalism have likewise long meant more than mere economic or productive position—and under the conditions of late capitalism this is ever more the case. Within late capitalism, social class is experienced, indeed constituted, as much by affective affiliation, leisure aesthetics, and collective consumption as by income or employment (see e.g., Hayward and Yar, 2006). The cultural theorists and "new criminologists" of the 1970s first began to theorize this class culture, and likewise began to trace its connection to patterns of crime and criminalization. As they revealed, and cultural criminologists have continued to document (Hayward, 2001, 2004; Young, 2003, 2007), predatory crime within and between classes so constituted often emerges out of *perceptions* of relative deprivation, other times from a twisted allegiance to consumer goods considered essential for class identity or class mobility (e.g. Featherstone, 1991; Lury, 1996; Miles, 1998). And yet, even when so acquired, a class identity of this sort remains a fragile one, its inherent instability spawning still other crimes of outrage, transgression, or predation. If crime is connected to social class, as it surely is, the connective tissue today is largely the cultural filaments of leisure, consumption, and shared perception.

Crime, Culture, Resistance

In the same way that cultural criminology attempts to conceptualize the dynamics of class, crime, and social control within the cultural fluidity of contemporary capitalism, it also attempts to understand the connections between crime, activism, and political and cultural resistance under these circumstances. Some critics argue that cultural criminology in fact remains *too* ready to understand these insurgent possibilities, confounding crime and resistance while celebrating little moments of illicit transgression. For such critics, cultural criminology's political focus on everyday resistance to late capitalism presents a double danger, minimizing the real harm done by everyday crime while missing the importance of large-scale, organized political change. Martin O'Brien, for example, suggests that "cultural criminology might be best advised to downgrade the study of deviant species and focus more attention on the generically political character of criminalization" (2005: 610; see also Howe, 2003; Ruggiero, 2005). Steve Hall and Simon Winlow (2007: 83-84) likewise critique cultural criminology's alleged tendency to find "authentic resistance" in every transgressive event or criminal subculture, and dismiss out of hand forms of cultural resistance like "subversive symbol inversion" and "creative recoding" that cultural criminologists supposedly enjoy finding among outlaws and outsiders.

In response, we would note that cultural criminology doesn't simply focus on efflorescences of resistance and transgression; it also explores boredom, repetition, everyday acquiescence, and other mundane dimensions of society and criminality (for example, Ferrell, 2004a; Yar, 2005). Cultural criminology's attention to meaning and micro-social detail ensures that it is equally at home explaining the monotonous routines of DVD piracy, or the dulling trade in counterfeit "grey" automotive components, as it is the sub rosa worlds of gang members or graffiti artists. As cultural *criminologists*, we seek to understand all components of crime: the criminal actor, formal and informal control agencies, victims, and others. In this context, we urge also the continued development of a cultural criminology of the state (e.g. Wender, 2001; Hamm, 2004, 2007; Ferrell et al., 2008: 75-6). Hayward and Young, (2007: 113) note that "there would be no contradiction" between 'cultural criminology' and 'the realist square of crime' [offender, victim, state, society]; rather, that realism, by being overly and simplistically rationalistic in its conception of agency, is not realistic enough." A fully social and cultural criminology must incorporate notions of agency and meaning which can account for crime and crime control, criminal energy and tension, illicit emotion and alternative rationalities, resistance and submission, transgression and enforcement.

Then again, it is probably the case that we and other cultural criminologists do take special pleasure in moments of subversive resistance; as Jean Genet once admitted to an interviewer, "obviously, I am drawn to peoples in revolt... because I myself have the need to call the whole of society into question" (in Soueif, 2003: 25). But maybe it's also the case that illicit cultural practices like "subversive symbol inversion" and "creative recoding" *do* in fact constitute a growing opposition to capitalism's suffocations—and have done so in the past as well. Long before capitalism's late modern liquidity, back in the period of nuts-and-bolts industrial capitalism, for example, one group most clearly and courageously engaged in organized, in-your-face confrontation with capitalism's predatory economics: the Wobblies, more formally known as the Industrial Workers of the World. Indeed, the Wobblies were known for their ability to organize itinerant and marginal workers, for their dedication to direct economic action—and for their facility at subversive symbol inversion and creative recoding. In fact, it was just this sort of symbolic sleight of hand that allowed this ragtag group of low-wage outsiders and peripatetic outlaws to organize, fight—and often win—against the robber barons and deputy sheriffs of industrial capitalism. Looking to create a culture of union solidarity, the Wobblies converted well-known church hymns into rousing union anthems. Facing legal injunctions against advocating sabotage or organizing, they posted "silent agitators" (union organizing stickers), published notices that spelt out "sabotage" in code, and issued communiqués that surely seemed to support the legal authorities—since these communiqués provided such detailed instructions to IWW members regarding what forms of sabotage they should (not) employ. Like other progressive groups of the time, the Wobblies were animated by—in many ways *organized by*—shared symbols, subversive recodings, and semiotic inversions of the existing order (Kornbluh, 1998).

If, then, we can find illicit symbolic subversion and cultural recoding sparking "authentic resistance" even in an early capitalist period characterized by material production and circumscribed communication, what might we find under the current conditions of late capitalism, with its environments of swirling symbolism and pervasive communication? To start, we would find the women's movements, gay/lesbian movements, and anti-war movements of the past few decades, staging illegal public spectacles, confronting mediated representations of women and men and war, and recruiting members through channels of alternative communication. We would spot activists on New York City's Lower East Side, recalling the Wobblies as they organize opposition to the Giuliani administration's criminalization of informal public notices by distributing informal public notices saying, "Warning! Do Not Read This Poster" (Patterson, 2006). With the historian John Bushnell (1990), we would find a parallel dynamic outside the bounds of western capitalism, noticing how the emergence of street graffiti in the Soviet Union exposed the totalizing lies of the Soviet authorities, and ultimately helped organize successful resistance to them.

And if you're a cultural criminologist, you might pay particular attention to the ways in which new terms of legal and political engagement emerge from the fluid cultural dynamics of late capitalism. To summarize some of our recent studies in crime and resistance: when gentrification and "urban redevelopment" drive late capitalist urban economies, when urban public spaces are increasingly converted to privatized consumption zones, graffiti comes under particular attack by legal and economic authorities as an aesthetic threat to cities' economic vitality. In such a context legal authorities aggressively criminalize graffiti, corporate media campaigns construct graffiti writers as violent vandals—and graffiti writers themselves become more organized and politicized in response. When consumer culture and privatized transportation conspire to shape cities into little more than car parks connected by motorways, bicycle and pedestrian activists create collective alternatives and stage illegal public interruptions. When late capitalist consumer culture spawns profligate waste, trash scroungers together learn to glean survival and dignity from the discards of the privileged, and activists organize illicit programs to convert consumer "trash" into food for homeless folks, clothes for illegal immigrants, and housing for the impoverished. When the same concentrated corporate media that stigmatizes graffiti writers and trash pickers closes down other possibilities of local culture and street activism, a micro-radio movement emerges—and is aggressively policed by local and national authorities for its failure to abide by regulatory standards designed to privilege concentrated corporate media (Ferrell 2001/2002, 2006).

In all of these cases easy political dichotomies don't hold. These aren't matters of culture or economy, of crime or politics; they're cases in which activists of all sorts employ subversive political strategies—that is, various forms of organized cultural resistance—to counter a capitalist economy itself defined by cultural dynamics of mediated representation, marketing strategy, and lifestyle consumption. Likewise, these cases don't embody simple dynamics of law and economy, or law and culture; they exemplify a confounding of economy, culture, and law that spawns new forms of illegality and new campaigns of enforcement. Similarly, these cases neither prove nor disprove themselves as "authentic" resistance or successful political change—but they do reveal widespread, if scattered and as yet largely unconnected, cultural opposition to a capitalist culture busily inventing new forms of containment and control.

Most importantly, the cultural criminological analysis of these and other cases neither accounts for them as purely subjective moments of cultural innovation, nor reduces them to objective by-products of structural inequality. Among the more curious characterizations of cultural criminology and its politics is the contention that it has abandoned structural analysis and "criminological macro-theories of causality" in favor of "subjectivist-culturalism" (Hall and Winlow, 2007: 83, 86). In reality, since its earliest days, cultural criminology has sought to overcome this very dichotomization of structure and agency, of the objective and the subjective, by locating structural dynamics within lived experience. This is precisely the point of Stephen Lyng's (1990) "edgework" concept, embodying both Marx and Mead in an attempt to account for the interplay between structural context and illicit sensuality. Likewise, Jack Katz's (1988) "seductions of crime" are meant as provocative engagements with, and correctives to, "criminological macro-theories of causality." As Katz argues, a criminology lost within the abstractions of conventional structural analysis tends to forget the interpersonal drama of its subject matter—or paraphrasing Howard Becker (1963: 190), tends to turn crime into an abstraction and then study the abstraction—and so must be reminded of crime's fearsome foreground. Clearly, cultural criminology hasn't chosen "subjectivist-culturalism" over structural analysis; it has chosen instead a style of analysis that can focus structure and subject in the same frame (Ferrell, 1992; Young, 2003; Hayward, 2004). Perhaps some criminologists only recognize structural analysis when encased in multi-syllabic syntax or statistical tabulation. But structural analysis can be rooted in moments of transgression as well; it can show that "structure" remains a metaphor for patterns of power and regularities of meaning produced in back alleys as surely as corporate boardrooms.

The Politics of Resistance and Romance

Engaging in this way with the politics of crime, resistance, and late capitalism requires yet another turn as well, this one toward a central irony of contemporary life: the vast potential of late capitalism to co-opt illicit resistance into the very system it is meant to oppose, and so to transform experiential opposition into commodified acquiescence. This homogenizing tendency constitutes an essential late capitalistic dynamic, and the most insidious of consumer capitalism's control mechanisms. The ability to reconstitute resistance as commodity, and so to sell the illusion of freedom and diversity, is powerful magic indeed. Because of this, a number of cultural criminological studies have explored this dynamic in some detail. Meticulously tracing the history of outlaw biker style, Stephen Lyng and Mitchell Bracey (1995) have demonstrated that early criminal justice attempts to criminalize biker style only amplified its illicit meanings, while later corporate schemes to incorporate biker style into mass production and marketing effectively evacuated its subversive potential. More recently, we have outlined the ways in which consumption overtakes experiences of resistance—indeed, most all experiences—within the consumerist swirl of the late capitalist city (Hayward, 2004). Likewise, Heitor Alvelos (2004) has carefully documented the appropriation of street graffiti by multi-national corporations and their advertisers; as the illicit visual marker of urban hipness, graffiti is now incorporated into everything from corporate theme parks and Broadway musicals to clothing lines, automobile adverts (Muzzati, 2009), and video games (Ferrell et al., 2008: chapter 5). When it comes to the politics of illicit resistance, death by diffusion—dare we say, impotence by incorporation—remains always a real possibility.

And yet again, a dichotomized distinction between authentically illicit political resistance and commodified market posturing does little to explain these cases, or the fluidity of this larger dynamic. From one view, of course, this dynamic would suggest that there can be no authentic resistance, since everything—revolutionary tract, subversive criminality, labor history—is now automatically and inescapably remade as commodity, re-presented as image, and so destroyed. A more useful view, we think, is to see this dynamic as one of complexity and contradiction. As insidious as it is, the late capitalistic process of incorporation is not completely totalizing; it is instead an ongoing battleground of meaning; more a matter of policing the crisis than of definitively overcoming it. Sometimes the safest of corporate products becomes, in the hands of activists or artists or criminals, a dangerous subversion; stolen away, remade, it is all the more dangerous for its ready familiarity, a Trojan horse sent back into the midst of the everyday. Other times the most dangerously illegal of transgressions becomes, in the hands of corporate marketers, the safest of selling schemes, a sure bet precisely because of its illicit appeal. Mostly, though, these processes intertwine, sprouting further ironies and contradictions, and often bearing the fruits of both "crime" and "commodity."

A new generation of progressive activists born to these circumstances seems well aware of them, by the way (e.g.., The Billboard Liberation Front, The Bubble Project, and Reject False Icons)--and because of this, well aware that the point is ultimately not the thing itself, not the act or the image or the style, but the activism that surrounds and survives it. So, anti-globalization activists, militant hackers, and urban environmentalists project images onto governmental buildings, throw adulterated representations back at the system that disseminates them, organize ironic critiques, recode official proclamations, and remain ready to destroy whatever of their subversions might become commodities. Even within late capitalism's formidable machinery of incorporation, the exhaustion of meaning is never complete, the illicit subversion never quite conquered. The husk appropriated, the seed sprouts again.

Our political hope for cultural criminology—that it can contribute to this sort of activism, operating as a counter-discourse on crime and criminal justice that shorts out the circuitry of official meaning—is founded in just this sensibility. We don't imagine that cultural criminology can overturn the accumulated ideologies of law and crime—but we do imagine that these accumulations are never fully accomplished, and so remain available for ongoing subversion. In fact, the logic of resistance suggests that it is the very viability of crime control as a contemporary political strategy, the very visibility of crime dramas and crime news in the media that make such subversion possible, and possibly significant. In a world where political campaigns run loud and long on claims of controlling crime, where crime circulates endlessly as image and entertainment, we're offered a symbolic climate ready made for a culturally attuned criminology—and so we must find ways to confound those campaigns, and to turn that circulation to better ends. And as those in power work to manage this slippery world, to recuperate that meaning for themselves, we must remain ready to keep the meaning moving in the direction of progressive transformation.

This hope for social and cultural change, this sense that even the sprawling recuperations of late capitalism can be resisted, rests on a politics that runs deeper still. Certainly the "cultural" in cultural criminology denotes in one sense a particular analytic focus: an approach that addresses class and crime as lived experience, a model that highlights meaning and representation in the construction of transgression, and a strategy designed to untangle the symbolic entrapments laid by late capitalism and law. But the "cultural" in cultural criminology denotes something else, too: the conviction that it is shared human agency and symbolic action that shape the world. Looking up at corporate misconduct or corporate crime, looking down to those victimized or in revolt, looking sideways at ourselves, cultural criminologists see that people certainly don't make history just as they please, but that together, they do indeed make it.

For this reason cultural criminologists employ *inter alia* the tools of interactionist and cultural analysis. From our view, notions of "interaction" or "intersubjectivity" don't exclude the sweep of social structure or the exercise of power; rather, they help explain how structures of social life are maintained and made meaningful, and how power is exercised, portrayed, and resisted. To inhabit the "social constructionist ghetto," as Hall and Winlow (2007: 89) have accused cultural criminologists of doing, is in this way to offer a radical critique of authorities' truth claims about crime and justice, and to unravel the reifications through which progressive alternatives are made unimaginable. That "ghetto," we might add, also keeps the neighbouring enclave of macro-structural analysis honest and open; without it, such enclaves tend to close their gates to the ambiguous possibilities of process, agency, and self-reflection. And so an irony that appeals especially to "ghetto" residents like ourselves: the categories by which serious scholars deny "culture" and "interaction" as essential components in the construction of human (mis)conduct are themselves cultural constructions, shaped from collective interaction and encoded with collective meaning.

And deeper yet into the politics of cultural criminology, and into some controversial territory indeed. As already seen, cultural criminology is sometimes accused of political "romanticism," of a tendency to embrace marginalized groups and to find among them an indefatigable dignity in the face of domination. As regards that critique, we would begin by saying...yes. A sense of human possibility, not to mention a rudimentary grasp of recent world history, would indeed suggest that human agency is never completely contained nor defined by dominant social forces, legal or capitalist or otherwise. The Warsaw ghetto, the Soviet gulag, the American slave plantation—not even the horrors of their systematic brutality was enough to fully exhaust the human dignity and cultural innovation of those trapped within their walls. If law is the mailed fist of the ruling class, then those hammered down by that fist, those marginalized and made outlaws, carry with them at least the seeds of progressive opposition, offering at a minimum a broken mirror in which to reflect and critique power and its consequences. Marginalization and criminalization certainly produce internecine predation—but they also produce, sometimes in the same tangled circumstances, moments in which outsiders collectively twist and shout against their own sorry situations. From the Delta blues to Russian prison poetry, from the Paris Commune to the street art of the anti-globalization movement, there is after all a certain romance to illicit resistance.

Or is there? In common usage, "romanticization" suggests a sort of sympathetic divergence from reality; in the present context, it suggests that cultural criminologists create overly sympathetic portraits of criminals and other outsiders, glorifying their bad behavior, imagining their resistance, and minimizing their harm to others. Yet embedded in this criticism is a bedrock question for cultural criminologists: what *is* the "reality" of crime, and who determines it? After all, a charge of romanticizing a criminalized or marginalized group implies a solid baseline, a true reality, against which this romanticization can be measured. But what might that be, and how would we know it? As criminologists are well aware, police reports and official crime statistics certainly won't do, what with their propensity for forcing complex actions into simplistic bureaucratic categories. Mediated representations, fraught with inflation and scandal, hardly help either. And so another irony: given the ongoing demonization of criminals and dramatization of crime in the interest of prison construction, political containment, and media production values, it seems likely that what accumulates as "true" about crime is mostly fiction, and that "romanticism" may mostly mark cultural criminologists' diversion from this fiction as they go about investigating the complexities of transgression.

When critics chide cultural criminologists for romanticizing crime and resistance, then, they risk reproducing by default the manufactured misunderstandings that should in fact be the object of criminology's critical gaze. The same danger arises with criticisms of cultural criminology for allegedly focusing on "little delinquents" and "petty misdemeanors," on "graffiti writing or riding a motorcycle" (O'Brien, 2005:610), rather than on larger crimes of greater political import. Once again, we would counter that criminal acts are never quite so obviously little or large, never inherently inconsequential or important, but rather made to be what they are, invested with meaning and consequence, by perpetrators, victims, lawyers, news reporters, and judges, all operating amidst existing arrangements of power (see especially Ferrell et al. 2008, chapter 4). Delinquents and death row inmates, petty misdemeanours and high crimes all emerge from a process so fraught with injustice that it regularly confounds life and death, guilt and innocence–and so, again, this process must be the *subject matter* of criminology, not an *a priori* foundation for it. When urban gentrification is underway, little criminals like homeless folks and graffiti writers get larger, at least in the eyes of the authorities. When the Patriot Act passes, petty misdemeanors are reconstructed by some as terrorism and treason. With enough political influence, the high crimes of corporations can be made inconsequential, if not invisible. The key isn't to accept criminal acts for what they are, but to interrogate them for what they become.

Moreover, this sort of cultural criminological interrogation hardly necessitates that we look only at crimes made little, or only affirmatively at crimes of resistance. Mark Hamm's (1997, 2002) extensive research on the culture of right-wing terrorism; Phillip Jenkins' (1999) analysis of anti-abortion violence and its "unconstruction" as terrorism; Chris Cunneen and Julie Stubbs' (2004) research into the domestic murder of immigrant women moved about the world as commodities; Tim Boekhout van Solinge's (2008) ethnographic account of governmental complicity in the illegal logging trade; even our own work on pervasive automotive death and the ideologies that mask it (Ferrell, 2004b)—the lens used to investigate such crimes is critical and cultural, sometimes even condemnatory, but certainly not affirmative. As these and other studies in cultural criminology show, the politics of cultural criminology can be effectively aimed not only at crimes of illicit resistance, but at "serious" crimes of political harm and predation.

Conclusion

In its original manifestation in the United States, cultural criminology focused on "image, meaning, and representation in the interplay of crime and crime control," especially in relation to the "stylised frameworks and experiential dynamics of illicit subcultures," the "symbolic criminalisation of popular cultural forms," and the "mediated construction of crime and crime control issues" (Ferrell, 1999: 395). While these foci remain very much within cultural criminology's wheelhouse, in recent years we have sought to further develop cultural criminology by responding to the criticism that it lacks an overtly political critique. Certainly, as cultural criminology has gathered traction in the UK (and increasingly in Europe, see Bovenkerk et al., 2009), more and more attempts are being made to "inject a more materialist spine into cultural criminology's theoretical body" (O'Brien, 2005: 605; see also Carney, 2009). This chapter constitutes yet another step in developing within cultural criminology a politics that incorporates both a thoroughgoing critique of late capitalism, its market culture, and its hegemonic discourses, and an attentiveness to the illicit political practices emerging in opposition (see, e.g., Young, 2003; Hayward, 2004; Hayward and Yar, 2006; Hayward and Hobbs, 2007; Winlow and Hall, 2006; Hall et al., 2008).

It is essential that this process continue. Cultural criminologists are striving to (re)create a sociologically inspired criminology that is more critical, not less—a criminology capable of understanding contemporary conditions, and the social harms spawned by global economies running on the cultural creation of hyper-consumptive panic and the symbolic construction of insatiable wants and desires. They are attempting to build a criminology that can critique and expose both the social structures and the symbolic representations (see Hayward and Presdee, 2009) through which market discourses and power relations are enforced. Certainly they are working to confront the posturing of political neutrality that too often characterizes academic criminology and criminal justice—and to replace this fraudulent neutrality with a critical emphasis on the ideological terms by which we frame problems of crime, inequality and justice.

We find ourselves in mean times, and in such times there's no neat choice between political involvement and criminological analysis—only dangerous implications to be traced and hard questions to be asked. Pushed and pulled by the economic riptides of turbo-charged neo-liberal capitalism, increasingly overrun by the emerging police states of mass imprisonment and hyper-surveillance, we all struggle to frame these questions and trace these implications. But one thing is clear: The only time we have left to develop a critical cultural criminology is now.

4

White Collar Crime and Critical Criminology: Convergence and Divergence

David O. Friedrichs

Early in the twenty-first century, criminological interest in white collar crime is quite pronounced, with a steady stream of books and articles being published. The White Collar Crime Research Consortium now has over one hundred members. Critical criminology today has an even more pronounced presence in the field. The Division on Critical Criminology of the American Society of Criminology is a large and conspicuous entity. The present chapter offers a provisional exploration of the points of intersection between these two developments.

Radical Criminology and White Collar Crime

Mainstream criminology's traditional neglect of white collar crime is commonly acknowledged today. E. H. Sutherland's (1940) famous call for more attention to white collar crime was largely—although not wholly—disregarded for several decades. In the 1970s, this situation began to change, but the most common reading of Sutherland's original address seems to stress the need for more systematic study of white collar crime rather than a demand for transforming a system that both produces and indulges (or extends excessive lenience towards) white collar offenders. Most of the criminological writing on white collar crime today fits comfortably within a mainstream social science perspective. Sutherland himself was no radical in the conventional sense, but he identified with a Midwest populism that had affinities with progressive political movements. In an address given near the end of his life Sutherland (1973: 93) stated:

Author's Note: The original version of this chapter was presented as a paper at the Annual Meeting of the American Society of Criminology in Phoenix, October, 1993.

the interests of businessmen have changed, to a considerable extent, from efficiency in production to efficiency in public manipulation, including manipulation of the government for the attainment of preferential advantages.... We no longer have competition as a regulator of economic processes; we have not substituted efficient government regulation. We must go forward to some new system—perhaps communism, perhaps co-operativism, perhaps much more complete governmental regulation than we now have. I don't know what lies ahead of us and am not particularly concerned, but I do know that what was a fairly efficient system has been destroyed by the illegal behavior of Big Business.

Sentiments of this sort probably led Donald Cressey, his former student (and the reviser of later editions of his criminology textbook), to describe Sutherland as:

[A] radical in a quiet way. He also was very patriotic.
The *White Collar Crime* book is a reflection of both his
radicalism and his patriotism. (Cressey, in Laub, 1983: 138)

Sutherland has even been accused of being a Marxist (Orland 1980: 505). Gilbert Geis and Colin Goff (1992) discovered that Sutherland was put on an FBI "no contact" list, and had difficulty obtaining copies of the Uniform Crime Report, after he gave a 1938 speech critical of the FBI. But Sutherland defies facile labeling. His value system was a quintessentially American synthesis of entrepreneurial and progressive beliefs that were wedded to his professional commitment to detached social scientific inquiry.

The relatively few criminologists who initially took Sutherland up on his call to attend more fully to white collar crime—including Marshall Clinard, Donald Cressey, and Donald Newman—were not self-identified radicals in any sense. It is interesting to note, however, that Richard Quinney (1962), one of the very few Ph.D. criminology students of this era who wrote a dissertation focusing on a form of white collar crime (by pharmacists), emerged within a decade or so as the best-known American radical criminologist (Friedrichs, 1980; Martin, Mutchnick and Austin, 1990). The criminal behavior system typology formulated with Marshall Clinard (Clinard and Quinney, 1967; 1973) is one of the contributions to the field for which Quinney is best known and frequently cited. While this work is not specifically linked with Quinney's promotion of radical criminology, the separation of corporate crime from the broader category of occupational crime—a distinction which has come to be widely accepted—clearly reflected the radical influences Quinney was exposed to during this period.

During the 1970s, a clearly identifiable radical criminology emerged with far more extensive attention paid to white collar crime. This decade also witnessed, as I have observed elsewhere, the emergence of victimology and a victim's rights movement, and an autonomous field of criminal justice (Friedrichs 1983). These two developments were independent in more respects than not, although they also had some common roots. Both radical criminology and the intensified scholarly attention to white collar crime were in part responding to increased exposure of elite wrongdoing from the late 1960s on (with the Vietnam War and the Watergate Affair simply two of the more conspicuous such events in the political realm; Friedrichs, 1980; 2007a; Simon, 2006). The consumer and environmental movements that emerged during this period generated broad concern with some of the illegal or unethical practices of major corporations. During the 1970s and 1980s, a number of criminologists identified with radical criminology started writing quite extensively about white collar crime (especially its corporate and governmental forms). Harold Barnett, Steven Box, James Brady, William Chambliss, Ronald Kramer, Ray Michalowski, Frank Pearce, Jeffrey Reiman, and David Simon are among those who come most readily to mind in this context. Much of this work stressed the following:

- A capitalist political economy has structural attributes promoting high levels of exploitative and harmful activity by governmental and corporate elites;
- The activities of governmental and corporate elites cause far more harm than do the crimes of conventional offenders;
- These elites have sufficient influence over the law-making and criminal justice process to prevent much of this activity from being characterized or adjudicated as criminal;
- Distorted and unrepresentative media coverage of crime contributes to an attenuated public consciousness of and concern with white collar crime generally;
- Even when white collar offenders are prosecuted and punished they are subjected to significantly more lenient treatment than is true of conventional offenders.

Despite these contributions, it should be stressed that radical and critical criminologists have devoted much more attention to the analysis of oppressive features of the capitalist system (and some of the consequences for conventional offenders) than to white collar crime specifically (Lynch and Michalowski, 2006; Schwartz and Hatty, 2003). A significant proportion of radical criminological work of this period was taken up with broader theoretical questions pertaining to the relationship between the political economy and law and crime, rather than with focused analyses of specific forms of criminal law and criminal behavior.

The Emergence of Critical Criminology

If the radical criminology that emerged during the 1970s was never a unified enterprise, it became even more fragmented during the course of the 1980s (Anderson, 1991). From the late 1980s on the term "critical criminology" became increasingly the favored umbrella designation for a series of evolving, emerging progressive perspectives and theories. Critical criminologists are united in drawing basic inspiration from the conflict and neo-Marxist perspectives developed in the 1970s, in particular, in their rejection of positivistic approaches as a means of revealing fundamental truths, and in their commitment to seeking connections between theoretical and empirical work and progressive policy initiatives and action. If some critical criminologists continue to work within one or the other of the earlier conflict/neo-Marxist perspectives, many others have become more closely identified with critical perspectives that have emerged (or been applied to criminological phenomena) more recently. The following four perspectives are among the principal new critical criminological perspectives: left realism; peacemaking criminology; feminist criminology; and postmodernist criminology. My project here is somewhat limited in scope: What, if anything, have these perspectives contributed to the understanding of white collar crime?

Critical Criminology and White Collar Crime

Peacemaking Criminology

Although it has basic roots in an anarchistic criminological perspective that was promoted in the 1970s and 1980s *peacemaking criminology* has become a recognized perspective within criminology only since the early 1990s. The contemporary form of peacemaking criminology is principally the product of two well-known, prolific, and singular criminologists, Richard Quinney and Hal Pepinsky. They have collaborated to put together the premier reader on the subject, Pepinsky and Quinney, *Criminology as Peacemaking* (1991). The basic themes of a peacemaking criminology have been concisely identified as follows: connectedness, caring, and mindfulness (Braswell, 1990). Personal suffering and suffering in the world are taken to be inseparable. We should avoid personalizing evil and constructing false schemes that pigeonhole human beings, as honorable citizens and reprehensible criminals. Rather, we should focus on our common humanity, and choose affirmative ways of reaching out to and interacting with others. Responses to the problem of crime must begin with attending to ourselves as human beings; we need to suffer with the criminal rather than make the criminal suffer for us. According to John Fuller (2003: 86-88), a peacemaking criminology approach to the problems of the criminal justice system has the following six stages: nonviolence, social justice, inclusion, correct means, ascertainable criteria, and adoption of Kant's categorical imperative. Altogether, peacemaking criminology calls for a fundamental transformation in our way of thinking about crime and criminal justice.

Peacemaking criminology is by any measure a heretical challenge to the dominant assumptions of mainstream criminological perspectives. It can, of course, be criticized as a form of utopianism, but at a minimum it serves as a provocative antidote to the explicit or implicit cynicism or pessimism of other criminological perspectives. Although both Quinney and Pepinsky at earlier points in their respective careers have focused on some dimensions of white collar crime, their peacemaking criminological work has not, to date, addressed this type of crime to any measurable degree. It is perhaps ironic, however, that the reconciliatory approach favored by peacemaking criminology is quite consistent with a "compliance" or cooperative approach to corporate crime favored by many mainstream or conservative students of corporate crime. But the dominant cooperative strategy toward corporate crime is more rooted in pragmatic assumptions rather than universal principles, and is considered the most efficient and effective way of limiting the harm of corporate activities. Although John Braithwaite would be unlikely to identify himself as a peacemaking criminologist his promotion of "re-integrative shaming" (e.g., Braithwaite, 2003) would appear to represent a specific strategy toward corporate crime acceptable to both mainstream compliance advocates and peacemaking criminologists. The rapidly expanding "restorative justice" movement has many points of intersection with a peacemaking criminology (e.g., Sullivan and Tifft, 2006). A peacemaking criminology need not be seen as wholly at odds with a crime control agenda, but it does call for a radical transformation of both the method of crime control and its primary targets.

The work of peacemaking criminologists, to date, has been directed principally toward sensitizing us to counterproductive, inherently unjust responses to conventional forms of crime. The disproportionate power of at least the elite segment of white collar criminals to manipulate meanings of crime and responses to it looms as one of the larger questions about the application of the peacemaking criminological perspective to this form of crime: does it simply provide another forum wherein white collar criminals have an advantage over conventional criminals, and have broadened opportunities for denial and rationalization of intrinsically harmful conduct?

Postmodernist Criminology

Although a *postmodernist criminology* has been identified as one strain of critical criminology, it should be emphasized that postmodern thought itself is by no means necessarily linked with a progressive agenda; on the contrary, much postmodernist thought is viewed as either consciously apolitical, or inherently conservative and reactionary.

Any attempt to characterize a postmodernist criminology—or postmodern thought itself—encounters difficulties (Arrigo, 2003; Schwartz and Friedrichs, 1994). It can, perhaps, be best described as a loose collection of themes and tendencies. Postmodernists reject totalizing concepts (such as the state); they reject positivism; they reject the potential of collective action to transform society (Henry, 1991; Hunt, 1991). Postmodernism contends that modernity is no longer liberating, but has become rather a force of subjugation, oppression, and repression. For postmodernism, language plays the central role in the human experience of reality. The postmodernist "deconstruction" of texts exposes the instability and relativity of meaning in the world. Within critical criminology specifically Henry and Milovanovic (1991; 2003) have produced a pioneering effort—which they call *constitutive criminology*—to integrate elements of post-modernist thought with the critical criminological project. They are especially concerned with highlighting the role of ideology, discursive practices, symbols and sense data in the production of meaning in the realm of crime. We must, they contend, understand how those who engage in crime, who seek to control it, and who study it "co-produce" its meaning.

A fully developed application of postmodern thought to white collar crime has yet to be undertaken, although Henry and Milovanovic (1996) have taken some preliminary steps in this direction. First, they call attention to how white collar crime is defined as a "socially constructed" category, with corporations in particular positioned to "constitute law to reflect the legitimacy of their power and the illegitimacy of the power of others" (Henry and Milovanovic, 1993: 2). In a postmodernist reading, law and the formal institutions of social control must be understood in terms of their interconnectedness with the whole range of forms of social control; law and the legalistic definition of crime can be understood only as particular manifestations of power. Accordingly, the "truth" about crime is principally an artifact of interrelationships within society, with white collar crime a reflection of imbalances in power which preclude a full-fledged acknowledgment of the real consequences of harmful actions and policies.

A second dimension of a postmodern approach to white collar crime would emphasize the contemporary context within which such crime occurs. It is a shared premise of postmodernist writers that the present era represents a fundamental break with the conditions of modernity, although the full scope of this break is a matter of some dispute. The challenge here is to establish connections between such alleged postmodern conditions as the "hyperreal" and the contemporary character of white collar crime. Denzin (1990: 37), in a discussion of the film *Wall Street* (which dealt with insider trading), observed that "The postmodern moment not only commodifies information...but it com-modifies time, individuals, life styles, status and prestige, and human feelings." Illusions (including the ultimate illusion of money) replace a more substantial dimension of "reality." Wall Street itself—the locus of some of the largest scale white collar crime—is described in the language of postmodernist analysis as "A site where a political economy of signs ceaselessly circulates across an imaginary computerized space where nothing is any longer real"(Denzin, 1990: 40). Such observations are at least indicative of one form of a postmodernist approach to the understanding of white collar crime. More specifically, at least some forms of white collar crime—such as techno crime—can perhaps be more fully understood in the context of a society where ever-larger proportions of human transactions occur through some medium of symbolic transmission. Increasingly, crimes carried out through the application of sophisticated computer technology, involving electronic transactions, can be expected to overshadow traditional, interpersonal forms of crime such as bank robbery. Hypothetically, then, postmodernist thought provides us with metaphors and concepts especially appropriate for the understanding of such crime.

A final general theme of postmodernist analysis that is relevant in this context is the rejection of meta-narratives and holistic responses to social phenomena, including white collar crime. We can engage in the reading of "texts" (an inclusive term, referring to all phenomena and events) but cannot impose an over-arching meaning on events. Indeed, the postmodern perspective at least implicitly accords to victims a broad prerogative of assigning their own meaning to their victimization, although this is especially problematic in the case of victims of corporate crimes who are often unaware of their victimization. And the postmodernist propensity for "passive resistance" and localized responses may usefully challenge grandiose claims for fundamental reform or revolutionary change, but is also especially feeble as a response to the corporate forms of white collar crime.

Feminist Criminology

The white collar world has traditionally been predominantly a male world, and white collar criminals have been mainly white males, with middle- and upper-class and middle-aged and older males disproportionately represented relative to their involvement in other forms of crime. Males greatly outnumber females among white collar crime offenders. The male dominance of the corporations and outside-the-home occupations, especially the more powerful positions—or "the gendered structure of opportunity" (Braithwaite, 1993: 225)—is the single most important factor explaining this discrepancy.

White collar crime has not been a primary concern of *feminist criminology*. Such criminology has especially focused on exposing the overall patterns of patriarchy and male dominance in all realms pertaining to crime and the legal system. Whatever their differences, feminists have been quite united in their interest in identifying and opposing those social arrangements which contribute to the oppression of women (Miller, 2003; Schwendinger and Schwendinger, 1991). Inevitably, direct forms of male violence (e.g., rape and spouse abuse) targeting women have been a major preoccupation of feminist criminology. In a pioneering application of a feminist criminology to white collar crime Kathleen Daly (1989c) found that the female share of most forms of occupational crime and of corporate crime was low, and when females did commit white collar crimes the patterns were somewhat different from those of males, as were their motivations. In a more recent analysis Mary Dodge (2007) finds that while some of these trends persist, as females become more integrated into the higher echelons of the corporate world their involvement in white collar crime in this environment has increased as well.

On the other side of the crime/victim equation some work (reflecting a feminist influence) puts forth the claim that in certain respects women are especially vulnerable to being victims of white collar crime, at least in its corporate form (DeKeseredy and Hinch, 1991; Hinch and DeKeseredy, 1992; Gerber and Weeks, 1992; Szockyj and Fox, 1996). Over the past several decades there has been a dramatic movement of women into the outside-the-home workplace. As noted earlier, however, women are overrepresented in the lower-level jobs, such as clerical and assembly line positions. They are, accordingly, more vulnerable to harm in the form of repetitive strain injuries, exposure to video displays and toxic substances, brown lung disease, and so forth (DeKeseredy and Hinch, 1992; Gerber and Weeks, 1992). Women are also more vulnerable than men to sexual harassment and assault in low-level clerical and store clerk positions. As consumers, women have disproportionately consumed harmful pharmaceutical products, and are uniquely harmed by products such as intra-uterine devices (as in the Dalkon Shield case, which seriously injured thousands of women). Since women also disproportionately assume the burdens of housekeeping they are more fully exposed to harmful household appliances, cleaning products, and pesticides. Some students of this issue view the alleged greater vulnerability of women to corporate crime as a reflection of both capitalism and patriarchy, or male dominance (Gerber and Weeks, 1992; Hinch and DeKeseredy, 1992). Women are underrepresented in the corporate decision-making process, in this account, and their concerns for health and safety issues are not accorded a high priority.

The preceding argument can be overstated, and it goes without saying that many men are victimized in the same way as women, and are also overrepresented in some vulnerable positions (e.g., miners). But at a minimum a feminist criminology has promoted attention to various connections between gender and white collar crime. The policy implications of a feminist criminological approach to white collar crime are somewhat less than fully clear, however. One faction of feminists calls for much tougher enforcement of law, and harsher sanctions, for male victimizers of women, including pornographers and wife batterers (Schwartz and DeKeseredy, 1991). An ongoing tension on policy issues exists, however, between those who read the criminological evidence on women and violence as calling for advocacy on behalf of women and confrontation with male victimizers, and those who read this evidence as calling for a feminist-inspired transformation toward reconciliatory strategies. In a parallel vein, a feminist criminological perspective could be read to be supportive of either the punitive or compliance approach to corporate and other forms of white collar crime.

Left Realism

Left realism emerged largely in Great Britain and Canada in the period after 1985 as a response to the perceived analytical and practical deficiencies of radical criminology, especially in its neo-Marxist form (Young and Matthews, 1992). Left realists realized that right wingers were able to largely preempt the crime issue, because the fear of street crime is pervasive and intense and typically has more immediacy than fear of elite crime. Radicals who either ignore street crime, or even worse are seen as romanticizing street criminals, lose all credibility in the eyes of their largest potential constituency. Furthermore, traditional radical criminology does not attend to the fact that the principal victims of street crime are disadvantaged members of society, and that conventional crime persists in non-capitalist societies (DeKeseredy 2003; Matthews and Young, 1992). Left realists also reject one-dimensional interpretations of state crackdowns on street crime that characterize it exclusively as repression. But left realists vehemently deny that their work leads in the same direction as right realists, and they differ from them in many ways: they prioritize social justice over order; reject biogenetic, individualistic explanations of criminality and emphasize structural factors; are not positivistic, insofar as they are concerned with social meaning of crime as well as criminal behavior, and the links between law-making and law-breaking; and they are acutely aware of the limitations of coercive intervention, and are more likely to stress informal control (Matthews and Young, 1992; Young and Matthews, 1992). Left realist criminology insists on attending to the community as well as the state, the victim as well as the offender (Schwartz and DeKeseredy, 1991). It argues, furthermore, that at least some traditional criminological research methods can be used to generate research which can serve progressive objectives.

Although left realists have recognized the relative impact of corporate crime and its disproportionate impact on vulnerable segments of the community, it has not been a principal focus of their attention (DeKeseredy, 2003). If left realists have attended more fully to conventional crime, it is in part out of recognition that such crime is generally a more pressing concern of members of disadvantaged communities. But as Pearce (1992) has pointed out, members of such communities typically have a very narrow and limited conception of white collar crime, and are simply not conscious of much of their victimization from such crime. Some scholars who identify with a left realist perspective have examined corporate crime as well as crimes of the state and the legal response to such crime (Pearce 2007; Tombs and Whyte, 2007). They naturally argue against narrow conceptions of such crime that emphasize inter-subjective dimensions, and in favor of recognizing the influence of corporations in defining many harmful or questionable activities of theirs as "legitimate" (Pearce, 1992; McQueen, 1992). In this context, a fuller understanding of the plurality of interests informing corporate decision-making is necessary. Further, left realists call for some fundamental changes in law and regulatory policy relating to corporations. Rob McQueen (1992) calls for imposing much broader responsibility and accountability on corporations, with community representatives on corporate governing boards and mandatory annual audits. Frank Pearce and Steve Tombs (1992) contend that a realist agenda requires broader empowerment of workers and local communities against corporations, and they argue against the dominant "compliance" school in favor of tough independent regulatory control and effective criminal sanctions. It is, of course, something of a paradox (and conundrum) to have progressives arguing in favor of more substantial state intervention. At a minimum, it raises questions about implicit trust of government integrity and efficiency.

Recent Critical Criminological Initiatives and White Collar Crime

The foregoing discussion was limited to four prominent strains of critical criminology in the contemporary era. Some brief mention can be made here of some other strains—especially more recent ones—in relation to white collar crime, and some specific critical criminological initiatives on this topic.

Newsmaking criminology: This strain of critical criminology is primarily associated with Gregg Barak (2007), calling for bringing critical criminological perspectives to a broader audience through engagement with the mass media. It is well-established that corporations exercise a greatly disproportionate influence in the mass media, both as a function of ownership and sponsorship. Recent calls for a public criminology dovetail well with the concerns of newsmaking criminology. In the realm of the corporate form of white collar crime in particular, the need to counter a mainstream emphasis on "bad apples" and individual miscreants needs to be countered at every opportunity by attention to the structural sources of such crime. Of course in an evolving generational shift away from the mass media as a primary source of news and information, critical criminologists will have to embrace new mediums through the Internet to reach a younger generation.

Cultural criminology: This new strain of critical criminology has been characterized by an interest in "the role of image, style, and symbolic meaning among criminals and their subcultures, in the mass media's representation of crime and criminal justice, and in public conflicts over crime and crime control" (Ferrell, 2003: 71). Most of the work done as cultural criminology focuses on such phenomena as graffiti artists, drug users, gang members and the like, as well as media representations of such phenomena. But certainly there is a considerable potential to apply a cultural criminological analysis to the worlds inhabited by white collar and corporate offenders, and representations of them in the popular culture and the media.

Green criminology: Ensuring a sustainable environment going forward is surely one of the principal challenges for the future. Some critical criminologists have embraced a "green" criminology that focuses upon crimes against the environment (e.g., South and Beirne, 2006). Of course, corporations have always been and continue to be among the entities causing the most destruction against the environment (Burns and Lynch, 2004). Crimes against the environment on all levels seem likely to be a growing area of concern in the years ahead.

Social harm and crime: Some critical criminologists have now adopted the view that a social harm framework better captures the pernicious range of activities of major corporations (and states) and other powerful entities than a criminological framework (Hillyard, Pantazis, Tombs, and Gordon, 2004). More specifically, Steve Tombs (2007: 531) argues that "criminological definitions of violence still fail to recognize offenses against workers and the public arising out of work." The fate of this initiative remains to be seen.

State-corporate crime: In 1990 Ronald Kramer and Raymond Michalowski introduced the concept of "state-corporate crime," to address crime that occurs at the intersection of the state and business, or as a cooperative venture between those acting on behalf of states and of corporations, and by 2006 this concept had become sufficiently influential that an anthology of some major contributions on the topic was published (Michalowski and Kramer, 2006). This initiative is certainly an important critical criminological contribution to the understanding of white collar crime, broadly defined.

State crime: The broad expansion of critical criminological attention to crimes of states has been among the most noteworthy developments of recent years, most comprehensively captured in Penny Green and Tony Ward's (2004) *State Crime.* Although Sutherland originally applied the concept of white collar crime to private sector activity, the generic relationship (and parallels) between crimes in the private and public sector has become increasingly recognized (Friedrichs, 2007a; Rothe and Friedrichs 2006). In this realm critical criminologists have played a central role.

Recent personal initiatives: On Crimes of Globalization and on Corporate Scandals: If Sutherland's original introduction of the concept of white collar crime was intended to contribute to an expanded criminological conception of crime, critical criminologists have been especially active in challenging the limitations of conventional criminological frameworks. I take some special pride in the increasing adoption of the concept of "crimes of globalization" as a significant form of white collar crime in a global context. My own promotion of this concept came about as follows: In 1999-2000 by daughter Jessica spent her junior year of college in Thailand. While there, she lived among river fishermen whose way of life was being destroyed by a World Bank-financed dam (at Pak Mun River). She became actively involved with their protest movement, and returned to the United States in April, 2000, to participate in an "anti-globalization" protest in Washington, D.C. Out of discussions with her—and as a product of my own interests in "macro"-level crime—an American Society of Criminology paper emerged, subsequently published as an article entitled "The World Bank and Crimes of Globalization: A Case Study" (Friedrichs and Friedrichs 2002).

The core claim here is that certain activities of international financial institutions such as the World Bank, the International Monetary Fund and the World Trade Organization, have immensely harmful consequences in developing countries, and should be recognized as a global form of white collar crime.

In the first years of the twenty-first century a new wave of "corporate scandals" broke out in the United States, beginning with the high profile Enron case. I subsequently published an article in *Critical Criminology* entitled "Enron et al.: Paradigmatic White Collar Crime Cases for the New Century" (Friedrichs, 2004), with an objective of recognizing the ways in which the Enron, World-Com and other crimes occurring today in the corporate world differ in certain dimensions from earlier forms of corporate crime, as well as the need to apply several levels of analysis to understanding and explaining these crimes. The structural level of explanation, with special emphasis on attributes of contemporary capitalism, has to be the starting point.

A third and related theme of my recent work on white collar crime calls for attention to the evolving context within which white collar and corporate crime today occurs: i.e., "White Collar Crime in a Postmodern, Globalized World" (Friedrichs, 2007b). Both mainstream criminology and critical criminology have principally adopted a "modern," national framework for the analysis of crime and its control, although critical criminology has collectively been more attuned to a global context. But traditional frameworks are increasingly inadequate for addressing many of the most significant forms of white collar crime and their control today.

Making Sense of the Critical Contradictions: Toward a Progressive Pluralist Criminology

Radical criminology was influential in exposing the inherent biases of law and the criminal justice system in a capitalist society, and played an instrumental role in directing attention to "crimes of the powerful." The newer versions of critical criminology have to date manifested variable degrees of interest in white collar crime; for the most part, white collar crime has not been at the top of the agenda of any of these critical criminological perspectives. I have sought to at least indicate some real or potential contributions of these perspectives to our understanding of white collar crime.

What, if anything, do these various critical perspectives have in common, at least in terms of an approach to white collar crime? First, they all challenge perceived distortions in conventional consciousness regarding crime, including white collar crime, although in quite different ways. Second, they all tend to take power differentials as quite central in understanding both crime and the criminal justice response to it. And third, they all seek to find ways to empower constituencies who are especially vulnerable to corporate crime (e.g., workers, consumers, women generally). Beyond these broad generalizations they cannot be said to advance a uniform response to white collar crime. Indeed, given the endless complexity of such crime, no uniform response is either feasible or desirable.

At the present time, early in the twenty-first century, it cannot be said that we have an environment that is manifestly receptive to any of the critical perspectives identified above. In terms of overall orientation toward a progressive agenda very small percentages of the population identify with a specifically leftist perspective, although of course a substantial plurality embraces some form of a liberal or reformist outlook. The collapse of various state socialist systems in the Eastern hemisphere has been widely celebrated as a fundamental repudiation of the basic tenets of Marxism and a vindication of free markets and Western democracies. But it is also evident that there are many sources of discontent, disquiet and frustration within our state capitalist system, and accordingly there is a considerable *latent* potential receptiveness to a persuasive critique coupled with a credible vision and program. Within criminology itself mainstream approaches remain dominant and critical criminology contends with various structural constraints, but there are recurrent indicators of significant dissatisfaction with the achievements of the mainstream approaches (e.g., Schwartz and Hatty, 2003). Despite a broad generalized resistance to critical criminological perspectives there is the sense of a begrudging curiosity about such perspectives and at least in some quarters some openness to what they might have to offer.

I favor what I call a progressive pluralist critical perspective that: (1) acknowledges the endless complexity, contradictions and conundrums characterizing the totality of social existence; (2) shares with postmodern thought a skepticism toward exclusive "truth" claims; and (3) concedes that many different perspectives (and methods) can advance our understanding of facets or dimensions of social reality. Nevertheless this perspective (at odds with one basic strain of the postmodern view) regards the critical tradition as "privileged" in the sense of offering a broader, more fundamental interpretation of social reality. It incorporates, on faith, the progressive belief that social transformation in a more positive direction (e.g., diminishing inequities, enhancing overall autonomy, improving basic conditions) is possible.

The most realistic and productive strategy for critical criminology in the present context is not to focus on structural inequities—which have been very thoroughly documented in the literature by now—but rather to attend to the sources of social consciousness that continue to "distort" understandings of crime and shape differential support for public policy. A critical criminology which aspires to make a difference must also identify factors that help contribute to a receptiveness to a progressive agenda. A progressive, pluralist perspective on white collar crime, then, while continuing to attend to the complex of structural factors explaining such crime and the responses to it, should more fully focus on the formation of conventional images of such crime as well as specific factors which open people up to counter-images.

5

Corporate Crime: A Panacea for Critical Criminology

Vincenzo Ruggiero

This chapter is an attempt to verify whether and how, in the current situation, a revitalization of critical criminological analysis is viable. I identify the area of study pertaining to corporate crime as the ideal area, within criminology, that lends itself to a radical approach. In the following pages, conceptualizations, causations, and prevention of this type of crime will be addressed through the tools offered by classical sociology as well as those made available by more contemporary analysis. The argument developed below is intended to suggest that corporate crime is a panacea for critical criminology.

Conceptualizations

Elaborations of Sutherland's (1983) seminal work focus, among other things, on the nature and definition of corporate crime. According to a relatively accepted formulation, this consists of illegal acts performed within a legitimate organization, and in accordance with the organization goals, which victimize employees, customers, or the general public (Schrager and Short, 1977). It has also been stated that, even when excluding from consideration many forms of business "malpractice" that are "either not criminal at all or whose criminality is ambiguous, the term corporate crime describes a number of very different sorts of activities" (Levi, 1987: xix). This refers to the circumstance that corporate crime may be perpetrated by individuals whose rank within organizations varies substantially.

If corporate crime embraces illegal behavior adopted within a legitimate enterprise, in effect, the degree of social and institutional power wielded by an enterprise varies significantly. However, if we associate corporate crime with high degrees of power, we have to limit our analysis to crimes committed by corporations and exclude those committed against them. The underlying premise of this chapter is that corporate crime is not an equal opportunity offence, hence the necessity, for any study of the subject matter, to clearly delimit the terrain to which the study itself is to be referred. My argument is confined to offences committed by actors such as states, corporations, financial institutions, and other similarly powerful organizations, namely offenders who possess an exorbitantly exceeding amount of material and symbolic resources when compared to those possessed by their victims.

I would conceptualize these as "power crimes," a phrase which in turn requires further qualification and precise connotation. The phrase should be located against the background of differentiated opportunities offered to social groups. Social inequalities determine varied degrees of freedom, whereby individuals are granted a specific number of choices and a specific range of potential actions they can carry out. Each degree of freedom offers an ability to act, to choose the objectives of one's action, and the means to make choices realistic. The greater the degree of freedom enjoyed, the wider the range of choices available, along with the potential decisions to be made and the possibility of realistically predicting their outcomes (Bauman, 1990). We can argue, with respect to the corporate crime, that criminal designations are controversial and highly problematic, due to the higher degree of freedom enjoyed by perpetrators. The capacity to control the effects of their actions allows those who have more freedom to conceal (or negotiate) the criminal nature of their actions. If we translate the notion of freedom into that of resources, we can argue that those possessing a larger quantity and variety of them also have greater possibilities of attributing criminal definitions to others and repelling those that others attribute to them. They also have greater ability to control the effects of their criminal activity, and usually do not allow this to appear and be designated as such. The notion of "power crime" is therefore referred to actors endowed with high degrees of freedom and resources, a notion that echoes Sutherland's variables "high status and respectability."

A different conceptualization of power crime is found in recent criminological contributions from control balance theory. Tittle's (1995) theory takes as its organizing theoretical variable the degree of control that actors exercise in relation to the amount of control they experience. According to his formulation, control surpluses (an excess of control exercised relative to control experienced) give rise to autonomous forms of deviance, namely deviance aimed at extending the existing control surplus. This includes offences which do not entail direct interaction with victims, ranging from acts of exploitation (corporate price-fixing, influence peddling by political figures) to acts of plunder (pollution, destruction of forests and animals, corporate manslaughter), and a variety of forms of indirect predation (Piquero and Piquero, 2006).

> An example of exploitative deviance [is] committed by corporate executives who authorize dumping of toxic waste into rivers after having carefully calculated that those who would be harmed most immediately – farmers and fishers along the rivers – will not be able to do much about it. Businesspeople do these things when they

become aware that they, through the corporate vehicle, enjoy a surplus of control, which can be extended by any means. (Tittle, 1995: 164)

Although perhaps still incomplete, the identification of corporate crime with power crime, namely illegal conduct by actors who enjoy an excess of freedom, resources and control may suffice for the purpose of this contribution.

It is now necessary to expand the concept I have just proposed. It has been widely argued that corporate or power crimes cannot be solely identified on the basis of a coded prohibition, because the law may fail to prohibit them clearly and strictly. Are these crimes narrowly definable in relation to a precise breach of rules and laws? In answering this question, some authors resort to different conceptualizations based on deviance rather than criminality. Quinney (1970), for instance, considers the correspondence between deviant and criminal behavior as crucial in the study of corporate crime. The question he poses is whether or not the behavior defined as criminal is also a deviation from the normative structure of the occupation: "If it can be established that the behaviors are regarded as deviant, as well as criminal, by the occupational members, the criminal violations can truly be studied as deviations from occupational norms" (ibid: 33). In brief, according to Quinney, the behavior studied by criminologists as criminal must be so regarded by the groups being studied.

This formulation raises old dilemmas and echoes the controversies engaging Sutherland and his critics. Sutherland holds little doubt about the criminality of powerful offenders, and stresses that the difference between these and their conventional counterparts has to be found in the responses they respectively elicit from institutional authority. Power crimes are socially injurious and can be legally so described, although the administrative procedure to which they are subject symbolically fades their seriousness. In a well-known diatribe around this specific view, Tappan (1947) retorts that crime entails an intentional will to violate norms of conduct prescribed by codes, jurisprudence, and custom, and as such prosecuted and punished by the state. Intentionality, a criminal mind, legally definable harm, along with successful prosecution and implementation of penalty: these are the legitimate requisites and by-products of criminal behavior: "In Tappan's view, it is illegitimate of Sutherland to describe people as criminal when they have not been successfully prosecuted for a crime and, moreover, he illegitimately extends the concept of crime to cover acts that do not violate the criminal law" (Slapper and Tombs, 1999: 6).

This long-running dispute illustrates the divergence between legal, social, and political definitions of criminality, simultaneously reminding us of the artificiality of all definitions of crime (Nelken, 1994). The concept of harm appears to rescue the debate, in that it allows us to identify a continuum linking administrative and criminal violations, *mala in se* and *mala prohibita*, ultimately: legality and illegality:

Once one extends the label crime beyond those who have been formally and successfully processed as criminals, one enters the sphere of normative reasoning, or moralising…the shift from a focus upon unequivocally defined criminal laws is a shift along a *continuum* which extends to social harms at the other extreme. (Slapper and Tombs, 1999: 6; my italics)

It is this *continuum* that deserves careful examination, in that subjectivity, social and intellectual identity and political strategy are engrained in the very process which extends the criminal label from clearly defined illegitimate acts to harmful acts. This process may cloud the very object of study it aims to clarify, for example, producing the simplification often needed in political campaigns but counterproductive in sociological enquiry. It should be noted, however, that this may result from the very nature and characteristics of corporate crimes, which are often, and rightly, described as hazy, evasive, invisible, thus inducing similarly hazy conceptualizations and suggesting nebulous categories or fields of study.

One of the crucial characteristics of corporate crime is part of what Nelken (1994) identifies as the fundamental ambiguity of these offences. The fact, for example, that the perpetrator has justification for being present at the scene where the crime takes place distinguishes this type of offending from conventional predatory crime (Clarke, 1990). On the surface, ambiguity makes this behavior very similar to ordinary legal behavior: "For example, for fraud to succeed, it must obviously succeed in mimicking the appearance of legitimate transactions, and it is not unusual for those guilty of this crime to remain undetected for years, even a lifetime" (Nelken, 1994: 373). In sum, difficulties in classifying corporate offenders are compounded by difficulties in discovering that an offence has been committed in the first place.

Invisibility, in turn, contributes to making the field of study indistinct, classification formless and typologies fuzzy. It has long been noted that invisibility describes the condition of both powerful criminals and their victims. The perpetrator is made invisible by the circumstance whereby the setting of the offence does not coincide with the setting where its effects will be felt. This is also the case because the time when the crime is performed and the time when the damage caused becomes apparent do not correspond. On the other hand, victims themselves can be described as invisible in that they are both absent from the scene of the crime and are frequently unaware of their own victimization.

It is time to take a reflective pause, and note that these controversies offer fertile ground to critical criminological analysis. For example, the very focus on power allows scholars to concentrate on the mechanisms leading to official definitions of what is to be regarded as crime. The study of such mechanisms and the institutional arrangements underpinning them may partly unveil harmful conducts that are commonly disguised behind what we call a dark figure. However, in this case radical analysis is not confined to revealing the dark figure of corporate crime, as detection would do for conventional crime. It also permits to draw attention onto harmful behaviors which are not designated as criminal. Radical analysis, in brief, may show that the purported universality of criminal definitions is, in fact, the result of conflicts between competing political identities and strategies. Let us now review further conceptualizations around corporate crime.

In the analysis of the moral and managerial component of human behavior within organizations, Punch (1996: 2) highlights the culture of competition providing opportunities, motivations, and rationalizations for rule-breakers. He also emphasizes the ambiguous and manipulative nature of management, matched by the incoherent character of organizations themselves, which may present a clear image of their objectives and practices to the outside world, but in fact operate in a contingent manner whereby the legitimacy of ends and conducts are constantly redefined. Summing up his argument: "the corporation, and the business environment, are potentially criminogenic." This statement is perhaps the clearest formulation we can find in the specialist literature of the legal-illegal continuum characterizing the practices of organizations and powerful actors. It is a statement, however, that perpetuates the vagueness of its object of study as much as it obfuscates the criminal nature of the conducts under scrutiny. A precise identification of the legality-illegality continuum requires the isolation of distinct practices and models of action, namely an empirical classification referred to specific conducts. The following may be one tentative such classification:

- *operative corporate crime*: this manifests itself when powerful groups and individuals violate their own rules and philosophies;
- *gangster corporate crime*: powerful actors committing conventional crime;
- *corporate crime by proxy*: this entails the use by official powerful actors of an illegitimate or clandestine strong arm;
- *corporate criminal partnerships*: crimes that are committed jointly by licit and illicit groups and individuals;
- *corporate philanthropic crime*: whose effects appear to benefit others than the perpetrators;
- *corporate foundational crime*: which possesses a de-criminalization impetus and establishes new favorable legislations (for a detailed discussion of these categories see Ruggiero, 2007).

There is a final, wider, area of corporate criminality that is located in the most extreme ring of the legal-illegal chain, namely in the area where criminal and economic behavior display intimate similarities. I am thinking of legitimate but harmful practices, and referring to conducts inspired by the cardinal values of market economies.

The study of these conducts is a panacea for critical criminology. As I have already stressed, it entails a shift of the analytical gaze from disadvantaged to powerful actors and groups. This shift, strongly promoted by Edwin Sutherland, allows us to address the murky boundaries between legitimate activity and entrepreneurial crime. But why is this shift so important? If we accept that by studying one phenomenon we contribute to its evolution, or even to its creation, subjective choice of the issues studied becomes paramount. Values and beliefs shape reality as well as human action attempting to change it. This is the conclusion reached, among others, by some historians, who claim that there is no contradiction, in their work, between the search for evidence and the use of rhetoric (Ginzburg, 2000). Sources, in their view, are neither wide-open windows, as realists and positivists believe, nor walls blocking the gaze: rather, they are very much like deforming glasses. The use of desire, without which any research is impossible, is not incompatible with the refutations inflicted by the principle of reality. Similarly, critical criminologists may stop thinking of themselves as solving social problems objectively defined. Rather, they may develop a sense of how subjectivity defines issues and, at the same time, may lead to possible solutions and to social change. Here the contribution of feminist criminology is paramount.

Some female criminologists advocate the need to oppose naturalism, and for that matter realism; they claim that reality and meaning are not there, in the world, waiting patiently to be recorded by objective observers. Criminologists, in brief, along with other external observers, contribute to the making of reality and meaning according to the ideological and cultural framework shaped by their role and occupation. We, as meaning-makers, are obliged to deal with meanings already constituted (by others) for us, but we also play an active part in reconstituting those meanings as we pass them on. Realism, while polemically advocating the concrete against the abstract, materialism versus idealism, implies on the one hand the impatience of one sense of practical, and on the other a tone of limited calculation typical of politicians and businessmen. The sense of practical and limited calculation, in their turn, may reduce the analysis to surface observation thus making realism prosaic, a device to evade the real. It is curious how some criminologists, while studying the conduct of others, find redundant the study of the way in which their perceptions affect the phenomena they observe, and how they neglect that by interacting with the subjects observed they actively constitute frames of meaning. These types of criminologists feel uncomfortable when facing the social mechanisms that produce what they regard as their knowledge. Critical criminologists should, on the contrary, feel comfortable when facing these mechanisms.

To understand crime is to engage in a positive act of creation—something requiring invention and imagination. Critical criminologists do not limit their work to reporting on the phenomenon of crime, but positively construct that body of knowledge; their understanding of crime depends on certain critical assumptions about the nature of social relations, and so their understanding is a product of a certain way of looking at the social system as a whole.

Causation

The second area in which the potential of critical criminology might be revitalized is the analytical area of corporate crime causation. As Cohen (1988) argued, there is a major distortion compounding the already distorting tendency in sociology to over-generalize. In his view, by concentrating on systems, structures, patterns and trends, by talking glibly of societies, systems, and epochs, sociological analysis is often quite insensitive to variations, differences and exceptions. Critical criminology may choose to reject generalizations, therefore rejecting the task of elaborating general, universal theories of crime, embracing, instead, variations and differences. In my opinion this might be achieved in a particular way, namely by focusing on the interpretative oscillations that often occur when we are faced with criminal activity. For example, I would suggest that each time we subscribe to one cause of crime we may realize that the opposite cause also possesses some reasonable validity. It is what I would like to term the *causality of contraries* (some examples later).

For now, let us observe that there is a sort of foundational curse, mixed with an un-confessed inferiority complex, which compels social scientists to constantly search for universal causations of phenomena. Giving up this search, many believe, would exclude them from the scientific community. Amongst sociologists of deviance and criminologists, this compulsion manifests itself in the attempt to identify a unified theory of crime. I am thinking in particular of scholars who focus exclusively on vulnerable sectors of the population, who may find that crime is the result of vulnerability or marginalization, and end up establishing an automatic association between illegitimate behavior and low social status.

The study of offending behavior adopted by powerful individuals shows that this automatic association can easily be refuted. Learning theories of crime possess an embryonic element of the *causality of the contraries* that I would like to endorse. Let us provide some examples.

A small company may adopt illegitimate procedures because it operates in a competitive business environment. In its case, criminal practices may grant a supplementary strength to be utilized in the market, and translate into a competing edge on competitors. On the contrary, a large company may adopt criminal practices because it operates in a monopolistic business sector: by virtue of its position in such sector of the economy this company may escape control by competitors and evade institutional monitoring. In the former case, the putative cause of criminal conduct is the competitive environment in which the company operates, while in the latter it is its contrary, namely the absence of a competitive environment. Similarly, companies engaged in long-term investments, which are forced to delay the enjoyment of profits, may be tempted to seek immediate returns through illegitimate practices. Conversely, one may suggest that companies engaged in the acquisition of rapid returns "learn" profit-making techniques so well that they are induced to apply such techniques in the illicit domain. This causality of the contraries, in a sense, throws doubt on the adequacy of a criminology devoted to the search for universal causes of crime. It is a type of causality that may be highly productive for critical approaches.

Critical criminology should abandon the search for omnipresent social conditions, for an "original sin," in brief, for a primary, universal cause of criminal behavior. How could we do otherwise? If we, for example, identify variables such as financial success, the pursuit of status, or the accumulation of resources as the primary causes of crime, we end up expanding the criminal label to cover all behavior. Success and financial gain, in fact, are also the main motivations of legitimate behavior. On the contrary, if we focus on variables such as lack, deficiency, *deficit* (of opportunities, socialization or resources), we end up excluding from the criminal rubric all those illegitimate practices caused by abundance, wealth and excess. Corporate crime, instead, may be aptly explained through "relative affluence," which is the contrary of relative deprivation. And the study of affluence, wealth, their effects and their criminogenic nature may be among the tasks of critical criminology. This leads me to the other area of potential development.

Prevention and Justice

After examining a number of "crimes of the elite," critical criminologists are bound to be tempted to conclude that the excess of resources and opportunities, rather than the lack of both, is the major cause of criminal activity. This conclusion may derive from subjective evaluation of the overall social damage caused by the two types of criminal behavior. But, against the backdrop of what I have termed the *aetiology of the contraries*, one should note that both the deficiency and the abundance of legitimate opportunities may lead to criminal activity (Ruggiero, 2000). Critical criminology, however, may analyze the selective processes that are in place whereby only some of those who are involved in such activity are also exposed to social stigma and institutional penalization, hence the formidable importance of the study of corporate crime.

Alternative conceptualizations and causations of corporate crime, however, may not be sufficient to reduce its incidence and social damaging effects without preventive strategies and action. In what remains of this chapter I would like to propose a notion of prevention as social action leading to change. In order to do so, I will make a brief excursus into classical social theories, I will attempt to trace ideas of social change and how these have been expunged from criminological analysis.

When we look at the sociological tradition from which criminology and the sociology of deviance originally take inspiration, we have to focus in particular on the sociological knowledge produced concomitantly with the expansion of urban settings. Throughout the twentieth century, the growth of cities was accompanied by the emergence of new forms of social conflict. It is true that students of urban settlements where obsessed by order and invoked innovative social processes which could strengthen it. However, early analysts of the city also focused on innovation and social change, as these were deemed essential for people to cohabit in the urban environment, and for groups to negotiate their respective role and degree of access to resources. Hence the emphasis on collective action, which shapes urban settlements, and through innovation establishes acceptable models of urban order. Hence, also, the attention placed on innovation that disrupts unjust social order and aims at creating a new one. There is, therefore, something dynamic in early studies of urban settings: there is a sense that collective interests and group action, through negotiation or conflict, may determine social mutation. Preventing corporate crime may require exactly such group action, although it remains to be seen how and what type of social mutation this is likely to produce.

For now, let us note that the simultaneous development of the sociology of deviance was the result of a radical shift, whereby collective action and innovation were abandoned as analytical issues and the focus placed on antisocial behavior, fear, and disorder (rather than order, or potential new order). Transitional hells and criminal zones became the central scene of enquiry, with the sociological gaze being diverted from more general conflicts.

An overview of some classics of sociology would help identify which tenets were retained and which eschewed, and how the conflictual nature of societies as depicted by the very pioneers of urban studies was distilled into an essentialist notion of conflict as deviance and crime. One of the tasks of contemporary anti-criminology might be that of analytically revisiting these aspects, which are neglected by mainstream analysis, and re-focus attention on collective action and social change.

Classical sociology does contain conceptual traces of "social movement," though such traces form a vague corollary to its central concern around social change. However, both the concept of "movement" and that of "change" are hidden behind, and coalesce with, notions of instability and incumbent menace. Exclusive attention to the latter notions was part of the cost the sociology of deviance had to pay for its ambition to achieve independence. Ultimately, confronted with unprecedented economic growth, the sociology of deviance alimented its independence with what I would term a deep sociological "fear of living together." It is among the tasks of contemporary critical criminology to resist this process and, paradoxically, to restore forms of theoretical dependence, rather than independence, from the sociology of social change.

Some examples. Many sociologists of deviance were deeply influenced by the views of social theorists such as Tönnies (1955), who described modern societies as "dysfunctional mechanic aggregates." This description was translated into that of social disorganization. In sum, the sociology of deviance uncritically embraced the ideas of Tönnies, who lamented that "people are all by themselves and isolated," and relationships are segmented and transitory. People were not expected to encounter each other as whole persons, because their relationships were deemed merely instrumental: "every person strives for that which is to his own advantage and affirms the actions of others only in so far as and as long as they can further his interest." Relationships in industrial societies, in brief, were viewed as more likely to generate predatory conducts than collective action for change. In studying corporate crime, critical criminological analysis is committed to shifting the focus from the former to the latter, therefore re-appropriating a crucial area of critical enquiry and practice.

Let us take the example of Durkheim. The concept of anomie was comprehensively adopted by the sociology of deviance, in that it describes an exceptional situation hampering the normal functioning of society. In Durkheim (1966), however, the polarization between a condition of stability and one of anomie is only apparent, because groups of individuals may challenge a specific form of stability without throwing the collectivity into a normless condition. The division of labor in society may be altered with a view to increasing consensus, a suggestion implying Durkheim's belief in subjectivities bringing change. The division of labor produces solidarity, he stresses, only if it is "spontaneous" and not forced.

According to Durkheim there is a "social force" in complex societies that manifests itself when the division of labor is perceived as highly unjust. Again, while completely ignored by mainstream criminology, this "social force" could be one of the areas of enquiry and action in which critical criminologists might engage.

Official criminology ignores similar pointers that we also find in some of Max Weber's contribution. Weberian societies are extremely conflictual due, mainly, to two orders of circumstances. First, conflict arises from the co-presence, in the same social setting, of people endowed with different power and resources. These people, Weber (1960) fears, live elbow to elbow, and become aware of their respective condition. This is Weber's way of arguing that relative deprivation, especially when persistent and visible, may trigger conflict. Second, conflict emerges when groups become aware that economic and political power, unlike in the city-states of the Renaissance that Weber idealizes, are concentrated in the same people and even in same physical settings. All these concerns tend to disappear from the criminological discourses inspired by Weberian thought. In this way, Weberian sociologists of deviance fail to observe how the elites can be contested and social change triggered. An intellectual selective process brings them to overlook what is perhaps the core of Weber's thought, namely that sociology is the science of social action, therefore of social change. The analysis of action, in Weber, addresses not what people might do but what they do purposively to achieve common aims. Actions may be, first, non-rational, inspired by tradition, following custom or meeting everyday expectations; second, they may be emotionally driven, acting upon impulse or the expression of feelings. Third, actions may be instrumentally rational, when directed towards attaining some specific objective, and, finally, value rational, when expressing political choice. It is rare to find these notions in analyses of contemporary society among disciples of Weberian sociology of deviance. Again, an analytical revitalization of "action" could inform contemporary efforts of critical criminology.

Let us now consider the legacy of Simmel, which we find in some of the work of the sociologists of the Chicago school. These sociologists were very receptive of Simmel's idea of so-called "extreme phenomena" generated by modern life, an idea that the author associated with the desire of individuals to distinguish themselves in a "colorless and uniform world." Did the late arrival of the sociology of deviance on the academic scene force this discipline to take as its subjects "the leftover materials of human behavior"? (Berger, 1995: 24). With the Chicago school, the study of the city started becoming the study of the real or imaginary fear caused by urban crime. This became manifest in the somewhat obsessive attention devoted to dangerous eruptions of conflict and particularly to the urban mob. Park and associates (1925) drew a parallel between fluctuations of markets and movements of crowds, both being characterized by a condition of instability in the form of permanent crisis. Although he stressed that, often, such movements could be controlled, urban populations were said to be in a state of perpetual agitation; the community itself was in a chronic condition of crisis, because casual and mobile aggregations in the city cause a condition of unstable equilibrium. Park and his colleagues wondered to what extent mob violence, strikes, and radical political movements were the results of the same general conditions that provoked financial panics, real estate booms, and mass movements in the population generally.

In brief, sociologists of deviance inspired by Simmel's (1971) thought were initially in search of the rationality guiding organized city life; they were fascinated by the opportunities arising from urban aggregations, but ended up devoting much of their analytical work to the mechanisms of disorganization. Park was adamant on this point: he saw deviance, urban riots, and "radical political movements" as forms of social pathology resulting from the unequal distribution of opportunities. A radical rereading of Simmel's thought would revitalize notions of conflict which are so central in his work.

Similarly, it is illuminating to observe how even the thought of one of the most celebrated figures influencing the sociology of deviance is selectively taken on board. When presenting his analysis of deviant adaptations, Merton (1968) argued that, along with individuals pursuing legitimate aims through illegitimate means, consideration should be given to individuals and groups who pursue new, unofficial, social aims with completely new means. This creative overturning of official aims and means he described with a type of deviant adaptation termed rebellion. By excluding such variable, sociologists of deviance rule out the possibility that their objects of study may, through collective action, modify their social condition. The inclusion of this variable in its theoretical and practical work is among the features denoting what might be termed a new critical criminology.

Examples of this reorientation include studies of collective action carried out by victims of violence, rather than studies of violent behavior; of initiatives set up by illicit drugs users, rather than of institutional initiatives addressed to them; studies of campaigns against corporate misconduct, rather than analysis of that conduct; finally, studies of movements against the crimes of the powerful, including conventional forms of organized crime, rather than studies of those crimes (Santino, 2000). This process of refocusing would fight what Pareto (1980) described as the "instinct for the persistence of aggregates," whereby individuals, and for that matter academic disciplines, are inclined to maintain established structures of ideas and action, and continue with familiar routines. It is how we cope with the inherent unpredictability of life. Our instinct is to make the world seem familiar and therefore more manageable. A task of critical criminology is that of analytically spreading notions of unpredictability and that the world is less familiar and manageable than we are prepared to believe.

Critical criminology can be inspired by social movements fighting against corporate crime, such as the environmental movement and the consumers' movement. It can also find a natural ally in the transnational movement fighting for global justice. Although the specific character of this movement is still open to interpretation (Ruggiero, 2005; Ruggiero and Montagna, 2008), it is now widely accepted that it has already had an effect on the policies implemented by international financial institutions, and that "it has the potential to influence the response to corporate forms of white-collar crime, especially the activities of transnational or multinational corporations" (Friedrichs, 2007: 174).

Conclusion

The study of corporate crime is a panacea for critical criminology. First, it allows us to shift the analytical focus from crime as the result of marginalized conditions to crime as the result of affluence and power. In doing so, it encourages the formulation of alternative aetiologies that run counter the conventional wisdom that crime is caused by a social or psychological deficit. Second, it paves the way for the exploration of conducts which are harmful but not, or not yet, criminalized. In this sense, the study of corporate crime amounts to the study of the philosophies underpinning economic activity and the institutional policies accompanying it. A crucial critical aspect of this study, in sum, resides in its transcending the conventional confines of criminological analysis and accessing other fields of knowledge. Third, when prevention of corporate crime is addressed, scholars are forced to re-visit notions of social change and collective action that form a large part of classical sociological thought. Such notions have been expelled from criminological reasoning as a consequence of conventional criminologists striving for the independence of their discipline. Their re-vitalization will be beneficial to critical analysis. While paying particular attention to preventative and regulatory measures, critical criminology addressing corporate crime is compelled to examine (and at times, make alliances with) the strategies of groups fighting against it.

Traditional popular culture offers numerous examples of how difficult it is to distinguish between those who accumulate wealth legitimately and those who do so illegitimately. Cervantes is never sure whether his characters epitomize entrepreneurship or fraud. The heroes of many popular songs possess such fuzzy features that one is never certain whether theirs is a form of criminal honesty or law-abiding criminality. Such popular tradition may provide the ideal backdrop for critical criminologists explaining and challenging corporate crime.

6

Toward a Supranational Criminology

Christopher W. Mullins and Dawn L. Rothe

Despite a decades-long focus on the intersection between social power and crime, to date critical criminologists have yet to focus much attention on some of the most serious crimes and atrocities which emerge from the imbalance of social power within societies. Genocides, war crimes, and crimes against humanity—fundamental violations of international humanitarian law—tend to have all of the core characteristics which would attract critical criminological attention. They are often organized and carried out by social institutions wielding immense power (e.g., states, militaries, etc.), they are often directed along ethnic or socio-economic class lines and are often driven by some of the rawest forms of destructive ideologies which arise in human societies. Yet, they are all but ignored in the field.

As such, our goal with this chapter is to firmly place international criminal atrocities on the criminological agenda by generating awareness of and interest in the most massive, systematic, and gruesome types of crime: genocide, crimes against humanity, war crimes, crimes of aggression and other gross human rights violations—an area of inquiry which has recently begun to be referred to as supranational criminology.

We define supranational crimes as violations of international criminal law that cause large amounts of human suffering and misery (i.e., genocide, crimes against humanity, war crimes, crimes of aggression and other gross human rights violations) by government actors acting in the name of or on behalf of a state, paramilitaries, or militias. Our definition of supranational crimes mirrors previous definitions of state crime and such crimes are clearly closely related to sorts of offenses discussed by state crime scholars. Yet, these phenomena do not always fit neatly into the category of crimes of the state. For example, Kramer and Michalowski (2005) defined state crime as any action violating public international law, international criminal law, when these actions are committed by individuals acting in official or covert capacity as agents of the state pursuant to expressed or implied orders of the state. However, in many of these atrocities paramilitaries and or militias play a central role. They are, quite simply, not agents of the state. While there are cases of militias working for or with governmental support (e.g., the Janjaweed and the Sudanese government—see Mullins and Rothe 2007, 2008; Rothe and Mullins, 2007), we cannot ignore those that do not (e.g., Lord's Resistance Army in Uganda, or the vast variety of militias in the Democratic Republic of the Congo (DRC)—see Mullins and Rothe 2008) nor should we misclassify them as state crimes. Other situations arise where the government is simply too weak to engage in systematic criminality. Still, other supranational crimes are produced by the actions of transnational organizations, with little state involvement. For example, AngloGold Ashante negotiated mineral contracts with militia groups in the Ituri region of the DRC in direct violation of numerous international laws and treaties.

In this chapter, we provide an overview of supranational crimes and a *supranational* criminology. We begin by surveying the key categories of the crimes we consider supranational, and their position under international law. We then provide a discussion of methodological issues surrounding the study of these acts. We close with a discussion of the common social elements and experiences in states that suffer from these phenomena.

War Crimes

European-based cultures have been formally developing and refining the notion of war crimes—illegal actions which occur on the field of battle—since the 1800s. As technologies of warfare became increasingly lethal, and civilians increasingly victimized, Western nations moved to limit the types of weapons and tactics used. The late 1800s and early 1900s saw numerous multilateral treaties entered into, only to be violated in subsequent conflicts. The end of World War I saw these laws first coupled with enforcement mechanisms, though the tribunals were piecemeal and largely symbolic. After World War II, the Nuremberg and Tokyo tribunals set the international standard for the convening of special courts to try cases of war crimes and crimes against humanity. These tribunals were initiated by, and governed under, the Nuremberg principles, whose primary purpose was to establish a set of guidelines for defining and identifying war crimes. Principle VI (b) defines war crimes as:

> Violations of the laws or customs of war which include but are not limited to, murder, ill-treatment or deportation of slave labor or for any other purpose the civilian population of or in occupied territory; murder or ill-treatment of prisoners of war or person on the Seas, killing of hostages, plunder of private or public property, wanton destruction of cities, towns or villages or devastation not justified by military necessity.

While these principles were designed *post hoc* to try German Nazi and Japanese Imperial leaders they form the bedrock of later United Nations and the International Criminal Court's definitions.

Following the Nuremberg principles, a complex set of definitions and rules of warfare were codified. Today, the term "war crime" typically refers directly to a violation of the *The United Nations Convention for the Amelioration of the Condition of the Wounded and Sick in Armed Forces in the Field* and its attendant protocols. These laws are applicable to every state, as recognition by the United Nations requires ratification of the UN Charter and the ratification by the applicant state of these conventions. Geneva governs the ways in which armed forces are allowed to operate within theaters of battle and occupied territories. Specific laws govern weapons and tactics, allowable targets, treatment of medical and religious personnel, the treatment of prisoners, and how an armed force is to interact with non-combatants.

For our purposes, the general rules of allowable targets are highly relevant, as most parties involved in the incidents target civilians and civilian areas. The rules of war also constrain the ways in which occupying forces are to administer, conquer and/or otherwise occupy territories. For example, an occupying force is not allowed to press civilians into labor, plunder, or loot the conquered territory. Any army must administer such resources in the best interests of the civilian population. While Geneva rests at the core of laws governing armed conflict, the twentieth century has seen wide expansions of this legal code, with new crimes being defined to cover gaps or vagaries within the Geneva Conventions.

Crimes against Humanity

The international arena's early attempts to develop humanitarian law during the nineteenth and early twentieth centuries wholly focused on war crimes. The term "crimes against humanity," however, originated in the 1907 Hague Convention preamble that codified extant customary law of armed conflict.[1] This was based on existing state practices derived from the values and principles deemed to constitute the laws of humanity (Bassiouni, 2006). After World War I, in connection with the 1919 Treaty of Versailles, and relying upon the 1907 Hague Convention, a commission to investigate war crimes was created. In addition to war crimes committed by the Germans, the commission also found that Turkish officials committed crimes against the laws of humanity for killing Armenian nationals and residents during the period of the war (Bassiouni 2006:2). Such investigations set the framework for legitimating the *idea* of an international criminal law; a process that was to become codified after the next global conflict.

In 1945, the United States and Allies developed the Agreement for the Prosecution and Punishment of the Major War Criminals of the European Axis and Charter of the International Military Tribunal (IMT), which defines and delineates crimes against humanity in Article 6(c). The Nuremberg Charter was the first document to establish the legal category of crimes against humanity in order to prosecute Nazis and Japanese warlords for the atrocities of World War II that were outside of the existing 1907 Hague Conventions. Acts like the Nazi Holocaust cried out for international legal action, but there was no international law to draw upon. As many of these actions were not committed by uniformed armed forces on the field of battle, existing war crimes laws did not hold jurisdiction.[2]

Initially crimes against humanity was an ad hoc concept developed in response to idiosyncratic sets of events; since, the category has, become one of the central bodies of International Criminal Law. Crimes against humanity have been included in the statutes of the International Criminal Tribunal for the former Yugoslavia (ICTY) and the International Criminal Tribunal for Rwanda (ICTR), and the Rome Statute of the International Criminal Court (ICC). Specifically, Article 7 of which states that crime against humanity means any of the following acts when committed as part of a widespread or systematic attack directed against any civilian population, with knowledge of the attack:

> (a) Murder; (b) Extermination; (c) Enslavement; (d) Deportation or forcible transfer of population; (e) Imprisonment or other severe deprivation of physical liberty in violation of fundamental rules of international law; (f) Torture; (g) Rape, sexual slavery, enforced prostitution, forced pregnancy, enforced sterilization, or any other form of sexual violence of comparable gravity; (h) Persecution against any identifiable group or collectivity on political, racial, national, ethnic, cultural, religious, gender; (i) Enforced disappearance of persons; (j) The crime of apartheid; (k) Other inhumane acts of a similar character intentionally causing great suffering, or serious injury to body or to mental or physical health.

Indeed crimes against humanity have come to "mean anything atrocious committed on a large scale" (Bassiouni, 2006:1). Further, this body of law governs the behaviors not only of states and state actors, but also of quasi-military bodies (e.g., militias), transnational organizations and of individuals.

Genocide

The term genocide was originally coined by Raphael Lemkin in 1933. Lemkin suggested a treaty should be created to make attacks on religious, ethnic, or national groups an international crime. He called this genocide: from the Greek word *genos*, meaning race or tribe, and *cide*, the Latin term for killing. Four years passed before genocide was recognized as an international crime by treaty. However, the legal foundation was first put in place during the 1945 Nuremberg Trials and subsequent Nuremberg Charter. Genocide was used in the indictment against the Nazi war criminals that stated that those accused "conducted deliberate and systematic genocide...the extermination of racial and national groups, against the civilian populations of certain occupied territories in order to destroy particular races and classes of people and national, racial or religious groups" (Orentlicher, 2006:2). Nuremberg prosecutors also invoked the term in their closing arguments. While the Nuremberg Charter did not use the term genocide per se, its definition of crimes against humanity was very close to the idea of genocide Lemkin proposed. The difference was the requirement of specific intent in the case of genocide, which is lacking in the definition of crimes against humanity.

In 1946, the United Nations General Assembly adopted a resolution establishing genocide as an international crime, defining genocide as "a denial of the right of existence of entire human groups, as homicide is the denial of the right to live of individual human beings" (Resolution 95 [1]). In 1948, *The Convention on the Prevention and Punishment of the Crime of Genocide* was adopted by the United Nations. Article 1 states that "the Contracting Parties confirm that genocide, whether committed in time of peace or in time of war, is a crime under international law which they undertake to prevent and to punish" (General Assembly resolution 260 A [III]). Thus genocide may be committed by an individual, group, or government, against one's own people or another, in peacetime or in wartime. This last point distinguishes genocide from "crimes against humanity," whose legal definition specifies wartime. Additionally, the Convention obligates state party members to "prevent and punish" genocide.[3]

Since its development in 1948 there has been a dearth of precedents that enforced the Convention. Specifically, it was not until the 1990s that the international arena prosecuted acts defined as genocide: the establishment of the 1993 International Criminal Tribunal for Yugoslavia and 1994 International Criminal Tribunal for Rwanda. In 1998, with the development of the Rome Statute, the crime of genocide was again reaffirmed as an international crime with the requirements of both a physical element (comprising certain enumerated acts) and a mental element (intent). Specifically, Article 5 of the ICC lists genocide (and crimes against humanity) as a crime of "most serious crimes of concern to the international community as a whole." Genocide is then defined in Article 6. Both the physical and mental requirements of the 1948 Convention were carried over and included in the Rome Statute.

Methodological Issues

Key issues with studying supranational crimes include (1) access to materials; (2) availability of resources; (3) availability of victims' accounts; and (4) an understanding of the totality of the event. No different than traditional street crime, the issue of knowing the actual numbers of victims and perpetrators can be problematic (Bijleveld 2007). As we know, with street crime there is a dark figure. Yet, criminologists attempt to get beyond this and attain estimates that are more reflective of crime by using, though imperfect, the multiple venues available (e.g., self report surveys, the U.S.'s National Crime Victimization Survey, and the British Crime Survey are well known examples). However, with international crimes this dark figure is a "doubly-dark figure" (Bijeveld, 2007: 4). In part this can be due to a state's unwillingness to disclose the information for multiple reasons, victims' desires to remain silent, lack of survivors, lack of pre-conflict census data, lack of post-conflict citizenry data, significant population displacements, and a score of other variables. As such, supranational criminologists must attempt to use multiple methods to make the doubly-dark figure of the crimes at best, a dark figure of the crimes. In part, this means attempting to find or arrive at a valid task of finding some sort of number precision.

The important task of counting the precise number of victims remains an arduous task, yet it is not only important but also speaks to the difficulty of quantitative methods for these types of crimes. For example, the death toll in Darfur has been estimated to be between 60,000 and 160,000, according to Deputy Secretary of State Robert B. Zoellick. However, the Coalition for International Justice[4] reports estimates near 400,000. The number of victims from the genocide in Rwanda is estimated at between 500,000 and 1,000,000. The mortality rate of Pakistan, due to the conflict in 1971 varies by a threefold variation, between one and three million and estimates of the death toll in Congo, between 1964 and 1965, vary tenfold (Bijeveld, 2007). As you can see, such figures display enormous variance leaving several problems. Such margins lend to the figures becoming at "best a mere statistic" (Bijeveld, 2007: 4). With these margins, the figures can also be trivialized or make it even easier for the perpetrators to use the uncertainty to dispute estimates as "overstatements" or "imprecise."

Further, finding a sound method to attain these statistics is important for prosecution and could include not only direct killings, rape, looting, and infrastructural destruction, but also deaths caused by specific groups indirectly. As Bijeveld (2007:6) noted,

> For Congo it was estimated that mortality due to preventable causes such as malnutrition and infectious diseases was many times the so-called 'direct mortality'.... famine and other preventable disasters are often used by governments as a cheap and efficient way to get rid of certain segments of the population. To establish this pattern is necessary to document and understand the patterns of gross human rights violations, as well as to be able to assess in what ways the scale of the damage could have been mitigated and can be mitigated in similar circumstances in the future.

There are various forms that can be used to attain statistics, no different than those used for traditional street crime, namely victim surveys. These have been used for estimating mortality. Yet, in situations of these types of crime, significant portions of the population may have left the country making it more difficult to account for the doubly-dark figures or if entire families have died such a method would underestimate mortality.

An additional barrier to attaining exact numbers or using victimization surveys is the inability to often go to the regions affected if the conflict is ongoing. Security issues can affect access to areas and thus the representativeness of the total numbers of victims. Further, some victims may not be willing to open up and share their experiences. This is often particularly the case with victims of genocidal rape.

An alternative method is collating information from several sources, also called triangulation. This can include using non-governmental organizations reports, United Nations Human Rights Commission Reports, other scholarly sources, and newspaper accounts (although this presents other problematic issues if used alone it can be used in combination with several other sources). Essentially, this includes combining many pieces of data to attain, (1) a more holistic view of the crimes; (2) arrive at some sort of "truth" through confirming and reconfirming information via several sources; and (3) repetition wherein you can feel confident you have received all available information. Nonetheless, we must acknowledge that this to can have limitations, namely that many of the reports that will be available may be regional or contain, as all research does, biases. With the case at hand this may be more a result of the emergency situation or the regional biases.

While we do not deny the importance of obtaining accurate counts of victims within such events, they are not essential to theorize these crimes. There are numerous other approaches to the study of atrocity, including case studies built upon media reports, survivor accounts, archival data, and court transcripts. Further, as the ICTR, ICTY, and now the ICC begin trying cases, they are secondarily producing a wealth of data in the form of intelligence analysis, victim testimony, and trial exhibits that can also be analyzed criminologically.

The Social Context

We now turn to a broad overview of the general social conditions that have produced widespread atrocities in the region and the most typical forms and elements these crimes take. Civil wars, genocides, and crimes against humanity do not merely appear; they are produced by a complex intersection of historical, social, political, economic, and cultural factors in a specific time and place. To fully understand the etiology of these phenomena, we must thoroughly understand the broader structural contexts out of which they emerge. We must also understand the basic forms which these events take. In this section, drawing on our broader work, we examine the macro-structural commonalities of Central African countries that developed into internecine conflicts resulting in international crimes. Specifically, we address a few of the common elements: global economics, social disorder, political instability, economic collapse, and ethnic tensions.

Global Economics

International commodity markets have been less than stable during the past five decades. Post-colonial African economies are fundamentally dependent upon export economies; fluctuations or collapses in specific commodity markets can have drastic effects on national and local economies. Compared to Western, and many Asian, economies, those of Central Africa are less diversified, which amplifies the influence of the drop in value of a given product on the economy as a whole. Such circumstances are typically a holdover result from the colonial period, where dominating powers set up colonial economies to be focused on the exportation of one or two commodities back to the "motherland." Political self-determination and international recognition of national sovereignty did nothing to alter existing economic organizations. For many African states, essential participation in international markets required maintenance of the old colonial cash-crop economies. For example, both Rwanda and Cote D'Ivoire suffered substantially due to the collapse of international coffee markets. As the price of coffee beans fell, peasants in the rural areas found their primary source of economic revenue tighten; states received less tax monies from this now debilitated sector of the economy. Such global forces enhance criminogenic factors experienced both by individuals in the poorer areas and the politico-social elites. Additionally, by the 1960s and 1970s these countries found themselves enmeshed in debtor relationships with institutions of international finance—the World Bank Group (WB)[5] and International Monetary Fund (IMF) and the states which head those organizations.

In return for debt reallocation or admission into forgiveness programs, the WB would demand that macro-structural political and economic changes occur within the debtor nations. Often the Bank also required recipient countries to adopt certain political measures, such as allowing multiple political parties to operate in a state, and also demand that state transfer publically owned property to private ownership.

Like the World Bank, the International Monetary Fund[6] is central in global economic development policies. Many international observers have been questioning the effectiveness of the remedies embodied in IMF-supported adjustment programs--especially those backed by the Enhanced Structural Adjustment Facility (ESAF), established in 1987 through which the IMF provides low-interest loans to poor countries with specific demands that must be followed. These policies are accompanied by specific requirements for the "borrowing" country (e.g., currency devaluations and/or pegging the value of a nation's currency to the value of another nation's currency, cuts in social programs and spending on civil works, opening state run industries to private, international investment). As noted by the IMF (1999:1), "some even described these remedies as part of the problem rather than the solution." In part, the remedies for countries' economic hardships are ideologically placed in a global capitalistic vacuum that ignores the primacy of citizens' human rights and the overall social, political, and economic health of a nation.

Political Instability

Political institutions are essential structural aspects of a society's macro-level conditions and often frame meso-level conditions. Post-colonial states often entered the world community with underdeveloped and ill-functioning social institutions. With indigenous lifeways subordinated, and to a large degree lost, during colonization and many aspects of the colonial order dismantled, newly independent peoples were confronted with having to rebuild a meaningful social order from the ground up, often with little to build upon. Political institutions simply have not been stable save under a one-party state which rules often through fear and force. Absolute control provides ample opportunity for the state or state actors to engage in criminal behaviors. Such states[7] often strongly benefit only a portion of the population. The nature and direction of control and stability is typically in the direction desired by the ruling elite. As long as the charismatic leader can control the military and structures of political authority, there is a veneer of stability and order. Yet, by these very policies, the seeds of discontent and insurrection are often sown by the processes that bring temporary stability—providing motivation for opposition groups that can be lured toward criminal behaviors or atrocities if seen as needed. As consequence of the nature of a one-party state, as well as the Western colonial model, many state actors became quickly corrupt, using the states' resources for their personal gain and that of their kin and allies (e.g., Amin and Obote in Uganda, Habyarimana in Rwanda, Bede in Cote D'Ivoire).

The history of central African political conflicts is filled not only with coups d'état, but counter-coups designed to remove despots from power. These wars too frequently become international affairs as opposition groups that initially fled the coup found safe haven in neighboring counties where they may have ethnic or linguistic ties. Given aid, training, arms and frequently supported by the harboring state's army, the refugee military forces reorganize, plan, and eventually execute an invasion (e.g., Rwandan Tutsi refugees and Museveni and the National Resistance Army in Uganda). Foreign powers often assist these groups directly or indirectly for several reasons (e.g., Sudan's support of Kony's Lord's Resistance Army and their fight against the standing government in Uganda). They may be just as apprehensive of the dictator as the refugee army is; if a leader will use systemic violence in all its forms against its own citizens, what promise can be made to satisfy a neighbor that the sovereignty of a shared border will be honored? Further, in light of the arbitrary nature of colonial territorial lines, and their reinforcement in the post-colonial period, the neighboring power may have strong ethnic or other cultural ties to the refuge population. Such connections often provide encouragement to get involved with a neighbor's internecine struggles.[8] Backing a neighboring rebel army can bring territorial or other natural resources to the sponsoring state. For example, Rwanda and Uganda both invaded the DRC, in part to obtain control over mineral rich areas of the DRC's northeastern territories (see Mullins and Rothe, 2008; Rothe and Mullins, 2006).

As political orders become less stable and more corrupt, existing social control mechanisms are reduced in their effectiveness. State-level law and law enforcement ceases to operate in any acceptable manner—it becomes little more than a tool of the social elite and is often turned towards political opponents.

Such conditions of impunity not only enhance opportunity for offending but can also provide additional motivation via the alteration of worldview of core actors within a criminal government or regional militia.

Economic Collapse

Economies in this region have been problematic throughout the last half of the twentieth century. Underdeveloped and overly controlled by foreign investment, local peoples, and institutions have difficult reaping the rewards of even a functional economy. Even where certain economic sectors (be they agrarian, mineral, or industrial) are healthy, the revenues are rarely spread through the entire population. Such cases typically can be traced back to colonial authorities' preferential treatment of one geographic area wherein monies and a strong economic foundation were seeded in a regionalized area at the expense of other regions within the country (e.g., Darfur, where the south was ignored in favor of the northern lands around the capitol). In other cases, economic collapse can be precipitated by ecological factors including desertification and long periods of drought bringing additional hardships and tensions to bear on an already tumultuous economic situation. Such factors enhance motivation for forming criminogenic groups as well as motivating the commission of atrocities themselves.

When state economies are overly controlled by foreign investors and/or the global market they are reliant upon the decision-making by commodity market leaders or foreign investors. When drastic fluctuations occur or when a commodity is forced to crash for economic gain of those in control of the market, weak economic states find themselves in dire conditions, socially and economically. Especially among those individuals living in communities involved in the production of the said commodity, such economic lapses increase both motivation toward criminal behavior and provide opportunity via the enhanced social disorder created and the illegitimate opportunity structures which frequently emerge. Such was the case with the coffee market crash in Rwanda that further facilitated the instability of the ruling regime and fueled already tense ethnic divisions (see Rothe, Mullins, and Sandstrom, 2008). Further, transnational corporations are often directly involved in black-market and/or illegal export and importing of state resources. As Human Rights Watch and the United Nations have reported, numerous transnational corporations have traveled to the Ituri region of the Democratic Republic of Congo to directly negotiate with warlords controlling the mines. From there, agreements are reached to transport the minerals across the border into Uganda, which then exports the minerals typically in the European markets and exchanges. Particularly, these strategies take advantage of the Swiss freeport system, which allows for the open and anonymous importation and sale of commodities from around the globe. Such activities exasperate the already tumultuous economic conditions of states.

Ethnic Tensions and Divisiveness

A central element within these atrocity-producing environments are a set of intense ethnic rivalries and tensions often—at least in the contemporary post-colonial environment—focused on resources access, be it political, social or economic. Despite the way in which these issues are typically covered in the media (e.g., as longstanding, pre-colonial disputes—see Western media coverage of Rwanda and Darfur), many of these nations did not begin their post-colonial experiences with deep divisions built along tribal or ethnic lines. While coloniz-ers in many cases (e.g., Rwanda and Burundi) drew arbitrary divisions amongst peoples and reinforced those splits via their political and economic policies, at the moment of liberation these tensions were rarely forefront in the society.

In the period leading up to the civil wars, and the associated crimes, political parties often played up these tensions in order to create a power base both within the governments and within the citizenry (see Rothe and Mullins 2007). Due to long periods of colonial domination, there were few natural lines along which political parties could be formed and fewer pre-existing bases of political power for a party to mobilize. In fact, the most "natural" divisions leading to party formation in newly democratic states was geographic in nature and rooted in the existing resource base (be those resources mineral, agricultural, or human capitals). While there was some general correspondence between peoples and territories, these early geographic divisions often cut across ethnic lines. The result was a political scene with dozens of parties possessing unarticulated goals, visions and motives. While all wanted a share of the new political power, a lack of general political drives, positions and ideologies produced hosts of parties indistinguishable from each other save by name. Such political hyper-plurality produced more disorganization than organization; many of these new governments were dissolved in coups d'état that established one-party states, that exacerbated the increasingly important ethnic divides to cement power (e.g., Rwanda and Cote D'Ivoire). Motivated to maintain power, leaders often began to generate public discourses of racial and ethnic differences and exclusion. Identity became a political tool to stabilize a government and as these states weakened under their own weight of corruption inefficiency, ethnicity became a polarizing force dividing the societies as they moved toward violent civil wars or, in the case of Rwanda and the Sudan, genocide.

Scholars of genocides and other war crimes have long pointed toward the "otherizing" effects of ethnic polarization and dehumanization as facilitating violence in general and wide-spread lethal violence in particular. Just as colonial powers dehumanized the peoples of Africa to legitimate colonial domination, ethnic groups dehumanized each other facilitating political and economic sub-ordination as well as wanton violence and destruction (e.g., Rwanda Hutus). Such divisions operate on the micro level to facilitate the wide-spread abuse and slaughter of targeted peoples. In ethnic-otherizing processes the humanity is removed from the targeted group which in turn facilities and legitimates violence against them. Ethnic polarization and identity creation processes are central in militia formation as well. At the international level the discourse serves to negate the responsibility of political and social authorities for creating, stimulating and continuing the conflict.

Conclusion

In this chapter we have provided a general overview of supranational criminology, the law that governs the acts, and a brief overview of common macro social elements that aid in or produce the offences. By bringing mass atrocities to criminological attention, we hope to not only more full explore the boundaries of the discipline itself but shine light on the nature of these mass violations of human life, security and dignity. While these crimes may be more difficult to study than other crimes, there are still numerous ways to gather and analyze data on these atrocities. Complex statistical analyses are not yet possible, but the compilation of data from existing sources provides hope for such work in the future.

Criminology as a disciple has shied away from the study of atrocity. Its self-definition has long been focused on street crimes and policies designed to curtail them. We see this as highly problematic. If criminology as a discipline cannot explain the worst crimes that humans commit, then it is not living up to its stated agenda. By bringing a criminological focus to these crimes we cannot only better understand the etiology of these events, we can better assess potential control modalities to reduce or eliminate future atrocities. In many ways, that is a much more essential task than mere academic explanation. Anything that can potentially reduce the amount of harm done by these crimes is well worth the effort and will go a long way to bringing more justice into the world.

Notes

1. The earliest use of the term we are aware of comes from the writings George Washington Williams, a minister and social critic who visited the Congo in 1890 (see Hochschild, 1998; Franklin, 1985).
2. While the creation and implementation of these tribunals violated many of the basic principles of Common and Continental Legal systems, especially *post hoc* prosecutions, this violation of basic legal human rights was largely ignored by the international political community due to the widespread pressure to bring war criminals to justice. Since, international tribunals have attended more closely to human rights issues, especially of *post hoc* and due process concerns (see Zappala, 2003).
3. This obligation is moral, not legal. As Bosnia, Kosovo, Rwanda, Burundi, East Timor, and Darfur have all shown, there is no real legal compulsion to intervene and no real consequences for ignoring a genocide in progress.
4. The Coalition for International Justice is a Washington-based nongovernmental organization that was hired by the United States Agency for International Development to try to determine whether the killing in Darfur amounted to genocide. The coalition also concluded that 142,944 people may have been killed by government forces or allied militias, the main groups ravaging the civilian population.

5. The World Bank is not a "bank" in the commonly-used sense of the term. Rather, it is a specialized financial agency, composed of 184 member countries. The World Bank, conceived during World War II, initially helped rebuild Europe after the war. Once its original mission of postwar European reconstruction was finished, the World Bank turned its lending practices to development issues. While its rhetoric is often focused on human rights, human dignity and infrastructure development, its operational concerns strongly focus on producing returns for investors and spreading the ideology of neo-liberal capitalist markets. Through the 1970s and 1980s, debtor nations were frequently unable to meet repayment demands. Therefore, during the 1980s, the Bank went through an extensive period focused on macroeconomic and debt rescheduling issues.

6. The International Monetary Fund is also composed of 184 member countries and is headquartered in Washington, D.C. It was established in 1945 to promote international monetary cooperation, to foster economic growth and to provide temporary financial assistance to needy countries. The IMF "is the central institution of the international monetary system—the system of international payments and exchange rates among national currencies" (IMF, 2006). Since the IMF was established, its above stated purposes have remained unchanged, but its operations such as surveillance (a dialogue among its members on the national and international consequences of their economic and financial policies), financial assistance (loans), and technical assistance (structural adjustment policies) have changed throughout its history.

7. The use of the term state may be questioned, as in some cases explored here; the organization which claims statehood only qualifies as such due to international recognition at the UN. Some would suggest the term "government" be used instead to indicate the limited and weak nature of the political apparatus. Additionally, the concept of state crime used broadly suggests the omission of militia behaviors within a case wherein the state is also actively engaged in illegal activities. As such, we consider both to be organizational offenders.

8. Such involvements are also different from interventions led by the international political society as the motivation for the intervener is directly for that state's (or that state's elite's) benefit. UNSC and other interventions are more complex with many more factors than self interest occasionally guides participants.

Part 2

Perspectives in Criminal Justice

7

Radical and Critical Criminology's Treatment of Municipal Policing

Jeffrey Ian Ross

Municipal policing in advanced industrialized countries is searching for a new paradigm. Traditional methods of administration, investigation, and patrol are often criticized for being outdated and ineffective, and the latest of experiments, community policing and Compstat, are encountering strong skepticism and even opposition in some policing circles and beyond.

This situation does not bode well for the current practice and future of law enforcement. What then shall we do to improve this state of affairs? We could conduct a multitude of studies, but there is no guarantee, however, that this information will be disseminated and integrated into the daily policies and practices of our police departments. Short of this option, among a variety of recommendations, perhaps the time is ripe to reexamine the ideological[1] foundations of policing research, writing, and commentary (hereafter research) to see if there are additional insights that can be gleaned in order make appropriate recommendations for changes in policing. Ideological biases, if left unchecked, produce poor or misguided policies and practices.

Policing is administered at different levels of government (i.e., federal, state/provincial, regional, etc.), but since the majority of people live in urban locales, municipal (or urban) policing is perhaps the most important type of law enforcement. Moreover, numbers alone justify the focus on local police officers and departments. In sum, there are more municipal police forces/officers[2] than state/provincial and federal forces in advanced industrialized countries, especially in Canada, the United Kingdom, and the United States.

Given the importance of this body of work for our understanding of law enforcement, I will briefly review the literature on municipal policing in these three Anglo-American democracies by arguing that it can be classified into three types; critique each of these approaches; and then suggest how a radical/critical[3] interpretation of the policing enterprise might be improved.

The Three Ideological Approaches to Municipal Policing

Introduction

Because of its applied and practitioner-oriented nature, theoretical studies of policing are rare (Leo, 1996). Certainly there are theories of police organization, behavior, and management (e.g., Bowker, 1980; Wilson, 1963, 1968; Worden; 1989; Worden and Brandl, 1990), but these are usually derived from the larger public administration/policy, and organization theory literature.[4]

Those interested in ideological approaches to law enforcement must infer it from the broad corpus of writing and research on policing. This literature can probably be divided into three categories: conservative/traditional, liberal/reformist, and radical/critical. Although conservative and liberal approaches to understanding policing abound, the radical/critical interpretations of policing are rarely employed and these approaches are generally unintegrated and/or marginalized in the study of law enforcement. To better understand this classification, I briefly review each subtype in terms of six factors: types of studies, their focus, where it has been disseminated, kinds of research methods utilized, their contribution to the literature, and difficulties with this approach.

Conservative/Traditional Literature

The majority of policing research and commentary is characterized primarily by its functionalistic and organizational behavior orientation (especially through its public administration and policy linkages). The conservative/traditional perspective basically argues that the way we currently practice policing is fine and/or suggests that the way we used do it is somewhat preferable. Predictably, this work is often written by current or retired police officers, trainers, or administrators.

Although a thorough content analysis of policing research has yet to be performed, with few exceptions, a healthy dose of the conservative/traditional approach can be found in the (now defunct) *Journal of Police Science and Administration*, *Canadian Police College Journal*, the United Kingdom-based *Policing*, and currently operating practitioner-oriented magazines such as *Police Chief* and *Law and Order*.

Additionally, with few exceptions, the majority of introductory textbooks on policing reflect a conservative bias. Classic books, such as Vollmer's *The Police and Modern Society* and O. W. Wilson and McLaren's *Police Administration*, fit the conservative/traditional model. This type of literature was typical of pre 1960s policing research and continues in most police learning contexts during the 1990s.

Even though understanding policing from this perspective is important, this approach suffers from a number of drawbacks. Much of this literature consists of descriptions of police activities, with occasional use of quantitative methods, in particular surveys, and leaves little room for analytical discussion. The conservative approach also tends to be either too narrow in focus, outdated, ethnocentric, primarily concerned with maintaining the status quo (vis-à-vis the power of the police to identify problems and propose and implement their own solutions), and/or improving the efficiency of policing. In short, the conservative approach also prevents students and observers from critically understanding and analyzing the police.

One reason why the conservative/traditional approach persists is because it is anathema to the typical undergraduate or current police officer, pursuing a degree either at the community college or university level, to challenge prior held beliefs they might have about the nature of policing. Concurrently, very often instructors in these environments are current or retired police personnel who have a vested interest in maintaining the real or imagined symbolic integrity of police departments and organizations.

Liberal/Reformist Literature

The liberal/reformist approach recognizes that the police have a difficult job to perform, and hence are a "necessary evil."[5] Solutions are aimed at improving police performance, by increasing efficiency, and improving recruitment and training procedures through the hiring of more visible minorities and women, by requiring longer police academy training, and advanced education, including bachelor's degrees. Five constituencies have concerned themselves with reforming the police: researchers, policy makers, police administrators, segments of the public, and activists.

By far the greatest concentration of liberal/reformist research on municipal policing was disseminated through three academic journals: the American-based (but now defunct) *Police Studies: The International Review of Police Development* (established in 1978), *American Journal of Police* (established in 1985) now consolidated as *Policing: An International Journal*, and the British based journal *Police and Society* (established in 1991).

Some of this literature has been reprinted, in whole or in part, as chapters in introductory readings books on the police (e.g., Klockars and Mastrofski, 1991; Kappeler, 1995; Dunham and Alpert, 1997). Occasionally some textbooks will have a liberal orientation (e.g., Berg, 1992; Alpert and Dunham, 1997; Walker, 1977; Robert and Kuykendall, 1993).

Moreover, during the 1960s, 1970s, and 1980s a number of academics (e.g., Banton, 1964; Skolnick, 1966; Wilson, 1968; Niederhoffer, 1969; Bittner, 1970; Goldstein, 1977; Muir, 1977; Klockars, 1985; Brown, 1988) wrote what can now probably be considered the classic liberal/reformist books on municipal policing. Additionally, we can probably characterize the reports produced by a litany of government inquiries, from the Lexow committee to the Mollen and Christopher commission findings as liberal/reformist tracts.

This research has focused on police deviance, patrol, cynicism, organization, change, control, discretion, police-community relations, and police and their families. It utilized reviews of the literature, personal experience, field ethnography, thick description, formal and informal interviews, and questionnaires/surveys conducted with police officers and administrators. It was performed in a variety of municipalities but primarily in the United States.

This body of work reflects the social and economic turbulence of its time, which provided fertile ground for understanding the racial, ethnic, and social parameters of policing urban communities. Some of this work was descriptive (e.g., Wilson, 1968), some was loosely causal in explaining why police behave as they do (.e.g., Brown, 1988). Still other researchers ventured into the area of theory development (e.g., Muir, 1977). During this time, the liberal/reformist approach was an improvement upon the conservative/traditional literature.

The liberal/reformist approach has sensitized a broad constituency to the need to reform the law enforcement profession and organization. It also presented a less biased understanding of the policing enterprise than was produced by conservative policing writers.

However, by today's standards this work can be criticized on its limited methodological sophistication; some of the samples from which researchers generalized were extremely small (e.g., Niederhoffer, 1969), and some of the ethnographies were conducted over an extremely short time period (e.g., Skolnick, 1966). Additionally, liberal/reformist research rarely advocates the use of alternative mechanisms (e.g., reform of criminal laws) that can accomplish many of the same goals (i.e., formal social control) that police are established to perform. It suggests that with some minor tinkering, the present system of law enforcement can be improved.

Frustration with both the conservative/traditional and liberal/reformist approaches generated a different ideological perspective.

Radical/Critical Literature

In essence, the radical/critical approach argues that modern-day policing has origins in private policing, which was established and continues to be for the protection of upper-class or elite individuals and their property. Inevitably this mission included "maintaining order" and controlling the lower and so-called dangerous classes (especially the poor, the disenfranchised, and the working class).

Additionally, police department policies and practices are not necessarily developed or sanctioned in consultation with the citizenry or street level officers; but because police departments are hierarchical paramilitary organizations, policy generally flows from the top management down and it is left to the individual line officers to interpret. This means that police are too often forced to break the law in support of the organization's mission. To radical/critical criminologists, this is robustly evident in the policing of strikes, racial riots, and student protests, and street stops. In these situations, police officers must maintain order and control (Van Maanen, 1978). According to radical/critical criminologists, police use a liberal/reformist interpretation of "reasonable use of force," and probable cause to accomplish this goal.

It should be acknowledged that the radical/critical approach is not monolithic. In other words, there is a considerable degree of diversity not only within the radical/critical area but inside its subcomponents. Marxists, for example, may be categorized into instrumentalists, structuralists, feminists, and so on.[6] Today a variety of interesting perspectives can be subsumed under this domain including, but not limited to postmodernism, left realism, feminism, and peacemaking criminology.

It is not easy distinguishing among literature written from a radical/critical perspective, research that others perceive to be aligned with a radical/critical perspective, and literature that is of interest to radical/critical criminologists. To be critical of the police or the conservative/traditional and liberal/reform literature and law enforcement practices does not necessarily mean that an individual and/or his/her work endorses radical/critical criminology. Many of the liberal/reformist analysts of the police are clearly critical of police practice, but their work falls short of using radical/critical criminology methods of analysis. For instance, Williams and Murphy (1990) suggest that Kelling and Moore's (1988) mainstream reading of police history is "disturbingly incomplete. It fails to take account of how slavery, segregation, discrimination, and racism have affected the development of American police department—and how these factors have affected the quality of policing in the nation's minority communities" (p. x).

Often there is the misperception that analyzing policing from a symbolic interactionist or social-action perspective amounts to taking a radical/critical perspective. This direction, tracing its roots to the "social construction of reality" approach (Berger and Luckmann, 1966), using ethnographic methods, has been used to understand police interactions with citizens, amongst themselves (Ericson, 1982; Manning, 1978), with police dispatchers (Manning, 1988), with the media (Ericson, Baranek and Chan, 1989: chapter 3), and police undercover work (Marx, 1980, 1981).

Although a small body of research has been conducted using this approach (e.g., Manning, Ericson), it is a research method, much as Liseral is a tool to measure the causal direction of effect. Additionally, examining policing from a journalistic or muckraking perspective, while important, does not provide the necessary analytic framework that would be characterized by the radical/critical perspective.

A piece of research is from the radical/critical perspective if it either uses, advocates, or tests a class analysis of policing; uses or tests the notion that policing is a manifestation of extreme power differentials; draws heavily on other radical/critical authors to support its argument or approach; recommends other forms of social control, formal or informal, to supplant law enforcement's intended mission (e.g., Black, 1980: chapter 6); and/or suggests the abolishment of law enforcement.

Since the late 1960s, there has been a steady production of radical/critical criminological treatments of urban policing. More often than not, radical/critical analyses of the police are found in journal articles (especially *Crime and Social Justice* and *Social Problems*), and chapters in books. Entire monographs devoted to a radical/critical analysis of the police are rare. The radical/critical pursuit has primarily been an American enterprise and it is only occasionally that British and Canadian researchers take this approach. Nevertheless, this body of work can be organized into two categories of topics: overviews, and specific studies.

Overviews

A number of studies present a broad overview of the radical/critical approach to policing then make a number of suggestions for improving research or policy. The purpose of this type of work, is to take stock of what radical/critical criminologists understand about policing, synthesize and categorize this information, offer a cohesive picture of this approach, and suggest directions for future research. Three authors accomplish this goal (Marenin, 1982; Das, 1983; Manning, 1974, 1979, 1988).

Although these works provide quick introductions to this body of work, primarily because of their brevity, these pieces do not capture the entire corpus of radical/critical research on policing. Additionally, none of these overviews tries to make cogent recommendations to policy audiences. Finally, these pieces are now dated.

Specific Topics

More common is research which focuses on a specific issue relevant to police that uses a radical or critical criminological perspective. This literature clusters into four areas, listed here in increasing order of scholarly output: the coercive capacity of the police, working conditions of police, police violence, and police history.

Coercive Capacity of the Police. The growth in the number of police officers per capita, increased law enforcement expenditures, and sustained public attention concerning police use of deadly force, has been interpreted by many radical/critical scholars as indicators of the nature and extent of the coerciveness of law enforcement officers. The bulk of studies examining the relations among these factors derive their hypotheses from conflict theory, and use sophisticated inferential statistical techniques (Jacobs, 1979; Jackson and Carrol, 1981; Nalla, Lynch, and Leiber, 1996; Jacobs and Helms, 1977; Jacobs and O'Brien, 1998).

The majority of this research is limited to the United States. Unfortunately, there is nothing in the literature to suggest that states and cities as the unit of analysis are an important indicator of inequality. Perhaps smaller jurisdictions (e.g., neighborhoods) are more relevant in terms of looking at inequality and police coerciveness.

Working Conditions of Police Officers. Radical/critical analysts have examined the increasing routinization of police work, reactions to the introduction of women on police departments, the de-radicalization of policing, and the class position of the police in the context of trade unionism. Five works fall under this categorization (Harring, 1981b; Hunt, 1990; Robinson, 1978; Reiner, 1978a, 1978b). This research has used archival materials, patrol observation, interviews, review of personnel files, and a critical analysis of extant literature.

Much of this research depicts a profession with worsening working conditions and hostile to women entering and staying in the field. It also documents "the contradictory place of the police in the class structure" (Reiner, 1978a). If radical change in policing is going to take place, some of these authors argue it will be over "bread and butter" issues and not any sort of class consciousness. Unfortunately, this work suffers from arrested development. Some of it is two decades old. It is also limited to a handful of police departments or countries.

Police Violence. Police violence and police paramilitarism has been a focus of attention for radical/critical analysts of the police.[7] Several independent variables have been examined as correlates of police violence, including violent crime rates, number of riots, change in population, inequality at the state level, racial and economic composition at the state level, and the rise of paramilitary policing both in the United Kingdom and United States.

Seven separate pieces of research fall under this rubric (Jacobs and Britt, 1979; Chamlin, 1989; Jefferson, 1987; Chambliss, 1994; Kraska, 1996; Kraska and Cubelis, 1997; Kraska and Kappeler, 1997). Much like radical/critical research on the coercive capacity of police, the lion's share of this research uses sophisticated quantitative techniques, some relying on official statistics, while others use surveys, with occasional case study analysis.

Police History. By far the most dominant types of studies from a radical/critical perspective are historical descriptive analyses. This body of work is generally country-specific and either is general in subject matter or focuses on municipal policing in the United Kingdom, Canada, and the United States. Some of the historical material tests Monkkonen's (1981) four theories (i.e., disorder, crime control, urban dispersion, and class control) to explain the development and growth of police departments. Other work is more descriptive of early policing from a radical/critical perspective. All of this research depends on the use of extant written documents, including archival materials (e.g., newspapers). This approach can be divided into two categories: general historical overviews and country specific research in Canada, the United Kingdom, and the United States.

First, several authors have supplied general historical overviews. A considerable amount of scholarship on the early development of policing in general (e.g., Philips, 1980) or in particular countries and cities (e.g., Lowe, 1984; Sharpe, 1980) has been produced. The majority of it documents the class nature of policing, but does not use per se a radical/critical analysis of law enforcement during this time period. Three exceptions to this state of affairs exist, which can be characterized as general historical overviews that document the rise of policing using a radical/critical analysis (Spitzer, 1993; Robinson and Scaglion, 1987; Robinson, Scaglion, and Olivero, 1994).

Second, country/city specific historical research has been conducted. With respect to historical studies of the rise of policing in Canada[8] in general, the underlying current in the historical analyses of processes in Canadian urban police forces seems to be evenly divided between examinations of the class-control and disorder control theses (Marquis, 1987; Boritch and Hagan, 1987). One of the pieces depends on a careful analysis of archival police records. The other uses police arrest practices and analysis of vice bylaws as categories of public order arrests. Most Canadian research that examines the class control thesis focuses on Toronto, which not only has one of the oldest police forces in Canada, but also a location where the greatest concentration of academics live and work.

Third, we have historical studies on the rise of policing in the United Kingdom. Three articles have been written from a radical/critical perspective (Silver, 1966; Robinson, 1979; Cohen, 1979). They discuss the class underpinnings of the emergence of police. Much of this is descriptive, depending on a careful reading of books, reports, and articles over a century old. Most English research on the rise of class-based policing focuses on London.

Fourth, the historical study of the rise of policing in the United States is divided between broad overviews and case studies of particular cities. A handful of sophisticated case studies from a radical/critical perspective on the rise of class control policing in selected cities in the United States have been produced (e.g., Harring and McMullin, 1975; Harring, 1982). The majority of these integrate an analysis of the urban power structure, the class backgrounds of the police forces, and the social histories—particularly of labor unrest, vagrancy, drunkenness, and workers' communities within the particular cities.

Four broad overviews of the rise of municipal policing have been written (Harring, 1976; Stretcher, 1991; CRCJ, 1977/1982; Harring, 1981a). Most lament the "ahistorical nature of most police history" (Harring, 1976). These authors present convincing evidence supporting the view that the police are and have always been a branch of government whose mission is to enforce the dominant power agenda. They suggest that the rise in the number of police departments and increase in the number of officers in existing forces in the United States was a product of class struggle.

Class bias usually manifests itself in six areas: controlling strikes; maintaining public order; policing working-class recreational activities (chiefly alcohol-related); controlling tramps and vagrants and unemployed members of the working class; monitoring vice, chiefly gambling and prostitution; and controlling most common types of felony crimes, the so-called "street crimes" (p. 557). Harring buttresses his arguments through analysis of the activities of the Buffalo, Chicago, Cleveland, Cincinnati, and Milwaukee police departments. Despite the considerable productivity in this area, the historical work does not look at policing cross-culturally or cross-nationally. Nevertheless, the historical approach best lends itself to a class analysis of policing.

Summary. Radical/critical approaches to municipal policing have advanced our thinking about the proper role of this publicly funded institution and provided an alternative conceptualization of law enforcement and the control of illegality. They have used a plethora of methods, from quantitative to qualitative, ranging from sophisticated interpretive statistics to field ethnographies to archival research.

However, radical/critical analyses of the police have a number of shortcomings, which include ignoring psychological factors, failing to adequately account for policing minority communities and policing by minorities, ignoring the radical/critical potential of community policing; neglecting to separate public from private policing; and failing to address the suitability of a class analysis for contemporary policing.

Quite understandably, the radical/critical perspective of policing is frequently criticized on its theoretical/ideological assumptions (Klockars, 1993). To begin with, psychological (i.e., individual-level mental processes) and structural (i.e., the economy, race/class, and gender) factors play a major role in the organization of policing. By focusing almost entirely on the structural factors, radical/critical analysts of the police take a narrow approach to their subject. For instance, structural factors, such as who is hired (particularly lower class and lower middle-class males) might be appropriate background reasons to explain how law enforcement agencies function. They do not, however, touch on the more subtle and intricate reasons of how decisions are made or implemented.

Additionally, a radical/critical approach to minority (visible or not) and female recruitment is lacking. This issue is inextricably linked to the examination of why certain individuals remain employed by police forces and others quit or are terminated. Noticeably absent, in this context, are feminist approaches to studying the police. Moreover, one of the more common questions periodically proposed is whether community policing is or can be a radical/critical approach?

With the current trend of paying lip service to communities, this question should have some appeals for conservatives, liberals, and radicals alike.

Furthermore, many of the writers merge both public and private police together or use broad definitions of the police in their analysis. Marenin (1982), for instance, suggests that "the police are the privately and publicly employed guardians of interest who are enlisted to use force to do whatever needs doing" (p. 252). Likewise, Spitzer (1993) argues that "policing will not be examined as a limited set of actions by a group of public (or even private) officials. It will be understood, rather, as a pattern of social development through which coercive regulation is established, decomposed, and recomposed in class societies" (p. 571). This makes the concept of the police and the practice of policing somewhat nebulous by minimizing conceptual clarity.

Also neglected is a radical/critical analysis of where and how police departments are funded. Understanding the resource base of law enforcement agencies is important to getting a sense of priorities concerning who is policed and why. Finally, although a class analysis may have been appropriate for the nineteenth- and twentieth-century policing, it is perhaps irrelevant today. As policing has changed considerably since the 1920s, a more state-centric theory, as Marenin suggests, could be applied. Given these difficulties, no wonder the theoretical/ideological and policy relevance of the radical/critical perspective is often neglected or marginalized in policing research and practice.

Conclusion

Some criminologists have argued that not only policing in general, but the radical/critical analysis of law enforcement can benefit from understanding policing in other countries and cultural contexts, particularly if these states have low crime rates or are experimenting with interesting programs. Marenin (1982), for instance, argues that "[t]he most useful methodological impact of critical thought on positivist science has been the resurrection of comparative research" (p. 245).

Knowledge about comparative policing (i.e., what happens in other countries)[9] can deepen our understanding, appreciation, and criticism of American and foreign police policies and practices. Comparative policing describes and (in many cases) explains the role of the police in different cultural, economic, ideological, and political contexts (e.g., Bailey, 1985; Findlay and Zvekic, 1993). Understanding these differences is crucial if we are to present a nonethnocentric view of policing.[10] Par of the answer to improving policing can be derived from how the profession has evolved and is practiced in other countries and cultural contexts.

This pursuit also calls attention to important gaps in our knowledge. For example, few police scholars or administrators really know what policing is or was like in socialist or communist countries? Efforts to design, implement and practice policing in such places as post-revolutionary China, Cuba, and Nicaragua where new models of humanistic concern were alleged to have developed, and where new types of policing were said to flourish, are poorly understood by academics, policymakers, and police professionals of all ideological stripes.

This approach is gaining more urgent support as our population diversifies and we police people with diverse cultural, ethnic, national, and racial backgrounds. If, in fact, less coercive methods of policing have been implemented in other societies, then this time they should be incorporated or at least experimented within the police departments of advanced industrialized democracies. Needless to say, this sentiment, however, is underscored by the understanding that comparative policing, while recognized as being important, is marginalized in typical American criminology/criminal justice departments (Ross, 1996).

During the 1990s and into the new century, policing will be affected by a number of current trends including: the so-called war on drugs, hate crime, the increasing transnational character of policing, and the fiscal crisis of the state. With the state's greater attention toward the use and sale of illegal drugs, and crime connected to that trade, police have found their roles change. This has led to an increase in emergency response SWAT teams, and the militarization of policing (Kraska, 1996; Kraska and Cubellis, 1997; Kraska and Kappeler, 1997). Although actions we now call hate crimes have existed since the dawn of time, since its criminalization, many big city police departments have developed teams or organizational units that monitor and arrest individuals with hate crimes. Policing expertise has become another commodity that continues to be imported and exported. For example, the United States and United Nations are sending police officers abroad in connection with multinational policing efforts, to police troubled areas (e.g., Haiti, Somalia, and Bosnia-Herzegovia). Additionally, the United States, through the Department of Justice's International Criminal Investigative and Training Assistance Program (ICITAP) is training police in a variety of countries.

Exploration of these areas will improve not only our general understanding of policing but also the radical/critical pursuit. The lion's share of radical/critical research has been published in academic journals, and rarely cited beyond radical/critical circles, a testimony of its marginalization in the field of policing, criminology/criminal justice, and beyond. As this chapter has argued, the radical/critical approach to policing is significant. Its place is central to any conceptualization of police and formal social control, and may actually help municipal policing reach the next paradigm.

Acknowledgements. Special thanks to Natasha J. Cabrera and Michael Vaughn for comments on this chapter.

Notes

1. Although some would argue with me, I do not separate theoretical from ideological interpretations.

2.   All future references to policing will imply municipal or urban policing.
3.   Although the author recognizes that there are subtle differences between radical and critical approaches, for ease of expression he amalgamates the two as radical/critical.
4.   Muir's (1977) statement on police use of coercion has been called a theory (e.g., Klockars, 1985: chapter 6) but I believe that it falls short of what many academics would classify as a theory. For an analysis of the paucity of theory in criminal justice see, for example, Hagan (1989).
5.   A related position, advocated by Menzies (1995), is responsible humanism.
6.   Albeit rarely does radical or critical approaches to the police the only exception I could find was Tift and Sullivan (1980) who suggest that "Anarchist utopias envision a society in which policing is interested only in protection; where the state has yielded to the cooperative efforts of all which promote peaceful interactions and progress. Policing is neither required or if deviance occurs, its correction is the responsibility of all" (Tift and Sullivan, 1980).
7.   There is a perception that radical and critical criminologists feel comfortable to use the term police violence. Those with strong connections to state funded agencies prefer to use the more neutral sounding term "police use of excessive force."
8.   For a review of the research on the history of municipal policing in Canada see, for example, Ross (1995).
9.   In general, research on comparative policing falls into two categories: descriptions and analyses of selected police departments outside of the United States, and theoretically based comparisons of two or more police systems selected based on some logical criteria. There is an abundance of the former type of research and a dearth of the latter. I argue for a greater emphasis on both approaches but with an emphasis on theoretically based comparisons.
10.   For a discussion of the obstacles in teaching a course like this see, for example, Ross (1996).

8

A House Divided:
Corrections in Conflict

Angela West Crews

In the first edition of this book, Michael Welch (1998) offered readers an alternative view of corrections within a social control context and distinguished between the text (rhetoric) and subtext (underlying principle) of American corrections. Welch argued that American society is increasingly reliant on the criminal justice system to deal with individuals who need to be managed (i.e., controlled). Due to correlations between unemployment, poverty, substance use and addiction, and the likelihood of incarceration, prisons and jails become storage facilities for poor, unemployed persons with significant substance abuse problems, and who most likely represent minority (black, Hispanic, native American) populations.

From a critical perspective, the rise in incarceration (as of 1998) clearly was a byproduct of the state's increasing reliance on corrections as *social control*. Welch stressed, however, that the "new penology" portrayed growing numbers of prisoners as a tactic of *crime control*. With an emphasis on actuarial assessment of risk, rather than on addressing problems (i.e., addictions, employment needs, education), the new penology incarcerated more and more members of "dangerous" and "high-risk" groups, who ended up being primarily young, poor, minority males who were under- or unemployed, and under- or uneducated. Essentially, the emphasis of the new penology was on potential crime control *through* social control.

In 1998, Welch cited statistics from Mauer and Huling (1995) that one in every three young (20-29 years old) black males was under some form of correctional control. Today, one in eight young black males is in *prison* or *jail* (Pew Center on the States, 2008), and if current trends continue, one in every three black men born today will be *imprisoned* (Bonczar, 2003). Hispanics also are increasingly being disproportionately sentenced to prison or jail, currently representing about 21 percent of the incarcerated population (Sabol, Couture and Harrison, 2007).

Welch and I share similar purposes in writing our respective chapters in *Cutting the Edge*. We both examine policies related to corrections, especially to incarceration. We both critique the ability of critical perspectives to impact those policies. We both advocate the development of alliances among critical criminologists and others to counter the overwhelming impact of conservative ideologies about crime and punishments. Finally, we both emphasize the critical perspective that social problems (lack of education, poverty, unemployment, economic and social inequality) are the primary contributors to crime and that failure to address these factors has (and continues to) drive incarcerated populations and incarceration rates upward.

I provide an extension of Welch's arguments by discussing some impediments to the effectiveness of critical policy (especially related to corrections). I also argue that incarceration as a policy response to criminal behavior and conditions of confinement are in desperate need of attention and action, not just from critical criminologists, but from anyone with an interest in social justice and humanity. Finally, I briefly review a couple of potentially promising developments, grounded in critical philosophy, that have been somewhat influential in correctional practice.

This chapter focuses on corrections (primarily prisons), but it is impossible to discuss corrections apart from the other components of the criminal justice system. The creation, enforcement, and administration of law obviously affect correctional policies, procedures, and outcomes. Less obvious, however, is that correctional policies, procedures, and outcomes affect the creation, enforcement, and administration of law.

It also is impossible to discuss corrections apart from society. The criminal justice system operates as an extension of society, ostensibly representing it in the following ways:

- by defining unacceptable behavior (legislation);
- by designating representatives to detect unacceptable behavior (law enforcement);
- by dictating the processes through which behavior will be adjudicated (courts);
- by devising responses to the commission of unacceptable behavior (punishment); and
- by developing rules to guide procedures throughout the system (policy).

Any critique of corrections must be circumscribed by an awareness of and appreciation for the larger systemic and societal contexts. What corrections does or does not do significantly impacts the system and society. Conversely, what the system and society does or does not do significantly impacts corrections.

This chapter affirms a critical commitment to social change, various types of which have been advocated at various times and to various degrees by various scholars (e.g., Barak, 1998; Braithwaite, 1989, 2002; Chambliss and Seidman, 1971; Davis, 2003, 2005; Marx and Engels, 1848/1992; Michalowski, 1996; Pepinsky and Quinney, 1991; Ross, 1998). On a micro-level, I examine incarceration and prisoner release, reentry, and recidivism, as examples in corrections wherein change is crucial, not only for the criminal justice system and corrections, but also for humanity. Finally, I discuss a couple of encouraging signs that critical criminologists are having some policy impact.

Correctional Policy and Practice: A House Divided?

During a campaign speech in 1858, Abraham Lincoln, who became the sixteenth president of the United States, paraphrased Jesus Christ (Matthew 12:25) and warned that "a house divided against itself cannot stand." Although Lincoln was referring to division among the states due to slavery, this warning is instructive for criminologists attempting to inform criminal justice policy, especially correctional policy. Clashing opinions about crime, criminality, and the criminal justice system and process, often lead to spirited ideological debates at professional conferences and in professional publications, but rarely to coherent or effective policies.

Unfortunately, a widely considered "defect" of critical perspectives is the perceived inability of the paradigm to spawn effective policy (Lilly, Cullen, and Ball, 2007). It is relatively easy to question, to challenge, and to point out flaws. It is much more difficult to develop effective and humane solutions. This is especially true when the problems are as complex as those related to crime and justice and not only affect individuals, but also affect, and are affected by, neighborhoods, communities, cultures, and societies. It precisely is because the problems are so complex, with human lives involved, that critically derived solutions are necessary.

Critics who claim critical criminologists "talk the talk" but do not (or cannot) "walk the walk" may have been correct at certain points in the historical and philosophical development of critical thought. Growth and evolution, however, have resulted in fewer theoretical perspectives with purely philosophical objectives. Even when perspectives are highly theoretical (or highly anti-theoretical or atheoretical) and speculative, such as postmodernism, abolitionism, and cultural criminology, implications for social and criminal justice policy are abundant, although sometimes not readily apparent or practically feasible within existing social, political, and cultural paradigms.

Most policies possibly derived from these perspectives have the same goals as other critical perspectives. These goals are:

- to develop a just legal system, criminal justice system and criminal justice process;
- to develop social structures that allow for just systems and processes;
- to develop ways to reduce inequalities among individuals and among groups in society;

- to develop ways to address unmet needs of individuals in society;
- to develop humane and effective ways of handling individuals accused of violating behavior standards; and
- to develop humane and effective ways to relate to individuals and communities harmed by the violation of behavior standards.

Many mainstream traditional perspectives neglect to consider policies related to these goals and focus instead on the enforcement of law, the breaking of law, and the punishment of offenders. In addition to being differentiated on the bases of our goals, we also are distinguished from conservative or mainstream criminology in our socio-legal, socio-political, socio-structural, and socio-functional approaches that embrace epistemologies from law, political science, philosophy, economics, feminism, gender studies, linguistics, sociology, psychology, and human services.

For decades, critical scholars (and others) have commented extensively on the relatively weak impact we seem to have on criminal justice policy (Barak, 1988; Barak, 1998; Hemmens, 2008). Rallying large groups of individuals (especially academic types) around any particular policy or position, however, is problematic because it demands taking a stand, a move that involves risk (Hemmens, 2008). As a result of unwillingness to take a stand, our secret policy desires remain hidden and useless.

Lilly, Cullen, and Ball (2007) argue that critical and conflict perspectives are most influential in public policy when they require "social reform" rather than "social revolution" (p. 176). Conflict or critical perspectives that enhance arguments of stigmatization and inequality in opportunity by emphasizing the role and interests of the powerful in the justice process can stimulate direct and measurable changes in policy. On the other hand, critical and conflict perspectives have little policy impact when they call for sweeping social, political, philosophical, and economic changes, such as the abolition of capitalism or the abolition of prisons.

Summarizing the sentiment of many critics, Lilly, Cullen, and Ball (2007) find that "criminological conflict theory...has had relatively little direct impact on social policy" (p. 176). It is not that radical and critical perspectives offer no policy implications (Barak, 1998; Braithwaite, 2007; Lilly, Cullen, and Ball, 2007)), and it is not that conservative perspectives offer more or better policy implications, it is that public policy is shaped by public opinion and public opinion is shaped by numerous influences other than informed research or theory (see, for example, Barak, 1988, 1994, 1995, 1998).

Whereas it is not difficult to see the impact of conservative criminology on current social and criminal justice policy ("three strikes" laws, mandatory sentences, sentencing guidelines, sex offender registration and notification laws, the continued reliance on incarceration and capital punishment), the impact of critical perspectives on current policies is more subtle. Although many critical perspectives support active policy agendas and many critical criminologists are active and vocal in their attempts to get those agendas transformed into actual policies and practices, the reality is that very few of our policy goals are realized. The most notable and most visible example of one such realized policy goal is the apparent widespread acceptance of restorative policies and procedures, briefly discussed later in the chapter.

Critical proponents face charges of utopian positivism, on one hand, and of negativism, on the other. Both derive from critical mandates to question and to challenge, primarily because what often is questioned or challenged commonly is portrayed as unquestionable or unchallengeable (i.e., the status quo), thus we appear negative. Questioning and challenging to reach a more utopian state of being is inherently optimistic, however, rather than pessimistic or negative. We believe our criminal justice system (and our society and our world) can be better and are unafraid to point out faults that need to be remedied. Questioning the status quo ultimately (hopefully) leads to change, especially necessary if the status quo is producing undesirable consequences. I discuss current incarceration rates and recidivism as two of these consequences later in this chapter.

A 2008 report issued by the Pew Center on the States (PCS) brought national and international attention to U.S. incarceration rates, one issue around which it is time we build a "house united" and address with swift action rather than continued debate. Although critical scholars have long questioned the utility of incarceration for most law violators, more mainstream proponents of incarceration also are beginning to voice their concerns.

Incarceration: Rates, Correlates, and Consequences

Incarceration as punishment may not be a uniquely American alternative to the use of torture and other forms of corporal punishment, but we wholeheartedly embrace it. Our current culture expects varying degrees of punishment as the proper response to law violation, and increasingly synonymous with the concept of punishment is the concept of incarceration. The historical expansion of incarceration as a penalty supports this statement (Gottschalk, 2006).

The United States recently observed a sobering milestone in the history of punishment. As of January 1, 2008, more than one in every hundred adults in the United States is incarcerated, with about one in every thirty under some form of correctional supervision (PCS, 2008). We incarcerate more people and have a higher incarceration rate than any other country in the world.

Interpreting official statistics on incarceration is tricky. The Bureau of Justice Statistics (BJS), for example, uses the entire population in the denominator when determining adult incarceration rates for their annual reports, rather than using the adult population. This has the effect of making the rates look much lower (about 35 percent lower) than they actually are (see figure 1).

As figure 1 depicts, 619 out of every 100,000 adults in the United States were incarcerated in 1990 (1,124,401/185,105,441) (Beck and Gilliard, 1995;

U.S. Census Bureau, 1990). The BJS estimate, however, was 460 per 100,000 (Beck and Gilliard, 1995). Ten years later, Beck and Harrison (2001) reported an incarceration rate of 699 per 100,000 in 2000, but using the adult population provides a more accurate estimate 939 per 100,000 (1,962,721/209,128,094) (U.S. Census Bureau, 2000). The BJS figures underestimate incarceration rates by about 35 percent for both decades compared to the more accurate estimations of incarceration rates.

Most recently, Sabol, Minton, and Harrison (2007) reported an incarceration rate of 750 per 100,000 at midyear 2006. However, when one calculates the rate with a midyear 2006 estimate of the total number of incarcerated adults as the numerator (2,292,359),[1] and a midyear estimate of the total U.S. adult population as the denominator (225,662,922),[2] the rate is closer to 1016 per 100,000 (or 1 in every 98 adults). Again, the BJS figure is 35 percent lower than the more accurate estimation.

The incarceration rate as of January 1, 2008 was 1,024 per 100,000 (1 in 98),[3] although the PCS reports it to be 1,009 per 100,000 (1 in 99). Their estimate of the incarcerated population is lower than it should be because they did not count "a significant number of inmates held in facilities other than federal and state prisons and local jails" (p. 25), excluding from their numerator prisoners held in territorial prisons, ICE facilities, military facilities, and Indian country jails. Although researchers at the PCS were well-intentioned, they commemorated the "One in 100" milestone more than a year too late; the United States actually reached "One in 98" sometime during 2006.

Figure 1
Comparison of BJS incarceration rates per 100,000 population and more accurate incarceration rates per 100,000 adults: 1990, 2000, 2006, 2008 (BJS estimates for 2008 are not yet released)

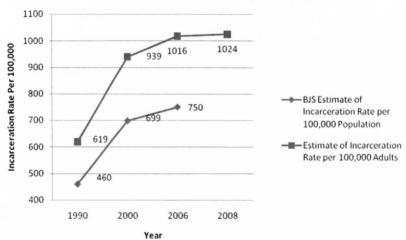

Figure 1 illustrates the discrepancy between "official" estimates of incarceration rates and actual incarceration rates. It also visually portrays the dramatic rise in incarceration rates between 1990 and 2000, with rates increasing a whopping 52 percent, followed by less drastic increases since 2000. Overall, incarceration rates increased about 64 percent between 1990 and 2006.

Rates of incarceration vary dramatically by sex, race/ethnicity, and age. The highest rate of incarceration is among black men, age 20-34, who have 1 in every 9 of their population incarcerated. One in every 15 adult black men and 1 in every 36 adult Hispanic men are incarcerated, compared to 1 in every 106 adult white men. For women, disparities by race/ethnicity in incarceration rates are similar. Black women age 35-39 are incarcerated at a rate of 1 in 100, Hispanic women in the same age group have an incarceration rate of 1 in 297, and for White women the rate is 1 in 355 (PCS, 2008, Sabol, Couture, and Harrison, 2007).

Perhaps increasing incarceration rates would make sense if crime rates were increasing or there were more people around committing crime, but according to both official data on reported offenses and victimization data, crime rates have decreased at greater rates than the population has increased. Between 1997 and 2006, for example, the population increased about 16 percent, reaching the 300 million mark in 2006 (CNN.com, 2006), while the violent crime rate *decreased* nearly 23 percent and the property crime rate *decreased* nearly 33 percent (U.S. Department of Justice, 2007). In fact, rates of violent crime known to the police are near record twenty-year lows and the reported property crime rate *is* at a record low (U.S. Department of Justice, 2007).

If increased incarceration rates are not linked to increased rates of crime, perhaps they are related to having more police, to the police clearing a greater percentage of reported crime, or to the police making arrests in a greater percentage of cases. Logically, having more law enforcement officers should result in clearing more crimes and/or making more arrests, which would in turn contribute to swelling prison populations.

Apparently, the answer is not that easy. The average number of sworn law enforcement personnel *decreased* from an average of 2.5 per 1000 citizens in 1997 (U.S. Department of Justice, 1998) to an average of 2.4 per 1000 citizens in 2006 (U.S. Department of Justice, 2007). Moreover, the clearance rate for violent offenses *dropped* from 48 percent to 44 percent between 1997 and 2006, and from 18 percent to 16 percent for property offenses during that same time (U.S. Department of Justice, 1998, 2007). Examining arrest rates was not much more illuminating. For violent crimes between 1997 and 2006, the arrest rate dropped from 274 to 207 per capita (a 24 percent decrease), and for property crimes, from 769 to 525 per capita (a 32 percent decrease) (U.S. Department of Justice, 1998, 2007).

The Pew Center on the States (2008) blames the burgeoning incarcerated population on "a wave of policy choices that are sending more lawbreakers to prison and, through popular 'three-strikes' measures and other sentencing en-hancements, keeping them there longer." Moreover, the "habitual use of prison stays" to punish those who violate the conditions of their probation and parole in some states also contribute to the problem (2008: 3-4).

This "wave of policy choices" at the state court level significantly impacts correctional populations although rates of reported crime have dropped, per capita representation of law enforcement officers has dropped, and the numbers of crime clearances and arrests have dropped. Some of these policy choices are illustrated below in Figure 2, showing the percentages of state felony de-fendants who were convicted and sentenced to probation, jail, or prison from 1994 to 2004, and the percentage of sentences that convicted felons actually served during those years.

While the percentage of those sentenced to prison actually has decreased since 1994 (and has remained relatively stable since 2000), the percentage sentenced to jail is subtly but steadily increasing and the percentage sentenced to probation actually is at its lowest point since 1994. In fact, for the first time, a greater percentage of defendants in 2004 were sentenced to jail (30 percent) than to probation (28 percent) (Durose and Langan, 2007). In addition, although there are fewer arrests, those arrests are more likely to result in conviction. In 2004, 31 percent of violent felony arrests resulted in conviction compared to only 23 percent in 1994 (Durose and Langan, 2007). More importantly, the percentage of imposed sentence that actually will be served by prisoners has increased from 45.8 percent in 1994 to 66 percent in 2004. With increasing probabilities that an arrest will result in a conviction, decreasing reliance on probation, 70 percent of convicted defendants sentenced to terms of incarcera-tion, and prisoners serving 66 percent of their sentences, the "wave" is quickly becoming a tsunami.

Some evidence indicates that decreased rates of crime are associated with increased rates of incarceration. Intuitively, this makes sense from an inca-pacitation perspective; the more incarcerated criminals, the fewer on the street to commit crime. Stemen (2007), however, argues that many prior studies at-tempting to link increased incarceration rates to reduced crime rates suffer from methodological issues related to *aggregation*, *simultaneity*, and *specification* (p. 5). Studies that aggregate data at lower levels (i.e., at county levels rather than at national levels), account for the simultaneous nature of the relationship between crime rates and incarceration rates, and specify other potential factors that may be related to crime rates, may "produce tremendous differences in results, leading researchers and policymakers to strikingly different conclu-sions" (Stemen, 2007: 5).

In a review of these methodological requirements in fifteen different stud-ies, Stemen (2007) determined that only three (Levitt, 1996; Spelman, 2000; Spelman, 2005) met the criteria above. All three were fairly consistent in their conclusions that a 10 percent increase in incarceration rates is correlated with

Figure 2
**Percentages of State Felony Defendants Sentenced to Probation, Jail or Prison,
and Percentages of Sentences Served Biannually from 1994-2004**

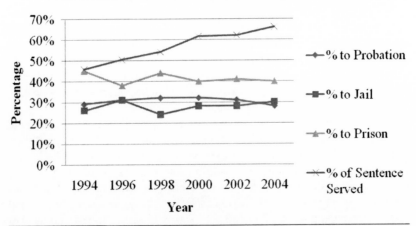

Data from biannual Bureau of Justice Statistics reports, *Felony Sentences in State Courts*, from 1994-2004.

a 2 percent to 4 percent decrease in crime rates (Stemen, 2007). As with most statistical information, both opponents and proponents of incarceration heralded this 2 percent-4 percent decrease as good news. Proponents of incarceration celebrated this news as evidence that putting people behind bars decreases crime. Opponents of incarceration pointed out that decreases of 2 percent-4 percent were too small to justify 10 percent increases in incarceration rates. William Spelman, one of the studies' authors considered an advocate of incarceration, noted the "fairly limited impact" of incarceration given the economic burdens imposed from such reliance (Stemen, 2007: 5).

This tenuous correlation between increased incarceration and decreased crime depends on the current incarceration rate and the size of the existing prison population. Liedka, Piehl, and Useem (2006) determined that increased incarceration rates in states with already large prison populations result in less of an impact on crime rates than increased incarceration rates in states with smaller prison populations. The authors define this "inflection point" as the rate at which higher incarceration rates (between 325 and 492 inmates per 100,000 people) result in higher crime rates. At the neighborhood level, Rose and Clear (1999) describe a similar "tipping point" at which increased rates of incarceration may actually contribute to increased rates of crime due to the destabilization of the community and the reduction of informal social controls.

State policymakers are beginning to realize this possibility. Maryland, for example, under Republican Governor Robert Ehrlich, passed "treatment not jail" legislation in 2004 and proposed the elimination or reduction of mandatory minimums, the expansion of "good time" credits and early release, and reform in sentencing guidelines (Lotke and Zeidenberg, 2005). Despite signs that these measures were having positive impacts on recidivism, the election of Martin O'Malley (Democrat) as Governor in 2006 seemingly has halted progress on some of these initiatives. For example, O'Malley recently vetoed a bill that would have abolished mandatory minimum prison sentences (ten years) for low-level, non-violent drug offenders and would have required short prison stays followed by parole supervision. Although the proposed measure would have saved Maryland taxpayers about $24,000 per year per released prisoner, O'Malley argued that drug-dealing was a "violent crime" requiring punishment ("Sentencing," 2007).

Kentucky, another state bearing the brunt of overreliance on incarceration, is a "truth-in-sentencing" state where prisoners must serve 85 percent of their sentences. It also retains indeterminate sentencing and a parole board reluctant to grant paroles. As a result, Kentucky's incarcerated population jumped 12 percent during 2007 (PCS, 2008). In an effort to alleviate the rapidly escalating numbers of prisoners, the Kentucky legislature approved a controversial budget provision allowing nonviolent prisoners to serve the last 180 days of their sentences on home confinement. The provision also gives the Department of Corrections Commissioner and the Justice and Public Safety Secretary the discretion to release other low-level felons who have more than 180 days remaining to serve. Most prosecutors in the state are vehemently opposed to such action because they fear it jeopardizes public safety in the interest of cost-savings (Riley, 2008).

States appear to be taking steps in the right direction. In the past few years, twenty-seven states have reformed their drug or sentencing laws ("Maryland Treatment Not Jail Bill Signed Into Law," 2004). Unfortunately, however, passage of law does not result in *de facto* change. Many proposed and actual "reforms" address only part of the problem and fail to consider other, more important contributors to violating behavior. According to Stemen (2007: 2), "policymakers with limited resources should weight the modest benefits of more incarceration against potentially greater reduction in crime that might be realized from investing in other areas."

Stemen (2007: 11) presented a summary of research related to these "other areas," contrasting the 2-4 percent reduction in crime rates for each 10 percent increase in incarceration rates with 10 percent increases in these "other factors." The studies he summarized found a 10 percent increase in unemployment associated with a 10 percent to 17 percent increase in property offenses (Gould, Weinberg, and Mustard, 2002; Levitt, 1996; Levitt, 1997; Rapheal and Winter-Ebner, 2001), a 10 percent increase in real wages associated with a 2 percent-25 percent reduction in various types of offenses (Gould, Weinberg, and Mustard, 2002; Rapheal and Winter-Ebner, 2001), and a 10 percent increase in the high school graduation rate associated with a 9 percent decrease in index offenses (Lochner and Moretti, 2004).

Apparently, policymakers notice correctional policies only when they affect the vote or the bottom line. Correctional policies that (purportedly) please the public (e.g., long-term incarceration, prompt probation and parole revocations, parole denials) cost the most, so policymakers must decide between being politically popular or fiscally responsible. In 2007, state spending of discretionary general funds (those primarily used for corrections) skyrocketed 127 percent over 1987 spending (adjusted to 2007 dollars), whereas education spending only increased 21 percent during the same time period (PCS, 2008). More telling is that from 1977 to 2003, state and local expenditures for corrections increased 1,173 percent compared to a 505 percent increase in education spending, a 572 percent increase in spending for hospitals and health care, and a 766 percent increase in spending on public welfare (Hughes, 2006).

Increasingly, incarceration as the best (most effective, most efficient) response to the problem of crime is being questioned. It is a very bad idea to all but the most conservative, most retributive among us. Clearly, it is a failure as a general deterrent, a rehabilitative agent, and as a facilitator of restoration, and provides questionable retributive benefits. In fact, evidence indicates that some people, particularly women (Bradley and Davino, 2002), may feel and be safer in the prison environment than they were on the street (Duncan, 1988). As a result, the only possible goal of punishment met with incarceration is incapacitation, or the "warehousing" of human beings (Irwin, 2007). Given that nearly everyone incarcerated is eventually released within three to five years, the incapacitation effect is limited. Moreover, given the short-sightedness of the incapacitative philosophy, released prisoners are no better equipped than before they were incarcerated. Recidivism rates are proof of that.

Lessons from Abu Ghraib and Guantanamo

As this chapter is completed, the Pentagon's first "war crimes" trial since World War II has reached deliberations in Guantanamo Bay, Cuba. Osama bin Laden's former driver, Salim Ahmed Hamdan of Yemen endured a ten-day trial by the Office of Military Commissions, charged with two counts of conspiracy and eight counts of aiding terrorism (Melia, 2008). Hamdan, along with approximately 265 other alleged terrorists, has been detained at Guantanamo since 2002 as an "enemy combatant" (Williams, 2008), although only about 80 of the detainees are slated for trial.

Detainees at Guantanamo claim to have experienced severe psychological and physical abuse at the hands of U.S. military personnel, claims that were confirmed by FBI eyewitness reports (Eggen and Smith, 2004). Allegations of detainee abuse also surfaced in 2003 and were confirmed in 2004 when Sergeant Joseph Darby provided photographic evidence of detainee torture by U.S. military personnel at Abu Ghraib (Hersh, 2004).

Maltreatment of individuals under custodial care is not unusual, especially when those individuals are perceived as threatening, dangerous, or subhuman.

The facilities at Abu Ghraib and Guantanamo housed individuals who came under American military supervision due to the "war on terror." Although the atrocities of Abu Ghraib and Guantanamo may seem distant from American corrections, our prisons house individuals also under supervision due to the conditions of war, the "war on crime," but more specifically, the "war on drugs." To partially justify inhumane treatment and torture, some may argue that the designation of individuals as "combatants," especially when they fit our perception of "terrorist," creates special situations regarding their confinement and treatment (Crews, 2008). Many may make the same argument regarding the treatment of individuals incarcerated in our jails and prisons.

In 2006, the Commission on Safety and Abuse in American Prisons released "Confronting Confinement," the result of a year-long inquiry into safety within America's correctional facilities. This report included an examination of four major areas within the American correctional system about which the Commission examined findings and made recommendations: (1) conditions of confinement; (2) labor and leadership; (3) oversight and accountability; and (4) knowledge and data.

The findings and recommendations on conditions of confinement primarily related to violence, medical care, and the use of segregation. Within the area of labor and leadership, the Commission emphasized the importance of training, leadership, and the establishment of a culture conducive to humane treatment of those under supervision. Report recommendations related to oversight and accountability stressed transparency in operations, a system that holds officers accountable, and a system in which complaints can be heard without fear of reprisals. Finally, the Commission highlighted the importance of knowledge and data, including base operations, programs, procedures, and the development of policies on research and data.

All of the Commission's concerns about the safety of American prisons are directly relevant to detained prisoners such as those of Abu Ghraib and Guantanamo Bay. The conditions of confinement (including the presence of violence), the attitudes of the administration and staff, the degree of oversight and accountability, and the collection and use of knowledge and data all contribute to an environment conducive to abuse of those in custody.

Environment may be everything. In *The Lucifer Effect: How Good People Turn Evil*, Zimbardo (2007) explains the factors that may contribute to certain behaviors. In the infamous "Stanford Prison Experiment," Haney, Banks, and Zimbardo (1973), evaluated the power of situational forces in shaping behaviors, determining that the situations can significantly shape behaviors. Zimbardo, an expert witness during trials resulting from Abu Ghraib, argues that environmental conditions create physical and psychological conditions that impact the abilities of those operating in such environments to rationally and humanely deal with those conditions. Dehumanization, lack of personal accountability, lack of surveillance, implied (or stated) permission to do acts normally prohibited, and social actions that indicate acceptance of these acts are the key factors that might make a good person do bad things, such as abuse another human being. These factors clearly are likely to exist within any prison environment.

Obviously, incarceration is not the answer to crime and other factors, more contributory to violating behaviors, remain unaddressed in the current crime control/warehousing model. As a result, we must examine alternatives to incarceration. The section below examines a few innovative and promising approaches that actually attempt to impact the significant problems that some people experience that continually land them behind prison walls. If we cannot or will not help people when they reach the point of "corrections," perhaps other parts of the criminal justice system can divert them away and keep them out of our prisons and jails.

Alternatives to Incarceration

Therapeutic Jurisprudence and Problem-Solving Justice

A few encouraging signs indicate growing recognition of law violations not as simply individual problems, but as social problems that require community involvement and systemic departures from "business as usual." One such indicator has been the evolution of "therapeutic jurisprudence" or "TJ" (Wexler, 1993; Wexler and Winick, 1996), a philosophy and practice based on the belief that law, in its various forms, affects the emotions and the psychological well-being of anyone who comes into contact with it.

This approach, modeled after Goldstein's (1979) conception of "problem-oriented policing," has been embraced by the court system. Rottman and Casey (1999) documented the impact of TJ on the emergence of problem-solving courts. They argue that the problem-solving approaches inherent in restorative justice and community justice models provide effective mechanisms to achieve therapeutic outcomes and to address the court system's lack of "a coherent strategy," such as the one inherent in community policing (p. 13).

The problem-solving approach, endorsed by the Conference of Chief Justices and the Conference of State Court Administrators, resulted in the development of the Problem-Solving Justice Toolkit (Casey, Rottman, and Bromage, 2007). The Toolkit encourages and instructs court personnel to integrate treatment and social services with judicial case processing and monitoring to address underlying social and medical problems faced by individuals who come before the court.

Specialized, problem-solving courts are popular judicial attempts both to avoid imposing sentences of incarceration and to provide defendants with treatments and services they need to reduce the probability of recidivism (Wolf, 2007). Although these types of courts began as programs to divert lower-level offenders away from incarceration, they now handle more serious offenders and are primarily probationary and post-plea. More than 3000 such courts are operating today in all fifty states (Huddleston, Freeman-Wilson, Marlowe, and

Roussell, 2005) addressing such problems as drugs, guns, domestic violence, mental health, homelessness, gambling, tobacco, elder abuse, DUI, sex offenses, truancy, license revocation/suspension, and child support (Center for Court Innovation, ND).

Drug courts are the most prevalent type of specialized court, with nearly 2000 in operation or being planned in all fifty states (Huddleston, Freeman-Wilson, Marlowe, and Roussell, 2005). These specialized courts are showing encouraging results. Finigan, Carey, and Cox (2007), for example, conducted a comprehensive ten-year (1991-2001) evaluation of the Multnomah County drug courts in Portland, Oregon. Compared to non-drug court participants, drug court participants experienced a near 30 percent reduction in recidivism (defined as re-arrest after drug court participation, not re-conviction) over a five year period. The study's authors calculated that investing in drug court participants cost $1,392 less than for participants who did not participate in drug courts and that outcome cost savings (avoided costs) were $6,744 per participant and $12,218 per participant if victimization costs are considered. All together, investment cost saving and outcome cost savings totaled approximately $88 million over the ten-year period.

Not all drug courts are so successful. A national study of 2,020 graduates from 95 drug courts across the country in 1999 and 2000 found widely varying recidivism rates (Roman, Townsend, and Bhati, 2003). Defining recidivism as "any arrest for a serious offense resulting in the filing of a charge" (p. 6), the authors determined that 16.4 percent of graduates recidivated within one year and 27.5 percent recidivated within two years after graduation.

Furthermore, the criminal justice field has not reached consensus about the utility of drug courts. Marlowe (2004) cited several studies as credible evidence that drug courts can provide significant benefits to participants in terms of alleviating dependence on substances and in terms of reducing violating behaviors associated with substance use. Whiteacre (2004), however, claims that "the jury is still out" as to whether drug courts are effective, questioning both the methodologies associated with many drug court evaluations and the conclusions offered.

In addition to drug courts, specialized "reentry courts" may facilitate and manage the transition of recently released prisoners. While courts that focus on a single problem (e.g., drug addiction) may be appropriate for some issues, Maruna and LeBel (2003) question whether this model can be applied to reentry, instead arguing for a "strengths-based" approach based on restorative justice principles rather than "risk-based" or "need based" strategies. They argue for a reentry narrative focused on restoration that revolves around the reentering individual's strengths rather than a control (risk-based) or support (need-based) narrative. In the restorative model, the community becomes more involved and the released prisoner assumes "active responsibility" for his or her own progress (Braithwaite, 2001).

Although some question the utility of the problem-solving approach, Wolf's six principles of problem-solving justice (2007), enhanced information, community engagement, collaboration, individualized justice, accountability, and outcomes, provide a framework within which to develop problem-solving tactics. These principles are broad, yet measurable, and apply to all types of problem-solving justice efforts, even those that have not yet been developed.

Clearly, an approach that favors community engagement, individualized justice, and outcomes over process is predicated on the recognition that individuals are products of their communities and that the criminal justice system and process, especially when it comes to "handling" violators, must be circumscribed around that recognition. For example, Glaser (2003) examined the potential utility of this approach in sex offender treatment programs and other "treatment-as-punishment" programs (p. 151), and concluded that therapeutic jurisprudence would "promote an acute awareness of the complex psychological and social processes" that characterize the legal system (p. 150). Modeled on this understanding, he proposed an "ethical code" for clinicians who counsel sex offenders emphasizing procedural fairness, proportionate sentencing, and the least punitive and restrictive punishment.

Restorative Justice

Therapeutic jurisprudence and problem-solving justice share many philosophies with restorative justice. Restorative justice aims to develop policies that promote conciliation and mediation as responses to law-breaking rather than punitive, "warlike" responses that contribute to the negative social consequences of our treatment of law violators (Braithwaite, 2007; Fuller, 2003; Pepinsky and Quinney, 1991). It also emphasizes the roles of government and of the community (Van Ness and Strong, 2002).

Although many perceive restoration as a "back-end" philosophy, constructed as a response to behavior and relevant primarily after incarceration (the "real" punishment), has been imposed, advocates of restorative justice have successfully pushed judges and sentencing authorities to offer more alternatives to incarceration (as exemplified in TJ, above). Despite the likelihood that use of these alternatives is the result of economic considerations related to overcrowding and budget cuts, rather than to any humanitarian concern, the effect is the same; people diverted from jail and prison are allowed to live and work in their communities among their friends and families.

While the unanimous passage in 2000 of a U.N. resolution for all nations to encourage restorative justice allows for some optimism that the world is ready for an approach contrary to the "get-tough" model, Braithwaite (2007) argues that support for such policies and processes, especially in the U.S., mostly is rhetorical. Restorative philosophies have the most power to impact policies that affect incarcerated individuals shortly prior to, during, and shortly after release.

Then, depending upon the jurisdiction, reentrants may be provided with programs or services to facilitate their transition from incarceration back into their communities. Again, the primary reason for focusing on reentry is probably to reduce costs associated with recidivism due to new crime and parole revocations rather than to repair reentrants and restore them and their communities.

Encouraging Policy Initiatives: Release and Reentry

Although change primarily is driven by economic concerns, the result of those changes may be improvements in the criminal justice system, especially in corrections. State governments and the federal government seem to be becoming more willing to re-examine legislation and the treatment of law violators. Particularly important to corrections is a recent spate of release and reentry policies and initiatives.

Since the mid 1990s, increased focus has been on released prisoners reentering society. This interest was partially stimulated by overburdened parole systems, longer sentences due to heavier reliance on determinate sentencing structures, untreated substance abuse and mental illness problems, less educated and less employable prison populations, and increased legal and practical barriers for released prisoners to obtain housing, jobs, and welfare assistance (Petersilia, 2004). Additionally, the increasing popularity of restorative justice brought communities and community groups in on efforts to keep recently released prisoners from returning to prison. These "grass-roots" efforts within communities are particularly important in preventing recidivism and include participation by Coalitions for the Homeless in various cities, churches, and other faith-based and community organizations (FBCOs).

Although historically involved with incarcerated populations (e.g., American Friends Society), FBCOs became more directly involved when serious discussions about reentry evolved during the mid- to late 1990s. In addition to providing counseling to prisoners and running traditional church services, FBCOs functioned as liaison between the prison and the outside, carrying from behind the walls the needs of prisoners who were getting ready to reenter their communities. Rallying the support of their members and affiliates, this network provided a strong impetus for assisting released prisoners in preparing for release and in rejoining their communities.

States also have made attempts to address prisoner release and reentry. The National Governor's Association (NGA), for example, seemingly has recognized the critical nature of the inmate release and reentry process. In 2002, the NGA developed the Prisoner Reentry Policy Academy for seven states (Georgia, Idaho, Massachusetts, Michigan, New Jersey, Rhode Island, and Virginia). The implicit goal of the Academy is to "help Governors and other state policymakers develop and implement statewide prisoner reentry strategies that reduce recidivism rates by improving access to key services and supports" (NGA, 2002: 1). The seven states involved created "interdisciplinary reentry policy teams" with representatives from the Governor's office and other integral state agencies, including corrections.

Although state attention to reentry would seem to be a good thing, it may just be more of the same old business as usual. To illustrate, the three foci of the 2007 "Fall Institute" of the National Governor's Criminal Justice Policy Advisor's Network (ostensibly focused on release and reentry) were sex offender management, illegal drug trends, and targeted violence reduction. These crime control mainstays illustrate the truth to Braithwaite's observation that support for restorative philosophies and policies is mostly rhetorical.

In response to demands for legislative involvement in release and reentry concerns, President Bush, in his 2004 State of the Union Address, proposed a four-year, $300 million "Prisoner Reentry Initiative" (PRI) for faith-based and community organizations to provide assistance to released prisoners returning to their communities. As a result of the PRI, the Department of Labor (in conjunction with the Department of Justice), awarded nearly $20 million to fund thirty reentry-focused projects in twenty states in 2005. Reports from these twenty states are promising. Recidivism rates among the 10,361 PRI participants are less than half that of released offenders who did not receive PRI assistance (20 percent versus 44 percent) (Department of Labor, 2008).

In April 2008, the Department of Labor, again partnered with the Department of Justice to provide nearly $3 million in grants for PRI. Grants of $130,434 to each of twenty-three criminal justice agencies across the country funded FBCOs in their communities to deliver employment services to reentering prisoners. These services include mentoring, job training, work readiness assessment, and soft-skills training. One of the requirements for participating in the PRI, however, is that the exiting prisoner had never have been convicted of a "violent" or "sex-related" offense, precluding a significant number of reentrants (arguably those who need the *most* assistance) from receiving any under the PRI.

Finally, at the national level, the Second Chance Act was signed into law by President Bush on April 9, 2008. This Act, introduced in 2007 as H.R. 1593 by Representative Danny Davis (D-IL), was co-sponsored in a bipartisan effort by ninety-two other representatives. The Act authorizes $330 million in grants to nonprofits groups and state and local governments for the provision of programs and social services to released prisoners in hope of reducing rates of re-offending and probation/parole violations. Regardless of Presidential approval and bipartisan support, however, the Act still needs funding to give it real life on the state and local levels. The congressionally approved budget appropriations for such discretionary spending in FY 2009 (and beyond) lack any mention of funding for the Second Chance Act (S. Con. Res. 70) and it is likely that no funding will be approved for such new programs until after the 2008 presidential election, if at all.

Although state and federal politicians promise real change in corrections as usual by developing initiatives, creating advisory groups and reentry policy teams, and passing legislation, they are just providing lip service if they fail to follow through with funding and support. This failure to follow-through only contributes to disappointments in correctional policy and practice, exemplified in rates of return to violating behaviors and to incarceration.

Recidivism

Recidivism is the red herring of corrections, distracting society from recognizing its own structural and functional maladies that contribute to violating behavior and to repeat violations and incarcerations. Instead, blame is leveled at corrections for failing to rehabilitate. Granted, correctional environments are not yet places where humans can reasonably be expected to transform, but release into a society that stymies reintegration only exacerbates the problem. However, examining rates of re-arrest and return to prison are the main way that most people judge the success (or failure) of the correctional process.

The most recent study of recidivism that approaches a national scope is rather dated (of prisoners released in 1994), but found that more than 67 percent of released prisoners are rearrested, about 47 percent are reconvicted, about 25 percent are resentenced to prison for a new crime, and more than 26 percent are sent back to prison for a probation or parole violation within three years of their release (Langan and Levin, 2002). These rates represent increases from a similar 1989 study of prisoners released in 1983, although the earlier study did not distinguish between returns to prison for new crime and returns for probation/parole violations (Beck and Shipley, 1989).

More recent estimates of individuals under probation or parole supervision indicate that only 57 percent of adults exiting probation and 44 percent of adults exiting parole in 2006 successfully completed the terms of their supervision (Glaze and Bonczar, 2007). In practical terms, this means that 43 percent of probationers and 56 percent of parolees failed on supervision, although only 18 percent of probationers and 39 percent of parolees actually were incarcerated as a result of their failure.

Some state studies provide more recent information. Connecticut, for example, conducted a five-year follow-up of 8,221 prisoners released during 2000 (Connecticut Statistical Analysis Center, 2007). Recidivism was measured as reconviction and resentence to prison for any crime. The study examined type of release from prison (expiration of sentence or community-based program), and type of community supervision the prisoners received before and after prison release (transitional supervision, parole, DOC community-based program).

The lowest reconviction rates (24 percent) were among those released from prison to a DOC community program, such as a half-way house, and the lowest rates of being resentenced to prison (12 percent) were among those released followed by a period of supervision on parole. The highest rates of reconviction (47 percent) and of resentencing to prison (26 percent) were found among those who were released with no supervision after serving their sentences.

A study of recidivism rates in Alaska indicated higher overall rates of re-cidivism (66 percent), but similar characteristics among recidivists as in Connecticut (Alaska Judicial Council, 2007). While 66 percent of Alaskan prisoners originally charged with a felony and released in 1999 were reincarcerated within three years after release, only 55 percent were reconvicted.

Property offenders consistently have the highest recidivism rates (re-arrest, re-conviction and re-incarceration) (Beck and Shipley, 2002; CSAC, 2007, Alaska Judicial Council, 2007), while sex offenders tend to have the lowest rates of re-arrest and re-conviction (CSAC, 2007, Alaska Judicial Council, 2007), but higher re-incarceration rates; 35 percent of Alaskan sex offenders were reconvicted but 63 percent were re-incarcerated (Alaska Judicial Council, 2007).

These discrepancies can be directly linked to increased rates of probation revocations resulting in the imposition of sentences to incarceration and to increased rates of parole revocations resulting in returns to incarceration. Clearly, punitive policies are more to blame for skyrocketing incarceration rates rather than any actual change in human behavior.

Conclusion

Corrections is out of control and the responsibility for reigning it in falls on all of us. Uniting over policy issues that have impacted imprisonment, conditions of confinement within prisons, release from prison, and reentry to society is a good way to start. Most of us recognize, however, that breaking the cycle of crime and punishment will take years of dedicated effort, targeted at changing the very nature of society. As many critical theorists argue, economic disparity is one problem on which reformers need to concentrate.

Economists agree. In a fall 2006 speech, Janet Yellen, president of the San Francisco Federal Reserve Bank, said that U.S. income inequality has risen to such a level that "there are signs that [it] is intensifying resistance to globalization, impairing social cohesion, and could, ultimately, undermine American democracy" (Kirchhoff, 2007). From 1997-2001, nearly 50 percent of productivity gains went to the top 10 percent of the income distribution (Gordon and Dew-Becker, 2005), particularly concentrated in the very top 1 percent of income earners (Piketty and Saez, 2006). In fact, this top 1 percent held 15.4 percent of total income in 2001.

Inequality has increased more in the U.S. than in most other advanced industrial countries in the Organization for Economic Cooperation and Development (OECD). Indeed, by most measures, the U.S. ranks near the top (some might say the bottom) in terms of household income inequality. The inequality gap in the United States is associated with higher levels of overall poverty and child poverty relative to a majority of OECD countries.

According to Yellen (2006), the high and growing level of relative inequality reflects, in part, differences in the "social safety net." Among the thirty OECD countries, the U.S. ranks above only three countries (Ireland, Korea, Mexico) in gross public expenditures as a proportion of gross domestic product spending. The U.S. also does the least to help move families out of poverty. As a result, life expectancy and infant mortality in the U.S. are worse than in most other industrial countries. Law violations and repeat offending are also worse than in most other countries. As critical criminologists continue to argue, inequality and individual and social problems are inextricably connected.

Incarceration is not a solution. It is a major concern that requires unifying divided houses, healing rifts among scholars dedicated to improving the criminal justice system, concentrated efforts to develop innovative and effective alternatives to incarceration, vigilance about the conditions within our prisons, and coordinated policies, programs, and services to assist released prisoners as they reenter society.

Corrections could take a cue from the courts by developing problem-solving approaches to the treatment of law violators. Assuming that the problem-solving approach in the courts is diverting more and more individuals from the formal criminal justice process (and not resulting in net-widening), corrections should welcome fewer and fewer prisoners behind the walls. Assuming that the revision of sentencing laws by states with overcrowded prisons and overburdened budgets will result in more flexibility in sentences, corrections should see more and more prisoners released within a reasonable time. Assuming that Congress will actually fund the provisions of the Second Chance Act, that state and local governments and non-profit agencies will begin to develop innovative social programs to proactively undermine the development of violating behaviors, and that communities and governments will continue to craft policies, programs, and services targeted at successful release and reentry, corrections should see fewer and fewer prisoners return once they have been released.

Utopian optimism? I prefer to think of it as optimistic realism. No matter what we call the perspective or paradigm, whether we think of ourselves as left realists, anarchists, Marxists, abolitionists, or social constructionists, we all have a common interest in justice for everyone involved in the process. Restorative philosophies, however, as progenitor of some of the more encouraging policies and programs described in this chapter, temper justice with mercy. This practice seems to be as instructive now as it was in the past when Abraham Lincoln advised that "mercy bears richer fruit than strict justice." Given the fruits of strict justice that our correctional system and out society now bear, a little mercy could benefit us all.

Notes

1.   This estimate was derived by using the total number of 2,385,213 individuals incarcerated in 2006 and subtracting the number of juveniles detained in juvenile facilities (92,854) (Sabol, Couture, and Harrison, 2007: 3).

2.   This estimate is the U.S. Census Bureau's official estimate of the U.S. adult population as of July 1, 2006, obtained by subtracting the population under the age of 18 (73,735,563) from the total population (299,398,484) (U.S. Census Bureau, 2007).

3. This figure was derived by using the total incarcerated population at yearend 2006 of 2,385,213, subtracting the 92,854 individuals held in juvenile facilities, and adding 2.6 percent (the average annual increase between 2000 and 2006) (Sabol, Couture, and Harrison, 2007). The denominator was the adult population estimate of 229,786,080 provided by the Pew Center for the States (2008: 27).

9

A Convict Criminology Perspective on Community Punishment: Further Lessons from the Darkness of Prison

Stephen C. Richards

Too often writing on community-based corrections (hereafter community punishment) is done from a managerial perspective. Rarely is the sanction approached from an alternative point of view. This chapter addresses this imbalance by introducing not only a critical and radical perspective on post-prison community punishments, but one that is informed by the convict criminology school. Why is this important? The traditional utilitarian correctional literature has failed to include class, race, gender, and correctional status in its theorizing. Instead, the discussion has been limited to administrative strategies to manage voiceless people. In contrast, critical and radical perspectives exploit this failure by exploring explanations rooted in societal contradiction. The following discussion compares utilitarian and critical and radical perspectives on community corrections, including research on how prisoners view community programs, and new directions for a critical theory of community punishment. From a convict criminology perspective, persons serving sentences in community custody, for example on probation or parole, or as what is now called "community supervision," may experience this as community punishment. The use of the term "community punishment" suggests that the following discussion will diverge from what is commonly known as community-based corrections. Unfortunately, many men and women experience community supervision as just more punishment.

Biographical Introduction

Intellectual integrity demands an honest accounting of from where we came, who we are, and what personal bias we retain in our research and writing. How we interpret what we study derives in part from our own personal location in social structure. Williams (1983: preface) reminds us that "More than we ever believe, we understand life from where we are." Biography as a "narrative of self-identity" (Giddens, 1991b: 189) is a record of how we are socially constructed (Berger and Luckman, 1966).

I am a felon and ex-convict (Richards, 1990, 2003, 2004a, 2004b) who knows the "degradation ceremony" (Garfinkel, 1956; Cohen 1980; Cosgrove, 1984) of trial, the "pains of imprisonment" (Johnson and Toch, 1982), and the "stigma" of "spoiled identity" (Goffman, 1963) experienced as an "invisible minority" reduced to "semi-citizenship." Prisoners remember the pinch of handcuffs, humiliation of strip search, the weight of leg irons and belly chains, and the cold winter nights in penitentiary cellblocks. It is from this perspective, combined with a Ph.D. in sociology, that I approach not only the academic fields of criminology and criminal justice, but the scholarly field of corrections.

Utilitarian Perspectives on Community Punishment

Sociology, criminology, and criminal justice have all contributed to the utility of community punishment. This utility is not "what works" (Blomberg and Cohen, 1995) to correct, habilitate, or rehabilitate, but what extends the realm of pain and punishment; what Cohen (1985: 30) termed "alibis for the exercise of power." Community corrections, as diversion or alternatives to incarceration, refers to pre-prison constructive custody including intermediate punishments and punishment packages (Morris and Tonry, 1990), court ordered probation (Byrne, 1986; Rosencranz, 1986; Vito, 1986; Lemert, 1993) house arrest (Petersilia, 1986; Lilly, Ball, and Huff, 1988), electronic home monitoring (Russell and Lilly 1989; Corbette and Marx, 1991; Walker, 1990; Lilly et al., 1993) community service, restitution schemes, and therapy protocols. These diversions, while alternatives to incarceration for some juveniles, first or misdemeanor offenders, also serve as dress rehearsal for millions of persons destined to experience prison and post prison custody.

The community corrections literature focuses on alternatives to incarceration, programs for men and women serving time in the community, and the rehabilitation of criminal offenders. The utilitarian literature on community corrections, despite its pretensions to be value-free covers the political spectrum, from liberal to conservative, left to right. It pretends to be value-free, as a means to appear scientific. The liberal-left domain can be characterized as humanistic, dedicated to reform policy that may increase pre-prison alternatives, and "saving" (Platt, 1969) the non-violent and correctable from the ravages of prison. The concern is with supplying political and administrative elites with pragmatic, piecemeal, policy options (Erickson and Carriere, 1994). This literature includes evaluations of cafeteria style judicial sentencing, discretionary release from prison, and innovations in community supervision. The liberal domain stresses civil and constitutional rights, and has advocated a "continuum of care" (Blomberg, 1995), employing different styles of compensation and conciliation.

The conservative right constituency (e.g., Alfred Blumstein, Mark Cohen, John Dilulio, Peter Greenwood, Shlomo and Reuel Shinnar, and James Q. Wilson) has recently been quite active. They have served the interests of correctional elites advertising old ideas as new developments including: privatization, boot camps, chain gangs, regional jails, shock incarceration, intensive parole supervision, split sentences, pre-trial detention, preventive detention, career criminals, mandatory minimum sentences, and informing victims and communities of the return of parolees. The literature focuses on deterrence, retribution, and incapacitation. They have published research studies and suggested numerous policies to extend and lengthen correctional punishments that have become law, including mandatory minimum sentences, longer sentences, so called "truth in sentencing," and "three strikes and you're out," that further punish so-called persistent offenders or career criminals (Austin, 2003:15-36).

In contrast, the liberal-left criminologists evaluate these reactionary ideas, attempting to challenge their political and bureaucratic implementation. The critical and radical literature characterizes this "care" of prisoners as "widening the net" (Binder and Geis, 1984; Cohen, 1985; McMahon, 1990), "wider, stronger, and different nets" (Austin and Krisberg, 1982; Cohen, 1985; McMahon, 1990), "accelerated social control" (Blomberg, 1977), "piling up of sanctions" (Blomberg and Lucken, 1994), "transcarceration" (Lowman, Menzies and Palys, 1987; Cohen, 1985, Faith, 1993), and transinstitutionalization (Cohen, 1985; Davis and Faith, 1987). Thus, the critical literature, while still utilitarian, tends to doubt the utility of more detention and harsher punishment. This left domain suggests that the criminal justice system has serious flaws, not the least of which is the way it has extended penal punishment into the community.

Advantages and Disadvantages of the Utilitatrian Perspectives on Community Corrections

The "panacea pendulum" (Dean-Myrda and Cullen, 1985) of community corrections swings from left to right, politicians dictating the budgets of research and practice, searching for the ultimate sanction, program, or routine supervision that will lower the recidivism rate. The pendulum meters the relative merit of incarceration versus community programs. This is mainstream criminology and criminal justice engaged in managerial research, policy debates, and program recommendations (Cohen, 1992: 19-20). The perspective is empirical, positivistic, piecemeal, and interdisciplinary, drawing from a number of academic fields, as well as criminal justice practitioners, providing breadth, if not depth, to the literature. The writing is functional, as it invariably supports and legitimates the existing social control infrastructure. The literature is well funded, with researchers building careers and academic programs working state sponsored agendas. This generally assures non-critical, carefully understated research with wide exposure, including textbooks, journals, government reports, and popular media. Many of the contributors to the literature are criminal justice personnel describing their pet projects and programs.

This utilitarian mainstream perspective is a dismal failure as the number of prisoners, parolees, and felons grow, low-income communities are transformed into felon ghettoes, populated by the victims of both crime and the criminal justice system. Recent scholarship refers to correctional populations that continue to grow at an alarming rate. Today, over 7 millions men and women live day to day in "constructive custody," confined in institutions or on probation or parole (Austin, et al. 2001).

Nevertheless, the criminal justice machine contains or controls even more people than correctional counts suggest. The state seriously under reports the total population in custody for two reasons. The numbers are growing so fast, and the Bureau of Justice Statistics fails to count significant numbers of persons. Cohen (1985: 7) stated: "We live inside Burroughs' (1959) 'soft machine,' an existence all the more perplexing because those who control us seem to have the most benevolent of intentions. Indeed we appear as the controllers as well as the controlled." In the shadow of the soft machine is the "semi-hard machine" of transcarceration/transinstitutionalization, a world of community based social control shelters, clinics, and services for marginal persons. Free persons (sic) live on the surface in the soft machine. Prisoners live below in the darkness of the really hard machine (prison), released at some future time to the semi-hard machine (community custody).

Government statistics only total the numbers of persons in official custody of the justice machine (jails, prisons, probation, and parole). Millions of people that have been processed through jails and prisons hide in the shadows, living in substandard housing, under bridges, or drifting from cheap hotels to community shelters. Many of these former prisoners are now street rabble (see Irwin, 1985), unemployed, living on the margins of society, with no permanent address, they may no longer be counted in government totals.

Correctional figures are also understated because the correctional net is so complex as to confuse the definition of terms. Juvenile justice may include diversion, probation, reform schools, teen court sanctions, drug courts, hospitals, substance abuse programs, jails and prisons. Probation may be granted as alternative to incarceration, as a split sentence (prison then probation), a second sentence to be served after prison. Parole refers to post-prison custody including life-time parole, intensive supervision, and special parole (Federal parolees upon revocation are returned to prison without credit for street time.). Jail figures are day estimates that do not include the millions of people arrested and released every year without being charged, charges dismissed, or bail granted. Lynch (1996: 297) estimates that the 300,000 day population turns over, like inventory in a parts warehouse or groceries on the shelf at Safeway, once every five days resulting in 22.5 million persons in local lock-up in the course of a year, with many persons jailed numerous times.

The 7 million in correctional custody does not include juveniles, military prisoners, and mental patients. Also neglected are the tens of thousands of men, women, and children incarcerated by the U.S. Immigration and Customs Enforcement (ICE) in the "Hot Gulag" (Kahn, 1996: 14, 70)[1] prisons. Many of these tent prisons, called service and processing centers by the ICE, have emergency capacities of 10,000 prisoners. Thousands of "Marielitos" Cubans without criminal convictions are being held indefinitely, some have been in custody for over twenty years "waiting for the end of the world" (Kahn, 1996: 139).[2] These prisoners drop out of the official census when moved from jails or prisons to ICE prisons. And, how do we estimate the number of felons residing in the community, living in the shadows, who have escaped the correctional net to be semi-citizens once again? We have little statistical work on the numbers of persons with felony convictions in the national population.

The utilitarian community corrections literature has other problems, less evident in the liberal-left domain, and more pronounced in the reactionary right domain. It does not examine underlying assumptions, is generally ahistorical and anti-intellectual, supporting law and order at the expense of social justice. There is little effort to penetrate the experience or identity of prisoners serving time in the community. For example, the conservative authors assume that crime is committed by criminals, and that prisoners are different from themselves (Miller, 1988; Pepinsky and Quinney, 1991). Unfortunately, only a few researchers write about how most prisoners and paroles do not consider themselves "criminal," usually hold normative values and aspirations, and may well themselves be victims of class- and race-based social disadvantage.

The writing is limited to individual and institutional levels of analysis. The conservatives like to theorize about how many people should be locked away in prison to lower the rate of crime. There is little thought as to how we might create legal opportunities as a means to reduce crime. For example, instead of conceptualizing community corrections as reforming individuals, we could be correcting communities (Currie, 1985, 1993; Mathiesen, 1990; Pepinsky and Quinney, 1991; Clear, 1994).

The most glaring disadvantage of the utilitarian perspective is the failure to consider the societal contradictions and consequences of social control technologies. Both liberals and conservatives assume that the criminal justice system is utilitarian when it beats the "dangerous classes" into submission. Meanwhile, every city in the U.S. has a growing felony ghetto as each year more convicted felons exit prison to return home. Vast urban areas, known for poverty and crime, have become depositories for felons. The criminal justice system is busy bagging and tagging felons. Criminal convictions and felony tags make sure they will never have a decent job. The contradiction may well be that social control technologies are creating a criminal class.

This utilitarian perspective does not think about the danger of chemical, computer information, and surveillance protocols used to control marginal populations. Today we have a growing number of "special needs prisoners" (mentally ill and mentally retarded) serving time in prisons and community corrections facilities who are controlled with medication (T.R. Young, 1996; Hassine, 1996).[3] Community prisoners are tracked with computer information systems and returned to prison when they fail to comply with court orders to pay restitution fines, or child support, take their medication, or complete their court ordered community service. Surveillance protocols now include reporting by employers, teachers, medical personnel, and neighbors. Chemical, computer, and surveillance protocols are now being used to monitor prisoners, community corrections clients, and employees in offices and factories; for example, drug and alcohol testing first used by criminal justice is now common corporate practice. Ironically, we are all now subject to the same testing.

Critical and Radical Perspectives on Community Punishments

The correctional continuum has contributed to the most perplexing problem facing policy makers, the public, and scholars: How do we reduce felony recidivism? Various proposals including get tough policies have been suggested at an enormous cost to the public. These get tough policies have resulted in what Irwin and Austin (1994) called "the rising tide of parole failures." Their research focuses on technical violations, drug test failures, parole officer close supervision, and parolee misconduct as the explanation for re-arrest and return to prison. Felony recidivism, whether as the result of technical violation, program failure, or criminal offense, has resulted in the construction of a "perpetual incarceration machine" (Richards, 1995; Richards and Jones, 1997, 2004) that recycles prisoners from prison to the street and back to prison. Today, nearly 50 percent of prison admissions are women and men being returned as the result of community failure.

Critical and radical criminology has contributed numerous discourses related to community punishments. Using Goffman's terms, Friedrichs (1996) suggested that critical criminologists have diverse methodologies, interests, and audiences. He identifies backstage, on-stage, and front-stage as theoretical work, empirical work, and efforts to introduce broad audiences to critical criminology. Many of the critical debates can be subsumed under three themes: First, social control has operated to defend upper class interests (Marx 1973, 1977, 1981; Greenberg, 1977; Foucault, 1977a; Schwendinger and Schwendinger, 1981; Takagi, 1981), to discipline the working class to menial and alienated labor, and in our time of structured unemployment to the fabrication of a growing under class (Moore, 1978, 1985; Wilson, 1978; 1987; Auletta, 1982; Irwin, 1985a; Currie, 1985; Miller, 1986; Irwin and Austin, 1994). The community correctional penal machinery, intended to support and assist, is now used to supervise and monitor, contain and control, a growing number of men and women released from prison.

Low-income neighborhoods are home to a proliferation of community punishment services operated by federal agencies, department of corrections, or private companies; correctional halfway houses, work release centers, parole offices, and substance abuse centers concentrated in urban ghettoes. This protects suburban citizens from struggling felons and parolees who need jobs and new opportunities. America is building a gulag to warehouse its surplus redundant population (Currie, 1985; Moore, 1978; Richards, 1990; Christie, 1993). As university professors, we are educating students to become the "officers" to manage this population.

Second, the "carceral archipelago" (Foucault, 1977b) is growing to encompass disadvantaged communities with deficient social and public institutions. This community gulag is the "hood" where children are raised by single parents (the other parent may be a correctional victim) in slums where the schools resemble prisons and police sirens wail through the night. The state creates social chaos by shifting fiscal resources from social-economic development and education to correctional containment of marginal populations. As factories close, public schools and low-income housing deteriorate, welfare assistance is terminated, and blue collar workers are forced, if they can find it, to take minimum wage service and retail employment. The state employs the war on drugs and war on sex offenders to manufacture rabble (Irwin, 1985a) out of the redundant working class, and invests in building and maintaining prisons and community punishment infrastructure.

Third, corrections and community corrections is an industry (Christie, 1993) feeding on public dollars and the fear of crime, operated as a business by an actuarial regime (Reiman, 1986; Simon, 1987; 1988) for corporate profit; the "commercial corrections complex" (Lilly and Knepper, 1993). There are now community punishment facilities concentrated in most low income neighborhoods, including facilities for day reporting, halfway-in and halfway-out houses, drug and alcohol treatment centers, work release centers, mental health facilities, and parole offices. Their clients supply the cheap involuntary labor for menial jobs washing dishes and autos, food service, cleaning retail businesses, and telemarketing providing profit for local entrepreneurs.

Correctional custody colonized the "free world" building a community juggernaut to supervise probationers, parolees and felons. Juggernaut is defined (*American Heritage Dictionary*, 1970) as: "Anything that draws blind and destructive devotion, or to which people are ruthlessly sacrificed, such as a belief or institution." The juggernaut may also be used as a metaphor for capitalism (Marx, 1977; Harvey, 1989), modernity (Giddens, 1990), or the legal and penal machinery of the panoptic criminal justice system (Foucault, 1977b; Gordon, 1990).

Gordon (1990) described the criminal justice system as a "justice juggernaut" rolling on two tracks; (1) capture and confinement, and (2) observation. The first practice refers to the dramatic increase in arrests and incarcerations as well as new developments in corrections, for example, warehousing prisoners in supermax penitentiaries (Richards, 2008), jailing defendants as pre-trial detention, or releasing them to serve years on bail supervision waiting for trial (common practice of federal courts), and monitoring community prisoners with house arrest and electronic shackles. Pre-trial supervision may include both jail time that does count and community bail supervision that does not count toward the completion of an anticipated criminal sentence. Prisoners released on bail may be ordered by federal courts to report to parole offices on a daily or weekly basis for months or years while they await the disposition of their criminal cases. These defendants are subject to the same rules and restrictions as probationers and parolees, including travel prohibitions, searches of their home, and association with persons in the community. Gordon (1990: 6) writes, "They blur distinctions that facilitate judicial regulation of criminal justice activity; when does punishment begin if someone has been under pre-trial supervision for six-months [or years] before guilt is determined." The question is not only when does custody begin, but when, if ever, does it end?

Felons are tracked by electronic record keeping that legally extends their punishment. The U.S. Department of Justice, state and local police departments and courts sell criminal history records information to the public. This information is used to do background checks for employment, licensing, and security clearances. This electronic tracking of criminal history records is facilitated by interlocking computer information systems. Gordon (1990:7) reports, "What is becoming a vast, national network, fed by smaller local tributaries, is both fundamentally changing the nature of police investigations and making tens of millions of records—many of them inaccurate, stale, and trivial—available not only to law enforcement nationwide but to employers and others outside the criminal justice system." These records, including pre-sentence investigations (PSI) and inmate central files, can be purchased at the local courthouse for a modest fee. In many states, criminal record information is sold by law enforcement agencies to employers, financial institutions, and landlords (Gordon, 1990).

Weber (1921/1968) asserted that records, files, and double-entry book-keeping were the basis for modern bureaucracies. Giddens (1984: 152) suggested that double-entry bookkeeping is a time machine which "stacks past events as well as anticipating future ones." He noted that "Language as Levi-Strauss says, is a time machine, which permits the reenactment of social practices across the generations, while also making possible the differentiation of past, present, and future" (Giddens, 1991b:23). Unfortunately, criminal records merge a person's past, present, and future together, imposing a perpetual and officially sanctioned stigmatization. Prisoners complain that these records are used to both enhance and sustain criminal sanctions; they are part of their punishment.

Gordon (1990) named this technological surveillance the "electronic pan-opticon" which extends the reach of criminal justice sanctions beyond prison walls into the community. Computer generated criminal justice data are used to systematically redefine the opportunity structure and create a permanent underclass of leveled aspirations. For example, while it is illegal to discriminate on the basis of race, it is legal to discriminate on the basis of criminal record, constructing biographical barriers to viable employment; the most apparent to felons, particularly the poor and minorities. These barriers are the invisible walls of urban ghetto, the secret stratifiers, that segregate and contain millions of ex-offenders, a sophisticated computer quarantine (Gordon, 1990).

We live in a computer age where social security numbers trace criminal records, credit histories, and insurance records. Ex-convicts are denied bank loans, credit cards, student loans, welfare assistance, as well as fair market insurance rates. Without credit, ex-convicts may be unable to purchase homes or a car, provide for their families, or pay for education. Even some universities are using criminal records to deny admission to undergraduate and graduate programs. Prisoners, upon release from prison, may encounter an opportunity structure limited by the rule of law that denies them access to employment and educational opportunities, the means to a new life.

Advantages and Disadvantages of Radical and Critical Perspectives on Community Punishments

The literature challenges existing social-economic relationships, class for-mations, and power differentials, demonstrating that social control serves the interest of political elites and the economically privileged. It is comparative, historical, intellectual, and multi-disciplinary, including research on social control practices, formal and informal, in different societies. The United States' experience with community punishments is often compared with the more benign examples of democratic socialist countries, for example Norway (Mathiesen, 1965, 1974, 1985, 1990; Christie, 1981, 1993), Sweden (Bondeson, 1994), the Netherlands (Hulsman, 1974; Tak, 1994), and Denmark (Bondeson, 1994).

This perspective does have disadvantages. Although the writing is eclectic, diverse, and creative, it tends to be too abstract and philosophical, without sufficient citation of empirical studies. Much of the existing work is armchair theorizing without reference to real life experience. One example is Cohen's (1985: 41-43) "fish story," wherein the criminal justice system trolls the free world netting millions of criminal fish. Small ones are thrown back, others are kept on a string or in buckets to clean, filet and eat, or used as bait for bigger catch. Some fish die or rot in the bucket, some jump out, most are released to be caught again. The metaphor brilliantly describes the criminal justice system, but fish and people are not directly comparable.

Most significantly, people have voices. Incorporating their voices into theo-retical discussions, not only acknowledges their social agency, but enhances our theorizing. While Marxists have placed social class as the center of the analytical focus, the critical literature, especially feminist criminology, has made progress in introducing perspectives on gender and ethnic differentials, adding voices of diversity. This attempt to simultaneously discuss gender, ethnicity, and class increases the complexities of theorizing. What remains is the need to restructure the relationship between theory and experience.

How do we develop the advantages and overcome the disadvantages of critical/radical perspectives on community punishments? First, we move beyond high level abstraction (Garland, 1990). Second, theory should guide and inform empirical studies, using both quantitative and qualitative methods (Blomberg, 1995). Third, we must learn to do "criminology from inside out rather than outside in" (Barak, 1994: 9; Ferrell and Sanders, 1995; Ferrell, 1994) by immersing ourselves in the cruel details of personal reality that can disrupt our sheltered comfort, by penetrating the gulag, interviewing prisoners on the inside, following them home to the free world (sic), and learning to incorporate their experience into our critical discourse.

Emerging Critical Perspectives on Community Punishments

Critical perspectives on community punishments include diverse analytical approaches, I have elected to discuss in turn Criminology as Peacemaking, Abolitionist, Peace Feminist, Restorative Justice, and Communitarian. Criminology as Peacemaking brings together interrelated religious and humanist traditions, including Abolitionist and Peace Feminist (Knopp, 1976, 1991; Harris, 1983, 1987; Rucker, 1991), Restorative Justice, and Communitarianism. Criminology as Peacemaking challenges the existing military structure of corrections. This is a promising new perspective that seeks to end the war on crime and war on drugs (Pepinsky and Quinney, 1991).

Will we be peacemakers or warmakers? The questions are many, troubled souls that we are, are we ready for restorative justice, mediation, and reconciliation? Or, is this just another, gentler style of liberal-left alternatives? Does the state want peace, or does this war on the people below serve the people at the top? Answers are difficult because they challenge are own privilege based on class, gender, race, and professional status. Making peace means coming to terms with the enemy within ourselves that seeks to discipline and punish (Foucault, 1977b) the deviant and nonconformist. If criminology as peacemaking is to flourish we need to learn tolerance of disorder and respect for non-intervention (Schur, 1973) and least possible intervention (Bondeson, 1994).

The Abolitionist tradition (Schur, 1973; Mathiesen, 1974, 1990; Christie, 1981, 1984, 1993; Rutherford, 1986; Bianchi, Herman and Swaaningen, 1986; Blad, van Mastrigt, and Uildriks, 1987) seeks to limit the use of prisons by closing penal institutions and providing alternatives to incarceration. Knopp (1976, 1991), a Quaker feminist and prison abolitionist worked for decades inside (Prisoner Visitation and Support) and outside of prisons (Safer Society Program) to challenge oppressive institutions of patriarchal punishment. She advocated mutual education/action strategies to address feminist and abolitionist issues, including consciousness raising, and a new system of justice based on a caring community where reconciliation prevails (Knopp, 1991: 183).

Knopp's action plan for gradually wearing away the use of imprisonment and building a caring community is the Safer Society Program "Attrition Model" (Knopp et al., 1976: 62-63; Knopp 1991: 184-186) that has four strategies; (1) moratorium on prison construction, (2) de-carceration-releasing prisoners from prisons, (3) ex-carceration-alternatives to prison including restitution, fines, community service, and mediation, and (4) restraint of the few.

The Restorative Justice perspective (Zehr and Sears, 1982; Zehr, 1985, 1990; Marshall, 1985; Umbreit, 1985; Van Ness, 1986; Wright, 1988; Van Ness, Zehr, and Harris, 1989; Wright and Galaway, 1989) is popular with religious communities because it includes a normative dialogue that is based on reparation of social injuries suffered by both victims and offenders. This approach emphasizes the needs of victims and the responsibility of criminal offenders to accept the consequences for their behavior by paying restitution, doing community service, encouraging a process of reconciliation based on repentance and forgiveness. Restorative Justice is experimenting with Victim Offender Reconciliation Programs (VORP) facilitated by trained mediators and sponsored by police and courts that "consists of face-to-face encounters between victim and offender in cases which have entered the criminal justice process and the offender has admitted the offense" (Zehr, 1990; 161).

Cordella's (1996: 379-392) Communitarian Theory of Social Order suggests that social and legal conformity are based on three distinct unity patterns, that correspond to three types of operational moralities. First, the Atomistic Unity Pattern is based on individualism and a rational calculus of coercion embodied in both criminal and civil law that mechanically defines and sanctions what is illegal: "The legitimacy of law in an atomistic context is dependent more on its uniform and consistent application than on its content or effectiveness" (Cordella, 1996: 380). Atomistic social relations are ruled by mechanical morality (i.e., law). Second, an Organic Unity Pattern is predicated on an understood interdependence that creates mutual obligation, and functions to maintain order and resolve conflicts through social morality. This pattern of social relations requires that people have roles that reward them for reciprocal cooperation, for example family or social membership, employment or careers. Third, a Personal Unity Pattern is conceived in terms of a communitarian concern for others for their own sake, a personal trust engendered not by a common purpose but by a common life and personal morality that is conciliatory with social harmony the primary goal. Communitarianism has long been practiced by communities (Hutterites, Amish, Mennonites) that employ restorative justice as a means to promote reintegration of deviant members. The process is group negotiation, apology, and forgiveness.

We can identify all three of the above unity patterns in our present society. Cordella (1996: 380) writes, "In any given society one or more of these unity patterns will become dominant as the other patterns become dependent." In our present society the Atomistic Unity Pattern is dominant, while both the Organic Unity Pattern and Personal Unity Pattern are dependent. For example, the legal system judges individuals, while people learn to cooperate in the workplace, and leave their personal concerns to family and friends.

Both the Restorative Justice Perspective and the Communitarian Theory of Social Order provide insight for community corrections. Convicts and parolees have lived lives beyond the law and outside of the accepted social-economic reward structure of legal employment. They lived on the margin as nonconformists or outlaws. Cordella (1996: 390) suggests:

> In an atomistic unity pattern, individuals conform either because they believe it is in their best interest to do so or because they feel powerless to do otherwise. Calculated conformity is an adequate way of maintaining order among those who are economically embedded. However, for those individuals with limited human capital and few material resources, conformity does not translate into continued material prosperity.

Therefore, the economically marginal do not risk reputation or resources when they commit crimes; when you have nothing you have nothing to lose. But, although a convict-parolee may have nothing or little materially to lose, he or she may still retain deep personal commitments to other people.

Ironically, many prisoners, while in the penitentiary, have experienced close face-to-face relations, not unlike that known by Old Order Anabaptist sects. Convicts live in an almost communal society where there is little social differentiation, no money other than rolls of coins (if the prison still sells coins at commissary) and cigarette cartons (if the prison still permits smoking), and little if any opportunity to escape each other. This is a world that is not atomistic or organic, but instead intensely personal. All conflict is personal, and differences are settled without recourse to legal remedy or contract. In prison, prisoners learn to negotiate or fight, to explain themselves or suffer retribution. These men and women have had years of experience with communitarian justice where your word is your contract and trust and obligation is confirmed by your day-to-day knowledge of one another.

A second irony about convicts is that, as expected, they have little interest in legal or social morality, but may have a well developed investment in personal morality. Criminologists (Sutherland, 1937; Riemer, 1937; Clemmer, 1940; Miller, 1958; Sykes, 1958; Irwin, 1970; Chambliss 1984) have written classic ethnographies about the moral codes of convict subcultures and professional thieves. I wonder if Chic Conwell and Harry King would have chosen to terminate their criminal careers if given the opportunity for restorative justice? But then, when the "bogeyman" (Irwin, 1985b) returns home from the penitentiary, it will take more than "reintegrative shaming" (Braithwaite, 1994) to restore his or her trust and mutual obligation, it will require employment, a home, a place in the community, and an end to the punishment.

A convict criminology perspective suggests that we need to rethink both prison and community punishments, as one leads to the next. The dramatic growth in American correctional populations is the result of the drug war. The drug war must end. Wars end with peace that provides amnesty for prisoners;

military prisoners are released from custody. The Convict Criminology Group advocates Amnesty for non-violent and drug prisoners after three years or less of incarceration. Prison should serve as a wake-up call to get their attention, dry out from substance abuse, and a letting go of criminal intentions. Men and women locked up for three years twenty four hours a day seven days a week (24-7 in prison or street talk) should be provided a correctional experience that prepares them for successful reintegration back into the community. Correctional officers should be "doing corrections" not performing like parking lot attendants; parking people in cells. Correctional camps with short sentences need fewer guards and no fences, and the correctional budget is spent on programs rather than security; education instead of cement and steel. These prisoners should be released with social security cards, driver's licenses, and sufficient gate money for rent and food for three months. They should be provided with voluntary services upon request (assistance with employment, personal and family counseling, drug and alcohol treatment programs, and medical services). They should return home to a community that welcomes them.

New Directions for a Critical Theory of Community Punishments

What must we do to help prisoners returning home to our communities? First, we must learn from men and women doing time in the community. We need to incorporate prisoners in our discussion of community punishments; only prisoners know the full punishment program. They experience custody as continuum of punishment without the artificial distinction accorded by theorists to the difference between incarceration and community supervision.

Federal and State law is replete with "repeat offender statutes." The severity of these statutes, as provided by either United States Code or various state codes, that dramatically enhance sentences for "career criminals," makes it imperative that the process of prison release and re-incarceration be addressed. As of the year 2008, more than 600,000 prisoners (U.S. Department of Justice, Bureau of Justice Statistics) will be released from prison, most of them with time to serve in halfway houses, work release facilities, and parole. A majority of them will be returned to prison within three years.

Second, we need to do more empirical studies of community correctional programs. This means interviewing men and women as they leave prison and struggle through community supervision. Critical criminology should be the eyes and ears of the oppressed that reports the cruel truth of corrections. The critical literature will improve as it uses theory to frame and explain what is learned from empirical observation of the journey prisoners travel from prison to home.

Third, we need to have higher expectations for the men and women leaving prison. Why do we assume they can only work menial low paid jobs? Instead, we need to encourage prisoners to use prison time to prepare for admission to college and universities. The Convict Criminology Group (Richards and Ross, 2001; Ross and Richards, 2003) will continue to help ex-convicts to enter universities, complete degrees, and then to help others. Our hope is that ex-convict and "non-convict" professors might create a "new school of criminology" to stem the tide of community punishments. Together, we can rethink reentry and community supervision. For example, by simply asking convicts and parolees what they want, what they think will help them, we might find a way to lower the rate of men and women returning to prison.

Recently, both the U. S. government and private foundations have opened conversation on the reentry problem. For example, the Soros Foundation has funded many projects to help former prisoners help others. Soros has funded the Convict Criminology Group with fellowships and research grants, ex-convicts operating shelters for ex-convicts, innocence projects at numerous law schools, the medical marijuana referendums in many states, and efforts to restore voting rights to felons.

Even President Bush recognizes the need to reduce community punishments. The Second Chance Act takes its name from the 2004 State of the Union address by President Bush:

> In the past, we've worked together to bring mentors to children of prisoners, and provide treatment for the addicted, and help for the homeless. Tonight I ask you to consider another group of Americans in need of help. This year, some 600,000 inmates will be released from prison back into society. We know from long experience that if they can't find work, or a home, or help, they are much more likely to commit crime and return to prison. So tonight, I propose a four-year, $300 million prisoner re-entry initiative to expand job-training and placement services, to provide transitional housing, and to help newly released prisoners get mentoring, including from faith-based groups. America is the land of second chance, and when the gates of the prison open, the path ahead should lead to a better life.

April 2008, the bill was signed into law. The question remains as to whether the funding will be used to help prisoners in our communities. At the very least, the federal funding will stimulate local interest in reentry issues. We hope it is not used for more supervision and surveillance.

Conclusion: Lessons from the Darkness of Prison

The darkness of prison has lessons to teach. In the movie *Shawshank Redemption* the convict Red (Morgan Freeman) goes to the parole board. The Parole Board Chair says, "Please sit down. Ellis Boyd Redding, your files say you've served forty years of a life sentence. You feel you've been rehabilitated?" Red replies, "Rehabilitated? Well now let me see. You know I don't have any idea what that means." The Chair says, "Well, it means you're ready to rejoin society." Red answers, "I know what you think it means, sonny. To me it's just a made up word, politician's word, so that young fellows like yourself can wear a suit and a tie and have a job."

After forty years in the penitentiary Red did not remember committing homicide, he did not even remember being a young man. Time had transformed young Red into old Red, the former a boy who made a tragic mistake, the latter man a pale facsimile of what he might have been. The boy sentenced to prison matured into a convict, learned the ways of the penitentiary, and found a home. Rehabilitation implies a program of education, therapy, and restoration, useful as correctional ideology or for a prisoner doing short time, an excuse for employment, or a rationale for institutional funding, but of little use to a man doing forty years inside the wall. Red knew what most prisoners learn after years in prison and a number of trips to the parole board, that rehabilitation is a word without definitive measure or relation to release. Prisoners know that parole release is determined by external factors such as the numbers of prisoners coming in, the daily count, court orders to reduce overcrowding, and current political fashion concerning time to serve on a given sentence.

As critical individuals we must learn not to use the words of politicians and state funded researchers. Prisoners of the state do not use these words, they know better. These are labels assigned by the state to punish, that do not do justice to the lives of men and women who may have had one bad day, a brief career, or periodic episodes with breaking the law. Rehabilitation, corrections, retribution, incarceration, incapacitation, abscond, and recidivism are all made up words. There are so many ugly words in criminology, criminal justice, and corrections. Traditional textbooks are filled with hate words used to generalize "them" as criminal offenders: Criminal, convict, parolee, jailbird, murderer, rapist, thief, armed robber, burglar, sex offender, child abuser, pedophile, pederast, embezzler, forger, drug abuser, drug dealer, career criminal, recidivist, the list is endless, all made up words loaded with prejudice.

The language used to critically describe and analyze crime, criminals, and corrections, has improved in the social justice, feminist criminology, and peace criminology literature. The literature has advanced with critiques of the state, feminist perspectives, and attempts to theorize about a demilitarized approach to community, but it is still a prisoner of privilege, written without the necessary anger and horror. Meanwhile, the men and women in the penitentiaries and the community dormitories tug on their chains and read worn and tattered copies of Chessman, Clever, Jackson, Davis, Malcolm X, Abbott, Mitford, and Fanon (Cummins, 1994).

It is safe to be white, polite, and ignorant of dirty and dangerous details. If you want to understand the reality of the correctional juggernaut then ask the men and women released from the penitentiaries and reformatories, juvenile and immigration detention centers, who are trapped in the community punishment infrastructure. In this sense, as we theorize about corrections and social control, "the heart of darkness returns home" (Cohen, 1992: 305).

A critical and radical perspective on community punishments cannot be written from the safety of distant debate. The community is filled with prisoners who have wandered home from our Western-style gulag (Christie, 1993) to sleep on our doorstep (and study in our classes). Victor Hugo wrote, "If a soul is left in the darkness, sins will be committed. The guilty one is not he who commits the sin, but he who causes the darkness." We have much to learn from the voices below, the convicts, men and women who wait to share the lessons of the darkness (Perrot 1986; Eribon, 1991).[4] The postmodern great incarceration of marginal Americans has begun; while we theorize, the clock ticks, the American gulag grows.

Acknowledgements: I would like to thank Bill Douglas, Don Gibbons, Michael Hirsch, Richard S. Jones, and Jeffrey Ian Ross for assistance with earlier drafts.

Notes

1.   Kahn (1996: 70) writes "The INS never executed Central American refuges directly, but a litany of abuses of law and human decency similar to what Aleksandr Solzhenitsyn reported about the gulag were repeated in U.S. Immigration prisons throughout the years of the Reagan administration."

2.   In 1980, more than 120,000 Cubans in the Mariel boatlift entered Florida. Most of them were given INS "special parole status" with 1,700 excluded and immediately imprisoned. Many of these refugees denied special parole were identified as criminals by the tattoos they wore; some of theses tattoos were marks made by the Cuban prison authorities to indicate specific crimes.

3.   Thousands of additional special parole Cubans would later have their parole status revoked for misdemeanors, failure to support themselves, or being a nuisance to local communities. By 1985 there were over 6,000 Marielitos in federal prisons. I served time in Atlanta (U.S.P.), Talladega (F.C.I.), and Leavenworth (U.S.P.) with Cuban prisoners. All Federal Bureau of Prisons (FBOP) prisoners have inmate numbers, for example 55555-021, with the last three digits designating the federal district court of sentencing. Many Cuban citizens incarcerated in the FBOP have 000 as their last three numbers, indicating that they are serving federal time without being convicted and sentenced. They are "waiting for the end of the world." This illegal incarceration of immigrant refuges in federal prisons led to a series of riots; Florence (AR.) INS Detention Center (1985), Miami (FLA.) INS Detention Center (1986), Oakdale (LA.) FBOP Detention Center (1987), Atlanta Federal Penitentiary (1987), and Talladega (AL.) Federal Correctional Institution (1991).

4.   "I think that, as the prison populations continue to grow and grow, and a younger and more violent crowd comes in, it will become harder and harder for the administration to control all the blocks. I think they are now learning that the best way to control inmates or pacify them is to totally medicate them. It may even become a reward system.... Just from the increasing size of the medication lines and the growing number of inmates doing the brake-fluid shuffle, I have observed that psychotropic medications [also known as "chemical shackles"] are defining the behavior of an increasing percentage of inmates in the general population" (Hassine, 1996: 83).

5.   Eribon's biography of Foucault contains a chapter entitled "Lesson from the Darkness" which refers to what he learned from Jean Genet, his own students, and French prisoners about his country's penal system. Foucault first became interested in prisons when a number of his students at the University of Vincennes were arrested in the Paris, May 1968 demonstrations, and later when the French police, 2,000 strong, arrested students at the university. In 1971, while at the College de France he would write *Discipline and Punish: The Birth of the Prison*. Michelle Perrot (1986: pp. 76-77) wrote, "A great book about society's dark side, it fed on this lesson from the darkness."

10

The Potential for Fundamental Change in Juvenile Justice: Implementing an Alternative Approach to Problem Youth

Preston Elrod

Apparently those responsible for juvenile justice policy have learned little from the history of juvenile justice. Many contemporary interventions for juvenile offenders are in most respects indistinguishable from those that existed over a century ago. Indeed, the history of juvenile justice policy development is one of resistance to fundamental change. In fact, the resistance of the juvenile justice system to alternative responses to the "delinquency problem" has led a number of writers to suggest a cyclical pattern in juvenile justice policy development (e.g., Albanese, 1993; Bernard, 1992; Ferdinand, 1989; Finckenauer, 1982; Gilbert, 1986; Miller, 1979; Schultz, 1973; Schwartz, 1989), where the same sequence of policy responses to juvenile crime are repeated during different historical periods (Bernard, 1992).

This chapter focuses on the development of more humane and effective responses to problem youth. I begin by examining the history of juvenile justice policy development. I argue that while some differences in liberal and conservative policy responses exist, there are important similarities between these two approaches that prevent them from fostering more effective responses to problem youth. I then examine conditions that may lead to the development of more humane, effective, and critically informed juvenile justice policy. I conclude by discussing the general political strategies necessary to implement more effective and humane approaches to problem children.

Changes in Juvenile Justice Policy: A Historical Perspective

There have been two major policy developments in the history of juvenile justice. The first major policy development produced the juvenile court; the second resulted in the conservative "get tough" approach to juvenile crime that began in the mid-1970s. By the time that the first formal juvenile court was established in 1899, doubts about the efficacy of existing juvenile justice interventions were already evident. These doubts were reinforced by new ideas that favored special treatment for many youths, and by emerging views of problem children as neglected but highly malleable human beings whose potential was still underdeveloped (Bernard, 1992; Empey, Stafford, and Hay 1999; Ferdinand, 1989). Although crimes committed by both juveniles and adults were seen as a significant social problem in urban areas throughout the 1800s, many youths who committed minor offenses were ignored by adult criminal courts. Indeed, the punitive responses available to adult criminal courts, such as jail and prison, were felt to be overly harsh; encouraging the types of behaviors that reformers hoped to prevent (Bernard, 1992; Lerman, 1977; Platt, 1977). Moreover, legal prohibitions in Illinois resulting from *People v. Turner* (1870) prevented efforts by liberal-minded reformers in that state to institutionalize youth without some due process considerations.

These legal proscriptions created the need for some mechanism by which control could be exerted over troublesome youth who were either outside the jurisdiction of criminal courts or ignored by them (Bernard, 1992; Ryerson, 1996). The result was a significant liberal reform, the juvenile court which was vested with broad legal authority over a range of neglected, dependent, pre-delinquent and delinquent youth (Bernard, 1992; Platt, 1977; Ryerson, 1996). Like earlier reforms directed at children such as the House of Refuge, the placing out system, and the reformatory, the juvenile court became one more institution designed to control troublesome youth. And like other reforms, the development of the juvenile court was made possible because of emergent conceptions of youth, prevailing ideas about the etiology of delinquency, and because previous efforts to effectively control youth appeared ineffective (Bernard, 1992). However, these reforms were also possible because they catered to powerful vested interests—the influential child-savers who desired to help and control children, the criminal courts who no longer had to deal with petty juvenile offenders, and conservatives who were also concerned about social control.

The development of the juvenile court represented a high water mark in liberal juvenile justice policy because it established what was essentially a child welfare agency that had broad legal powers to intervene in the lives of children (Bernard, 1992). However, while liberal juvenile justice policy was able to successfully dominate policy debates during the late 1800s and early 1900s, and has served as the cornerstone of juvenile justice practice throughout the first century of the juvenile court, since the mid-1970s liberal policy has been seriously challenged, and in many instances supplanted, by a more conservative stance toward juvenile crime. Since the mid-1970s "get tough" reformers have called attention to a new category of juvenile offender—the violent, serious offender; the superpredator. The picture of the new delinquent that began to emerge portrayed the juvenile offender as an urban, violent, hardened and often minority "criminal" who is not amenable to treatment by juvenile justice programs. According to the chief Administrator of the Office of Juvenile Justice and Delinquency Prevention (OJJDP)[1] during the Reagan administration and a leading proponent of the conservative perspective, the rehabilitative philosophy of the juvenile court had clearly failed and argued that "criminals should be treated as criminals" (Regnery, 1985: 1). Moreover, get tough reforms led to substantial changes in how juvenile justice agencies responded to juvenile crime. They also led to significant increases in the number of youths incarcerated in juvenile correctional facilities, as well as adult jails and correctional institutions, and increases in the number of youths transferred to adult courts for trial (Krisberg, 2005).

In support of their punitive policies, conservatives rely on explanations of delinquency and penal reform which collectively view crime and delinquency as a product of poor choices which are primarily influenced by individual pathology and poor parenting. Consequently, conservative policies are based on efforts to increase the "cost" of crime as the most promising crime reduction strategy (Currie, 1985; Miller, 1979; Wilson, 1975; Wilson and Herrnstein, 1985; Van den Haag, 1982). Unlike the reforms seen around the turn of the century, however, which were concerned with a wide range of neglected, abused, dependent, pre-delinquent and delinquent youth, the policy thrust of conservatives is directed at a narrow population of offenders—the violent and serious juvenile offender (Miller, 1979; Ohlin, 1983), the superpredator (Bennett, DiIulio, and Walters, 1996). However, the conservative focus on the violent and serious offender is not antithetical to liberal policies which have traditionally cast a broad net of social control. Also, like earlier liberal policies, conservative policies were innocuous to powerful economic, political, and juvenile justice interests. As a result, the shift to more conservative policies required few substantive changes by many juvenile justice agencies. Although this shift in focus was resisted by some, others embraced it and were happy to redefine themselves as warriors in the fight against crime; as law enforcers as opposed to social workers.

The Failure of Conservative and Liberal Juvenile Justice Policy

Although much of the debate over juvenile justice policy revolves around conservative or liberal views of delinquency and juvenile justice (Bernard, 1992; Miller, 1973), the shortcomings of juvenile justice policy are ultimately a product of the similarity in these two traditional approaches to problem youth. Although differences between liberal and conservative approaches to juvenile justice should be recognized, there are also similarities (Elrod and Kelley, 1995). For example, during the Clinton administration larger amounts of funding for a greater range of juvenile justice programs were made available to the states than under the George W. Bush administration (see Bilchik, 2007). Nevertheless, both conservative and liberal juvenile justice policies are based on a mainstream paradigmatic conception of crime and delinquency which views these phenomena as the product of individual and/or institutional pathology. Of particular significance to conservative and liberal policies is the role that family dysfunction and individual pathology play in delinquency. Clearly, individual, family, and other social institutions do play a role in youthful misbehavior. However, structural factors which are related to delinquency are almost always ignored by these approaches. By failing to recognize the salience of race and gender as well as economic, cultural, and social conditions that make crime an attractive choice for many youth, such reductionist conceptions of delinquency prevent the development of more effective juvenile justice policies.

Not surprisingly, the correctional focuses of liberal and conservative policies are also strikingly similar. Although conservatives and liberals may debate the differences in their theoretical approaches to crime and the nuances of effective correctional strategies, their policy responses have boiled down to one thing: a heavy reliance on formal, usually coercive, mechanisms of social control. What the history of actual conservative and liberal reactions to crime makes abundantly clear is that the real differences between these policies have more to do with the means by which formal control is exercised, than the ends of control (Ryerson, 1996). Indeed, it was the realization by many liberals that rehabilitation often meant punishment that helped lead to the demise in the rehabilitative ideal during the 1970s and 1980s (Cullen and Gilbert, 1982).

The fact that conservative and liberal policies are outgrowths of a mainstream paradigmatic conception of delinquency also results in similarities in the methods used by each of these perspectives to understand delinquency and the operation and effectiveness of juvenile justice. Both conservative and liberal policies are predicated upon and supported by a narrow range of methodologies that limit their understanding of delinquent behavior and the effectiveness of juvenile justice operations. This is not to say that the methods are necessarily inappropriate. Rather, it questions the extent to which "one shot" surveys and outcome evaluations as well as other types of quantitative methodologies that measure a narrow range of preconceived "realities" can capture the essence of delinquency from the perspectives of participants or understand the problems associated with the development, operation, and outcomes of juvenile justice interventions.

Another similarity between conservative and liberal approaches to delinquency is that they tend to draw attention to the differences between those youth who violate the law and their families, and those who are seen as "law-abiding." Consequently, both approaches target populations that require intervention or control. However, the tendency for conservative and liberal approaches to delinquency to differentiate and set apart the offender creates a troublesome paradox for juvenile correctional programs. By emphasizing how problem youth are different, and typically less deserving, children caught up in the juvenile justice process are confronted with a variety of obstacles that make law-abiding behaviors less likely (Cicourel, 1968; Garfinkel, 1956; Matza, 1974; Tannenbaum, 1936). Importantly, the very act of juvenile justice involvement in a child's life signifies an important difference between the juvenile offender and other youth which is often exacerbated by a process that fails to recognize their feelings or needs. Moreover, treating youth and their families as different has other consequences as well. As Miller (1998) and Krisberg (2005) have noted, the myth that most juveniles who violate the law are in some way fundamentally different from the rest of us serves as a pretext for treatments that would not be tolerated if they were seen as "our" children. By dealing with the offender, and often their family, in exclusionary as opposed to inclusionary ways, juvenile corrections often works against its stated mission of reintegrating youth into the community. Moreover, being singled out for juvenile justice processing is particularly acute for minority youth (Huizinga, Thornberry, Knight, and Lovegrove, 2007; Pope and Feyerherm, 1990; Krisberg, 2005).

Still another similarity between liberal and conservative juvenile justice policies is that they have served as the predominant frame of reference for the majority of juvenile justice practitioners since the 1800s. As a result, conservative and liberal policies are the status quo within juvenile justice which, due to the highly bureaucratic and conservative nature of legal institutions, displays considerable resistance to change. This tendency of both conservative and liberal policies to support the status quo is most clearly revealed in the consistency of juvenile justice interventions over time. For example, juvenile probation, presently the most widely used formal response to youth adjudicated in juvenile courts (see Puzzanchera and Kang, 2007), began in Massachusetts in the later half of the 1800s, and has changed little since that time. Although there appear to be new trends in juvenile probation (e.g., intensive, group, and wilderness probation), some programs, such as the use of volunteer probation officers and outdoor programs, have a long history (Lindner and Savarese, 1984; Schultz, 1973). Moreover, today, as in the past, probation often means "file drawer" or "token probation" where there is little, if any, contact between probation officers and probationers (President's Commission on Law Enforcement and Administration of Justice, 1967; Jacobs, 1990). Even electronic monitoring represents more of a technological than substantive innovation because it is intended to serve as an alternative to incarceration, reduce institutional overcrowding or costs (Vaughn, 1989), or increase surveillance, all of which are identical to the aims of traditional probation programs.

Likewise, the operation of juvenile institutions has been affected very little by shifts in conservative or liberal juvenile justice policies. Although there are purportedly "new" programs being implemented such as boot camps and outdoor adventure programs, these interventions are hardly innovative. Indeed, the belief that military regimen and discipline, removal of youth from the criminogenic influences of the city, and the rehabilitative potential of hard work were key principles which underlay the development of 19th century innovations such as the reformatory, cottage reformatory, and the placing out system (Platt, 1991; Roberts, 1998). Similarly, the development of forestry camps for juvenile offenders in Los Angeles County during the 1930s (Eldefonso and Hartinger, 1976; Siegel and Senna, 1997), wilderness adventure programs in the early 1960s (Golins, 1980; Winterdyk and Griffiths, 1984) are not unprecedented. Today, as in the 1800s, youth are incarcerated in a variety of institutional settings, including adult prisons, jails, and a variety of private institutional placements (Bilchik, 2007; Frazier and Bishop, 1990; Lerman, 1977; Schwartz, 1989; Krisberg, 2005) where they may get little real help and in many cases are actually harmed by the experience (Bilchik, 2007; Schwartz, 1989; Miller, 1998).

Indeed, the most significant similarity in conservative and liberal policies is their failure to grapple with the material and cultural conditions that produce juvenile crime and that serve as barriers to dealing effectively with it. As a result, they generally fail to adhere to a central element of successful correctional intervention—they do not address those factors that are strong predictors of delinquency (Gendreau and Goggin, 2000). Moreover, the actions they do take tend to be coercive; to involve orders. Further, they are usually effectuated by talking at, typically in a language that is foreign to their clients, rather than with the children and parents who come to their attention. Indeed, it is the development of highly bureaucratic and formalized mechanisms of problem solving that relegates youth, the family, and the community to the periphery of the juvenile justice process and represents the sine qua non of contemporary juvenile justice. As a result, both conservative and liberal policies fail to produce substantial reductions in juvenile crime because they contain within them contradictions that prevent them from either addressing the root causes of delinquency or implementing effective strategies for working with youths, families, and the community in developing collective responses to delinquency.

The Conditions that Influence Juvenile Justice Policy Development

A number of scholars have noted periodic shifts in juvenile justice policy (Albanese, 1993; Bernard, 1992; Elrod, 1998; Krisberg, Schwartz, Litsky, and Austin, 1986; Palmer, 1992; Ohlin, 1983; Weisheit and Alexander, 1988). For example, the development of the first formal juvenile court in 1899 represented a new attempt by powerful individuals to control an old problem—poor children who engaged in criminality or who were felt to be at risk of criminal behavior (Bernard, 1992; Platt, 1991). More recently, a shift away from the liberal policies that dominated juvenile justice from its inception until the mid-1970s to "get tough" policies that focus on the serious or violent offender (referred to by some as a "watershed in terms of reform"), has been well documented (Krisberg et al., 1986: 7). Presently, the juvenile justice policy debate continues. However, it is argued that the predominant liberal and conservative juvenile justice policies that have informed most responses to juvenile crime contain contradictions that severely limit their effectiveness. Consequently, it is reasonable to ask if it is possible to develop a more humane and effective response to juvenile crime, under what conditions could such a change occur, and what would be the general focus of such an approach to problem children?

Clearly, changes in juvenile justice policy are possible (e.g., Bernard, 1992; Elrod, 1998; Krisberg, 2005). The most recent of these changes was produced by the movement to "get tough" with juvenile crime. However, the get tough approach faces a number of serious challenges. These challenges include growing evidence that incarcerating youths and/or treating them as adults has limited utility as an effective response to youth problems(for a review, see Krisberg, 2005); that it is expensive (see Caldwell, Vitacco, and Rybroek, 2006); that it does not protect public safety (Bishop, Frazier, Lanza-Kaduce, and Winner, 1996; Fagan 1995; Steiner, Hemmens, and Bell, 2006), and that it is plagued with bias (see Free the Jena 6, 2007) that has resulted in disproportionate numbers of minority youth in the juvenile and adult justice process (Huizinga et al., 2007; Krisberg, 2005; Leonard, Pope, and Feyerherm, 1995; Poe-Yamagata and Jones, 2000). There is also growing evidence from research on human development that many adolescents do not possess the cognitive structures and abilities of mature adults which makes them ill equipped to effectively participate in and benefit from the adult criminal justice process (Burnett, Noblin, and Prosser, 2004; Griffin, 2003; Grisso et al., 2003). In fact, there is good evidence that adult correctional facilities are not healthy places for many adults, much less children (Ross and Richards, 2003). In sum, this evidence calls into question the viability of responses to juvenile crime that have served as the foundation of conservative juvenile justice policies since the mid-1970s.

In addition, there is some evidence that juvenile crime has been increasing in recent years after a steady decrease in violent juvenile crime between the mid-1990s and 2004. Since 2004, both the total numbers of arrests of persons under eighteen years of age and arrests of persons under eighteen for violent index offenses has been increasing (FBI, 2007). Although it is too early to determine if this increase represents a consistent upward trend in serious juvenile crime, statements given by former Attorney General Alberto Gonzales in 2007 to the Associated Press suggested that there was increasing concern about an upward trend juvenile crime. In speaking about a Department of Justice study of eighteen cities and suburban areas, Gonzales noted a surge in crime including violent juvenile crime (MSNBC, 2007).

The perception that juvenile crime is increasing once again (Bernard, 1992; Gilbert, 1986; Platt, 1991), coupled with the belief that existing policies are ineffective (Bernard, 1992) and costly, seriously undermine the credibility of the get tough approach. If these concerns continue to mount, they may provide a window for the implementation of alternative responses to problem youth, particularly at the state and local level where the possibility for innovative programming is more likely (Krisberg, et al., 1986) and the need to reduce costs is more pressing. Two important questions then are, what are the key ingredients of more humane and effective juvenile justice interventions, and what processes might be employed so that these interventions are adopted by juvenile justice policy makers?

The Key Ingredients of Humane and Effective Juvenile Justice Interventions

A humane and more effective approach to problem children is predicated on a critical approach to juvenile justice that seeks to respect the basic dignity of families and children, continually seeks to improve its operations based on "best evidence," and is reflexive. Conceptually, it is based on a different paradigmatic framework than traditional conservative and liberal approaches to juvenile justice, and it is built around the concept of social justice rather than deterrence and punishment (see Elrod and Kelley, 1995; Elrod 1998). Moreover, it employs a set of practices that are consonant with this critical framework. Rather than focus exclusively on the individual, critical juvenile justice is concerned with the social institutional and structural factors that place children and families at risk of various forms of victimization and of-fending. Critical juvenile justice strives to ensure that children's basic physical needs such as food, shelter and clothing are met; that youths live in healthy environments that are free from victimization; that youths receive a quality academic and vocational education; and that youths have viable age appropri-ate economic opportunities. In addition, it supports individual needs, and it is inclusionary and integrative as opposed to exclusionary and repressive; it limits involvement in the formal juvenile justice process; it ensures the protection of juvenile rights; it seeks to empower youth, families and community members; it reduces recidivism; it is accountable, and it engages in a regular process of program development and evaluation.

In terms of practice, an important component of critical juvenile justice is the development of a strong informal juvenile justice process. This process includes actions taken by citizens to respond to delinquency that do not involve formal agents of control such as the police, juvenile court personnel, or juvenile corrections officials (Elrod and Ryder, 2005). It is made possible by efforts to develop the human and social capital within communities that are capable of engendering a high degree of collective efficacy (see Sampson, Raudenbush, and Earls, 1997). It recognizes that many of the issues that are handled through the formal juvenile justice process can be dealt with as effectively or more effectively through informal processes where community members share responsibility for the socialization of youths and correcting problem behaviors. Moreover, critical juvenile justice is built on research that indicates that informal social controls represent a more effective prevention and response strategy to problem children than strict reliance on the deterrence-based strategies supported by get tough proponents (see Erickson and Gibbs, 1980; Pogarsky, Kim, and Paternoster, 2005; Sampson, Laub, and Allen, 2001).

Clearly, the most promising development in preventing and responding to a range of problem youth behaviors is the increasing use of restorative justice programs (for a description of different types of programs see Bazemore and Schiff, 2005). As Braithwaite (2007) notes, restorative justice has a number of advantages including its acceptability to policymakers who hold different political perspectives, its appeal to a wide range of citizens, its ability to empower those involved, and its ability to provide tangible benefits to victims. Other advantages include its ability to implement interventions that work, to reduce offending, and to satisfy citizens' perceptions of justice. It is not surprising then that there has been considerable growth in restorative justice programs both in this country and abroad.

An added benefit of restorative justice programs is that they can be employed at each stage of the juvenile justice process—at the informal stage, at the police and juvenile court intake stages as diversion programs, and at the formal stage of the juvenile justice process (see Bazemore and Schiff, 2005). For example, various types of interventions involving mediation and reconciliation between victims, offenders, and community members can be used as part of informal community responses to juvenile offending. They can also be used by police and courts in efforts to divert youths from the formal court process, and they can be used as post-adjudicative responses to delinquency. Moreover, restorative justice programs are consonant with a developing movement by some members of the legal profession and community activists to develop the concept of community courts and engage in therapeutic jurisprudence. These movements recognize that courts have traditionally been engaged in problem solving, but they seek to use courts in less formal and punitive ways to solve community problems.

The Politics of Implementing Critically Informed
Juvenile Justice Policies

The development and implementation of juvenile justice policy is an inherently political process that occurs at the national, state and local levels. At the national level, executive branch and congressional support for innovative responses to juvenile crime have been generally weak despite the passage of the Juvenile Justice and Delinquency Prevention Act (JJDPA) in 1974 and subsequent amendments to that legislation. As Krisberg (2005) notes, one important component of the JJDPA was the establishment of the Office of Juvenile Justice and Delinquency Prevention (OJJDP). OJJDP was important because its primary role was to encourage and support prevention and community-based efforts to respond to delinquency. In addition, it has served as a major source of funding for state and local juvenile justice efforts. However, despite substantial increases in funding for prevention during the Carter administration, funding was significantly curtailed by the Reagan and George H. W. Bush administrations (Krisberg, 2005), and similar policies have been adopted by George W. Bush. Indeed, all three of these Republican administrations have attempted to eliminate OJJDP. Moreover, conservatives in the executive branch and in Congress have played dominate roles in encouraging the get tough approach to juvenile crime. Sadly, the federal role in encouraging the development of effective humane responses to juvenile crime was less than stellar during the Clinton years as well. Although OJJDP did support the dissemination of information on a variety of juvenile justice interventions for youth ranging from youth oriented community policing to the development of effective residential interventions and aftercare during the Clinton years, during this same period the institutionalization of youth continued to grow and little was done to address the conditions of confinement in juvenile correctional institutions. Furthermore, while there have been some bipartisan successes (e.g., periodically saving the Office of Juvenile Justice and Delinquency Prevention [OJJDP] from elimination), the get tough movement in juvenile justice has received only tepid opposition from liberal members of Congress.

Similarly, conservatives within state legislatures and at the local level have led the movement toward the development of a range of punitive measures. These measures have resulted in the increased incarceration of youths, new options for trying youths as adults, and they have produced increases in the number of youths being transferred to criminal courts (Krisberg, 2005). Simultaneously, conservatives and many liberals have turned a blind eye to the quality of community correctional programs for youths and the overcrowding and inhumane conditions found in many juvenile and adult facilities that house juveniles. For too many politicians, appearing tough on juvenile crime has consistently trumped the growing evidence that effective interventions for problem youth do exist. It has also trumped the needs of families and children, and community safety.

Although the recent history of juvenile justice politics may lead to a less than sanguine view of the potential for substantial changes in juvenile justice policy in the short-term, there are signs that the regressive conservative policies of the past are vulnerable. This is because there is a growing body of evidence regarding what works in juvenile justice and the shortcomings of the get tough perspective. There is also growing documentation of the harm that results from a strict focus on punishment and the lack of accountability found in many juvenile justice and child welfare programs. In addition, there is increasing scrutiny of the juvenile justice process by individuals and groups who feel that inequality pervades juvenile and criminal justice operations in many communities (see Free the Jena 6, 2007).

Although the 2008 general election resulted in more progressive leadership at the national level and in many states, it will be important to understand the positions of political candidates and support those who take a more progressive stance toward issues facing families and children. However, voting for progressive candidates is only one of many steps that must be taken in support of a more critically informed version of juvenile justice. At the national level there is a clear need to develop an organization that has the express purpose of advocating for humane and effective juvenile justice policies. Such an organization should be comprised of diverse groups of individuals with backgrounds in law, juvenile justice, law enforcement, child welfare, the faith and business community, and it should include other citizens (including youths) interested in juvenile justice and child welfare issues. Representatives of this group should network with other child and family advocacy groups and should support legislation and policy initiatives related to primary, secondary, and tertiary delinquency prevention. It should also engage in educational projects for the general public and the press, and it should work diligently to educate political leaders on important issues and research on effective juvenile justice interventions.

At the local level there is also a need for advocacy groups that are actively involved with understanding local problems and engaged in activities designed to address problems related to child and family well-being and delinquency. These activities should include identifying and coordinating individuals and organizations and creating networks that are concerned with child welfare, and facilitating the development, implementation, and evaluation of evidence-based practices. These local organizations should also be involved in assessing the continuum of practices related to delinquency in the community, supporting effective practices, identifying gaps in services, and working to improve or replace practices that are ineffective or inhumane. They should also be involved in educating the public and the press about effective and harmful juvenile justice practices and developing relationships with local and state policymakers that support effective juvenile justice practice.

In addition to developing good working relationships with policymakers and lobbying for the implementation of critically informed policies, it should be recognized that there may be occasions when more confrontational strategies are needed. There may be situations where picketing, demonstrating, and actions involving nonviolent civil disobedience may be helpful in efforts to educate and mobilize the public and increase leverage on political figures. Recent examples of these types of actions occurred in Jena, Louisiana (Free the Jena 6, 2007) and there have been ongoing efforts in California to shed light on serious problems within that state's juvenile correctional system (Books Not Bars, 2008).

Finally, groups that advocate for more effective juvenile justice practices should keep in mind that there are potential supporters for children aligned with both of the dominate political parties in the U. S. Indeed, political party affiliation is not necessarily a clear indication of an individual's support for effective and humane juvenile justice and child welfare policies. Framed in the right way and bolstered by sound research and careful attention to the costs and benefits of effective and humane programming, there may be more support for a more critical justice process than many believe. To find out, however, will require many of us to engage in roles that are different than those we often occupy. It will require us to move away from the comfort of the university and our research agenda and to engage more actively in the life of the community. Moreover, it will require us to build upon our pedagogical skills so that we become effective organizers and advocates for children and families; for improving the quality of life in our community. It will require us to blend the theoretical world and the world of praxis. It will not be easy, but unless those of us who are concerned about the problems facing the juvenile justice process become actively engaged in the politics of change, we will be guilty of acquiescing to policies that harm children and families. For one, I find that unacceptable.

Note

1. OJJDP is a component of the Office of Justice Programs within the Department of Justice. Its stated "mission is to provide national leadership, coordination, and resources to develop, implement, and support effective methods to prevent juvenile victimization and respond appropriately to juvenile delinquency." Source: Shay Bilchik (n.d.) The Office of Juvenile Justice and Delinquency Prevention. Washington, DC: OJJDP.

11

Razing the Wall: A Feminist Critique of Sentencing Theory, Research and Policy

Jeanne Flavin

Most sentencing research and policy has been shaped by non-critical, non-feminist approaches. The "edge" which feminist criminologists are attempting to "cut" is more like a longstanding, well-defended wall; one constructed of androcentric, classist and racist assumptions that needs to be razed and replaced with (for lack of a better metaphor) a window framed by feminist principles.[1] Feminism attempts to describe gendered oppression, identify and explain its causes and consequences, and prescribe strategies for the political, economic and social equality of the sexes (Rice, 1990; Tong, 1989). Loosely defined, feminist criminology is criminological inquiry conducted using feminist theory and research.

In the United States, feminists have made significant gains in criminology. In recent years, scores of articles citing feminist principles have appeared in major journals, and two volumes have been published focusing specifically on feminist perspectives in criminology (Gelsthorpe and Morris, 1990; Rafter and Heidensohn, 1995). Much of this literature could be described as critical. Both feminist and critical perspectives object to mainstream criminology's claims to neutrality and objectivity, both are overtly political, and both strive to present a new vision of equality and social justice (Rafter and Heidensohn, 1995).[2] There cannot be *a* feminist criminology any more than there can be *a* critical criminology because neither perspective is monolithic.[3]

I agree with postmodern feminists that a "One and True" feminist theory is "neither feasible nor desirable" because women's experiences differ across dimensions of class, race, culture, age, and sexual orientation (Tong, 1989: 7). Nevertheless, the framework developed by McIntosh (1984) and others (cf. Anderson, 1988; Daly, 1995; Goodstein, 1992; McIntosh, 1984) suggests it is possible to use common feminist themes to locate gender and race in a discipline. Daly (1995) elaborated upon this work and delineated stages of curricular change and modes of feminist production of knowledge in criminology. The first two stages are pre- or nonfeminist. In Stage 1, minority men and all women are completely excluded from the discipline. In Stage 2, women and minority men are added to the discipline, but feminist perspectives are not used to shape the research or interpret findings. Daly and other scholars agree that criminology remains in this stage.

This chapter aspires to move the discussion of sentencing into Stage 3 by challenging existing theory and research on the sentencing of women offenders. The first part of this chapter critiques mainstream criminological approaches to the study of gender and sentencing and points out how these approaches have distorted our understanding of the judicial treatment of women, especially women of color. It also examines how nonfeminist biases have manifested themselves in sentencing policy.

In Stages 4 and 5 of the feminist production of knowledge, research, and policymaking efforts place all women and minority men at the center of knowledge, where they become the focus of research and are studied on their own terms. The second part of this chapter expands on feminism's potential to shape sentencing research and policy. This section will illustrate how sentencing research and policymaking might look from the fourth stage of transformation, where "all groups possess varying amounts of penalty and privilege in one historically created system" (Collins, 1991: 225).

The Bricks in the Wall: Non-Feminist Approaches to Sentencing

Women of color—like women of all races—are underrepresented in the American criminal justice system. Women comprise fifty-one percent of the United States population at large (U.S. Bureau of the Census, 1993) but only fourteen percent of all felony defendants in large urban counties, nine percent of jail inmates, five percent of state prison inmates, and seven percent of federal prisoners (Jankowski, 1992, Kline, 1992; Maguire and Pastore, 1994; Smith, 1993). The small numbers of women involved in the criminal justice system (relative to those of men) have contributed to an historic disinterest in the study of women offenders (Nagel and Johnson, 1994). Prior to the seventies, the few efforts that considered women's criminal behavior focused on physical or biological explanations of female criminality (cf. Lombroso and Ferrero, 1895, Pollack, 1950).

In the seventies, the women's rights movement, the rise in feminist scholarship (including feminist criminology), and the publication of Adler's *Sisters in Crime*, Simon's *Women and Crime*, and Smart's *Women, Crime and Criminology* stimulated interest in women offenders (Nagel and Johnson, 1994: 181). Since then, many scholars have acknowledged the importance of gender in studying women's criminality, including sentencing. Existing theories and methodologies have fallen short, however, in their attempts to advance understanding about the relationship between gender and sentencing. The literature reflects the enduring biases of a criminological tradition established largely by white male criminologists. For example, many researchers have explained their findings by citing notions of paternalism and chivalry without empirically evaluating the veracity of these assumptions. Another common analytical approach reduces the complexities of gender to a sex variable. While these studies frequently have established that gender differences in sentencing exist, they have done little to help us understand why differences exist.

Although women as a whole are underrepresented in the criminal justice system, black women (like black men) also are overrepresented in this environment. Between twelve and thirteen percent of all women and men in the United States are black (U.S. Bureau of the Census, 1993: 21).[4] Yet black women comprise 57 percent of female urban felony defendants, 40 percent of all female jail inmates, and 43 percent of female federal prisoners. For black men, the statistics are equally grim. Black men comprise 57 percent of male urban felony defendants, 47 percent of male jail inmates, and 32 percent of male federal prisoners (Jankowski, 1992; Kline, 1992; Smith, 1993).[5]

Although both black women and men are overrepresented as defendants and offenders, black women are caught in what has been deemed a "criminal justice double bind" (Richey Mann, 1989); black women (and other minority women) experience discrimination both because of their gender and race/ethnicity status.[6] The double bind has limited the study of black women offenders. Young noted, "[t]o say that the black female offender has been neglected in the study of crime and delinquency is to understate the obvious" (1986: 311). She also observes that the methodology of the few existing studies of black women offenders is flawed, resulting in conclusions that "are fragmented, speculative and lacking in adequate empirical bases" (1986: 318). Young's remarks were made a decade ago, yet the neglect persists. For example, Tonry (1995), purporting to examine "race, crime, and punishment in America," justified his decision to focus on blacks because they have experienced the sharpest disparities in the justice system. In the following paragraph, however, he excluded women from his study on the grounds that they constitute such a small percent of the total number of prisoners.

The sentencing literature focusing on race mainly has examined the experiences of black and white men, while that studying gender has assumed the experience of women is homogenous, disregarding the intersections of gender and race (Rice, 1990). In the past twenty years, feminist criminologists have focused on gender more than race and ethnicity. As is discussed later, more recent work conducted from a black feminist perspective offers significant promise for theory, research, and policy.

Theoretical Critique

MacKinnon proposes that the state is male because it sees and treats women the way men see and treat women (MacKinnon, 1989). The same could be said of criminology. While in recent years other fields (most notably, anthropology, history, and literature) have stressed the importance of employing nonsexist methods,[7] criminology has been slower to follow suit (Daly, 1995; Stacey and Thorne, 1985). This is unsurprising given that historically, the criminal justice arena has been dominated by men, pursuing questions of interest to men, focusing largely on aspects of men's criminality, from a male perspective.

Androcentricity permeates all aspects of scholarly inquiry, from theorizing and model-building, to data collection and analysis. The implications of theorizing in a field that has been shaped by androcentricity are significant:

> Scholarly research is supposed to be embedded within its appropriate literature. If an entire area has been shaped by androcentric research...it is necessary to consider the area carefully as a whole and ask oneself whether, for instance, the variables considered important include those that are particularly important for women. (Eichler, 1988: 42)

Admittedly, in the past quarter century criminologists increasingly have recognized the social significance of gender. A vast literature has emerged examining (if tangentially in some cases) gender and judicial outcome. The sheer volume of this literature gives the impression that we actually understand the relationship between the two. But as Sherif noted, "the `variable' called sex is like a railroad boxcar: everyone knows what it is called and what it is used for, but no one knows what is inside" (1987: 45).

The largest body of research suggests that female defendants are treated more favorably than male ones (Adams and Cutshall, 1987; Bickle and Peterson, 1991; Myers, 1987; Myers and Talarico, 1986a; Spohn, Gruhl, and Welch, 1987). A second, smaller body of literature finds that (at least for some offenses, historical periods, points in the system, and measures of outcome) women are treated more harshly (Boritch, 1992; Jamieson and Blowers, 1993; Myers and Talarico, 1986b; Wilbanks, 1986). Yet another group of studies suggests that no sex differences in judicial treatment exist (Crew, 1991; Curran, 1983; Phillips and DeFleur, 1982; Steffensmeier, Kramer, and Streifel, 1993). Daly and Bordt (1995) conducted the most recent and comprehensive review of statistical literature on gender and sentencing to date. Of the fifty datasets they reviewed and the 249 outcomes generated from these cases, 149 (60 percent) showed sex effects favoring women, ninety-eight (39 percent) showed no sex effects and only two showed effects favoring men.

The lack of conclusive findings in an immense literature illustrates the deficiencies of existing theories and methodologies in explaining the judicial treatment of men and women defendants. Only relatively recently have researchers given serious consideration to how extralegal factors may attenuate the relationship between gender and sentencing. Studies examining extralegal factors such as family status reflect a gradual shift away from "a search for direct gender effects, and toward the possible indirect gender effects and even interaction effects of gender with highly correlated social status variables" (Odubekun, 1992: 354). Models probing social factors (or "sociological models") are in the early stages of development and to date, remain largely unexplored.

The research examining race also is flawed. Since the sixties, sentencing researchers have concerned themselves with whether blacks and whites are sentenced differently, and whether discrepancies in treatment are discriminatory or merely disparate. As with studies considering gender, the findings have been mixed. One team of scholars concluded that "after fifty years of research on whether or not there are racial or ethnic disparities in sentencing, there is only one generalizable finding: Sometimes judges discriminate and sometimes they don't" (Unnever and Hembroff, 1988: 51). Just as the literature has failed to consider social characteristics attendant to gender that may influence sentencing, so too has race been reduced to a variable.

Two general models of sentencing can be identified: the jurisprudential model and the sociological model. Historically, the jurisprudential model (or "lawyers" model) dominated the study of sentencing. The jurisprudential model is one in which "the social structure of the case has no relevance at all.... Each case is analyzed in a social vacuum" (Black, 1989: 19). Social characteristics are not just overlooked in this model, they are excluded deliberately.[8] To consider social characteristics of the actors is to violate basic principles of the judicial process, to rebut the ideal of blind justice. Because social characteristics are not supposed to influence the handling of a case, the jurisprudential model assumes that they do not.

The jurisprudential model assumes law is constant and universal with the same facts resulting in the same decisions. Lawyers and judges presumably frame their arguments and decisions in terms of how the rules logically apply to the facts. If black and white women and men are sentenced differently for the same offense, it is because they differ on key legally germane characteristics, such as prior record and offense seriousness. Rules—and rules alone—determine how a case is decided. Consequently, when discrimination occurs it is considered an exception, not the rule.

To say that the judicial system is based on the jurisprudential model seems redundant. The recent enactment of sentencing guidelines, however, suggests that judicial officials recognize that social characteristics do play a role in judicial processing. Sentencing guidelines were developed out of increasing concern that social and demographic attributes influence sentencing. For instance, the United States Sentencing Guidelines (1992) specify that sex, race, and other characteristics such as pregnancy and primary parenting responsibilities are not to be considered when determining a sentence. Instead, the Guidelines emphasize the role offense and the offender's prior criminal record should play in sentence determination. In other words, sentencing guidelines demonstrate the legal culture's conviction that social characteristics should not influence sentencing while at the same time acknowledging that in reality, they have.

Later in this chapter, the ongoing debate over whether gender neutrality can be legislated will be discussed more fully.

Relative to the jurisprudential model, sociological models are recent developments (c.f. Odubekun, 1992). They acknowledge that technical or legal aspects of a case (such as prior record and offense seriousness) are important in explaining sentencing. Sociological models also assume that social characteristics influence case handling. Far from being constant from one case to another, law is assumed to be variable, changing with the social characteristics of the parties. Whereas the jurisprudential model is concerned with how cases should be decided, sociological models examine how they actually are.

While sociological models represent an improvement over jurisprudential models in their ability to further our understanding of gender and sentencing, many sociological approaches evince a number of shortcomings. Much sociology-based research on gender and judicial outcome is inherently flawed, because it is grounded in theory that is flawed (Daly, 1989a; 1989b). Or, as Harding notes, "Existing bodies of belief...distort our understanding of all of social life by ignoring the ways women and gender shape social life and by advancing false claims about both women and gender" (1987: 189).

Traditionally, paternalism-based theories have been used to explain gender differences in sentencing. These theories hold that women are punished more or less severely than men based on assessments of how deserving they are of "paternalistic" or "chivalrous" judicial treatment.[9] Preferential treatment models assert that female offenders receive less severe sentences than male defendants due to the court's "paternalistic" or "chivalrous" attitude (Pollack, 1950). Punitive treatment models come into play where female defendants have been found to receive more severe sentences. These models frequently cite the "evil woman" thesis which holds that the nature and seriousness of some women's offenses in effect will "cancel out" any chivalrous effects (Campbell, 1981; Casburn, 1979). Models predicting equal treatment of men and women offenders argue that the effects of chivalry and paternalism are diminishing as judicial attitudes and the social position of women change. Each of these types of paternalism-based theories is marked by a number of significant flaws, the most significant of which are summarized here.

Preferential Treatment Models

Paternalism-based models have been used as a common interpretation of preferential judicial treatment. However, in recent years they have been widely criticized on a number of grounds (Daly, 1987b; Kruttschnitt and Green, 1984). First, most studies asserting paternalism have not empirically evaluated whether it is in fact responsible for the differences (Daly, 1987b). If women are accorded leniency in judicial outcome, it does not necessarily mean that women are the objects of judicial protection. For example, other legal and extralegal factors (such as prior record or employment status) may account for the difference.

Second, chivalry has been called "a racist and classist concept . . . reserved for the women who are least likely ever to come in contact with the criminal justice system: the ladies, or white middle-class women" (Klein, 1973: 10, 13). There is ample reason to question whether all women have benefitted equally from judicial paternalism; indeed, whether black women have ever benefitted from it (Raeder, 1993; Young, 1986). Historical evidence of the lack of chivalry extended to black women includes their placement in chain gangs while white women offenders were placed in reformatories (Rafter, 1990). Similarly, white women's rebellion against gender roles may lead to psychiatric treatment, while black women are more likely to wind up in prison (Hurtado, 1989). Black women have been characterized by larger society as "welfare queens," "Mammys" and "Jezebels," tough, masculine "black Amazons" and castrating, dangerous "sinister Sapphires"—not the sorts of women upon which chivalry is generally bestowed (Mullings, 1994; Young, 1986).

Third, some critics argue that even if judicial attitudes result in the preferential treatment of women, one cannot assume these views reflect a paternalistic or chivalrous concern for the woman offender. For example, Daly (1987b; 1989b) and Musolino's (1988) interviews with judges suggest a concern for the children in the woman's care, not the women themselves.

A final objection to preferential paternalism models is raised against the framing of arguments in a way that suggests the treatment of male defendants is the "norm" or the standard against which women's treatment is to be measured. Asking "Why are men's sentences more severe than women's?" is as valid as asking "Why do women receive less severe sentences than men?" though it is the latter line of inquiry that permeates the literature. Our failure to formulate questions that do not assume a male norm obstructs our understanding of men's situation as well as women's. Perhaps the better question to ask is "What is it about men and women's social location (e.g., their roles as sole and primary parents and economic providers) that explains how they are sentenced?" As Daly notes, "feminist research need not situate women as `other' or men as `central' or `master-category' in order to compare the treatment of or the response to men and women accused of law-breaking" (1994: 126).

Punitive Treatment Models.

Sexual dichotomism exists when the sexes are treated as two discrete (rather than overlapping) groups (Eichler, 1988). In cases where human attributes are in fact identified solely with one sex or the other, sexual dichotomism is justified (such as females' unique capacity to bear children). Sexual dichotomism becomes problematic when referring to a concept that theoretically is present in both sexes but is linked to only one. Such is the case with the "evil woman" thesis.

The evil woman thesis predicts that women who commit crimes that are "unfeminine" or "masculine" will be sanctioned at least as harshly as men convicted of similar crimes (Bishop and Frazier, 1984; Crew, 1991; Nagel and Hagan, 1983; Parisi, 1982; Wilbanks, 1986).[10] Not only will a woman lose the benefits of chivalry and paternalism when her behavior falls outside the bounds of traditional sex role expectations, but she may be punished twice, once for the specific offense and once for transgressing against the expectations of "womanly" behavior (Simon, 1975).[11]

There is no corresponding "effeminate man" thesis predicting the treatment of male offenders who commit "feminine" crimes such as shoplifting and passing bad checks. Researchers' acceptance of the categorization of crimes by gender has resulted in the widespread acceptance of the sexist categorization of the crimes women (not men) commit as "masculine" or "feminine." Again, the male is assumed to be the "norm," the generalized criminal, the general human being. The evil woman thesis misspecifies the source of the problem which lies—not in women and the type of crimes they commit—but in the judicial system's selective attention to women and their crimes. Or, as Kruttschnitt observes, "the focus has been on explaining the offender and her conduct...rather than the legal system and its conduct toward women" (Kruttschnitt, 1980-81: 249). In sum, the "evil woman" proponents' characterization of the justice system in terms of chivalry is flawed. Critical feminist perspectives encourage us to consider that the legal system may be marked by social control and the enforcement of sex-role expectations rather than chivalry (Bowker, 1978; Crew, 1991).

Equal (or "Less Unequal") Treatment Models

A third approach proposes that gender is becoming less of a factor in the judicial treatment of women. Two explanations combine the concepts of women's emancipation and judicial paternalism, and are often categorized as the "liberation thesis."[12] Adler's "masculinity" thesis argues that as women are liberated and assume social roles historically held by males, they will become more like males—more violent, pushy, and crime-prone—and begin to commit traditionally male crimes, i.e., robbery and burglary (Adler, 1975; Daly and Chesney-Lind, 1988; Simon and Landis, 1991). Simon's work takes a more qualified view of the influence of social circumstances. Simon's opportunity thesis predicts that as women become increasingly self-supporting and enter the public sphere in increasing numbers, they will be subjected to less informal social control (by families and family responsibilities) and will encounter increased opportunities to commit crimes of fraud and embezzlement, forgery, counterfeiting, and larceny/theft. When extended to explain sentencing, Adler's and Simon's theories suggests that as more women commit more and different crimes, police, judges and other judicial players' chivalrous attitudes will diminish, and the treatment of women and men will be equalized (Krohn, Curry, and Nelson-Kilge, 1983).

Simon's and Adler's analyses have raised important questions regarding the influence on crime of women's changing socioeconomic status and their entry into previously male-dominated domains. At the time their work was published, it also addressed a deficit in knowledge of women's crime and gender differences in crime. Simon and Adler's scholarship has been credited with making inquiry into women and crime more acceptable and respected among some mainstream criminologists (Moyer, 1992).

Empirical support for Adler's and Simon's work has been mixed. Part of the problem stems from the difficulty in developing valid indicators of concepts such as "liberation" and "emancipation." More pointed criticisms take issue with the assumptions upon which the theories were based. Some of Adler's critics charge that predicting that women will think and act like men when they enter roles traditionally occupied by men reduces women "to mere imitators or mindless hedonists" (Box and Hale, 1984: 494). Additionally, any relationship between emancipation and crime may be spurious. The influence of potentially confounding factors must be considered, such as the public's increased willingness to report female offenders to the police, the increasing number of women police officers and court officials, the increasing professionalization of the police, and a greater willingness to categorize a woman's behavior as criminal even if she was merely an accomplice (Box and Hale, 1984).

Before conclusions can be made about gender differences and sentencing based on assumptions of increasing female criminality and diminishing judicial paternalism, it is important to establish that (1) a significant proportion of women offenders, in fact, are becoming liberated or emancipated; (2) women's criminal behavior is increasing and/or changing; and (3) judicial attitudes toward female criminality have been paternalistic and are becoming less so. Once we have empirically established these conditions exist, the task remains to consider plausible, rival hypotheses that may explain any observed relationships among emancipation, crime, and judicial treatment.

Methodological Critique

Feminist criminologists share with other critical theorists a concern with the "myth of objectivity." Methodological weaknesses undermine our understanding of gender differences and contribute to the propagation of misconceptions about gender and sentencing. There are two main reasons for criminologists' historical failure to consider the relationship between gender and judicial outcome as a subject deserving of scholarly inquiry. First, as demonstrated by the survival of paternalism/chivalry theory in the absence of empirical support, scholars have assumed for years that women receive less severe sentences than men. Researchers have not felt compelled to research a question to which the answer was already "known." Secondly, until recently, sex was considered a legally relevant factor in sentencing. If men and women received different judicial treatment, this was not viewed as a problem, but as the result of the system operating as intended (Crew, 1991).

Contemporary sentencing researchers rarely ignore the issue of gender altogether. More common are studies that acknowledge that gender may play a role in explaining judicial outcome but are deficient in its treatment. Studies involving only one sex are not necessarily unacceptable. The reasons for excluding women or men from the study vary, and some of the reasons given clearly are better than others. For example, studies excluding men may be necessary to compensate for inaccuracies and gaps in our existing knowledge of women's judicial treatment. Under these circumstances, one-sex studies are "perfectly acceptable" (Committees on the Status of Women in Sociology, 1986: 3). Some researchers, however, exclude either men or women from the study citing a desire for a more parsimonious model, even if it comes at the expense of understanding. One study dropped all cases with female defendants "[i]n order to avoid one possible source of variation" (Welch, Gruhl, and Spohn, 1984: 218). If reducing variation is the primary concern, male defendants could as easily be eliminated from the study, but they rarely are. Still other scholars do not acknowledge the exclusion of men or women or make it clear that women have been excluded from an analysis without providing any explanation for doing so. The consequences of these methodological deficiencies are exacerbated when the results of one-sex studies are then discussed in terms suggesting they apply equally to men and women.

Another standard approach is to include a sex variable in the analysis. Increasingly, scholars have acknowledged that "sex" is an important factor, and dutifully include a sex variable in their models.[13] In recent years, much criticism has been leveled against the "add-women-and-stir" approach. Stacey and Thorne (1985) note that gender is frequently:

> assumed to be a property of individuals and is conceptualized in terms of sex difference, rather than as a principle of social organization. Reducing social life to a series of measurable variables diminishes the sense of the whole that is crucial to theoretical understanding of social, including gender, relationships (1985: 307-308).

Hence, including a sex variable while ignoring social locations associated with sex is an approach only slightly more useful than ignoring gender altogether.

The problem of reducing gender to a sex variable is accompanied by a failure to consider extralegal factors that may account for differences in judicial outcome between men and women. The divergent findings reported earlier suggest that some researchers may be observing a non-causal correlation between gender and judicial outcome. That is, the statistical association reported between gender and sentence may in fact result from the relationship of gender and sentence with another variable. Such is clearly the case when key legal factors such as prior record or offense severity have been excluded from the model. Models based on legal factors hold that defendants will be treated and disposed of identically (Curran, 1983). There are two ways in which legal factors may account for some of the divergent findings regarding gender and sentence. Some studies have neglected to include in the model legal factors which are correlated with both gender and sentence. Many studies are concerned with identifying the influence of extralegal factors (such as gender, race, and socioeconomic status) on sentencing, not legal factors such as offense seriousness or prior record. The failure to control for relevant legal variables was documented at least as early as 1983 (Blumstein et al., 1983). Since then, most recent studies have included measures of offense seriousness and prior record.[14]

A second and more widespread problem is the failure to consider the implications of using various measures of prior record or offense seriousness. The findings of Welch, Gruhl, and Spohn (1984) and Steffensmeier, Kramer and Streifel (1993) demonstrate the importance of not only including key legal factors in the model, but also giving careful consideration to the way in which these factors are operationalized. Welch et al. (1984) compared eleven commonly used measures of prior record. Their findings suggest that the impact of prior record on sentence severity and the decision on whether or not to incarcerate varied depending upon which measure of prior record was used. Similarly, Steffensmeier et al. (1993: 416) argue that "[the] failure to differentiate grades of severity may easily confound gender-based comparisons in sentencing outcomes because female offenders tend to commit the less serious forms of crime within the broad category." The authors also looked specifically at gender and imprisonment decisions and concluded that "the studies with the fewest controls [for legal factors] are likely to report large gender effects, whereas those studies with more adequate controls find small, if any, gender effects" (p. 436).

Since the eighties, more theorists have examined how extralegal factors may enhance our understanding of the relationship between gender and judicial processing. Extralegal factors are those viewed as legally irrelevant but which may in fact be influential. They often are directly or indirectly built into aspects of criminal law (Hagan and Bumiller, 1983). Studies examining extralegal factors—such as economic or family status—reflect a gradual shift away from "a search for direct gender effects, and toward the possible indirect gender effects and even interaction effects of gender with highly correlated social status variables" (Odubuken, 1992: 354). Theories probing social factors, however, remain largely untested (cf. Kruttschnitt and Daly).

As Kruttschnitt notes, "[u]ntil we begin exploring precisely how a woman's status affects her treatment in a criminal courtroom, we cannot determine whether it is sex per se or the social locations attendant to a particular sexual status that affect any observed gender-related sentencing patterns" (Kruttschnitt, 1980, 81: 248). Kruttschnitt's position is an example of a "structural-contextual" approach to explaining judicial outcome. Such an approach considers the location of individual cases and courts in the larger social world. It places gender within a social framework and looks not just at gender itself, but the statuses associated with gender (such as parent and economic provider) that may influence judicial decisionmaking.[15]

Just as the current literature tends to reduce gender to a variable, so too does the literature downplay the social locations of minority women and men. Countless scholarly works purporting to examine some aspect of race and criminality point out the gross overrepresentation of blacks in the criminal justice system, yet fail to consider specific aspects of race that may be salient to sentencing. Race and gender are immutable characteristics; moreover, they are socially defined characteristics permeating every aspect of social life. Therefore, the influence of race and gender cannot be ignored, even when the sample is homogenous in terms of race or gender. To say that race is not a factor in a sentencing study employing an all-black sample is as wrongheaded as asserting that gender is not a factor when discussing judicial decisions made regarding an all-women sample. Therefore, one cannot "[avoid] the possibly confounding factor of the interaction between race and sex in sentencing patterns" by excluding people from the sample on the basis of race or gender (Welch and Spohn, 1986: 391).

As noted earlier, the need to focus on black women is especially acute given that they largely have been ignored both in the literature examining race and sentencing, and that examining gender and sentencing. The findings of the few existing studies that have examined race and gender simultaneously have come under fire for being "fragmented, speculative and lacking in adequate empirical bases" (Young, 1986: 318). Daly (1989a: 137) reported that gender differences (favoring women) are more often found than race differences (favoring whites) and asked, "What explains this pattern? And, how might race or ethnicity overlay gender and family in court decisions?" Of the multitude of possible answers to Daly's questions, only a few have been explored in the research.

Critique of Sentencing Policy

The biases which have shaped theorizing and research about sentencing also manifest themselves in sentencing policy, as is evidenced by the federal Sentencing Guidelines (1992). The primary goal of the federal Guidelines was to eliminate unwarranted sentencing disparity. In the mid-1980s, Congress directed the United States Sentencing Commission to create sentencing guidelines and policies that were entirely neutral with respect to the offender's race, sex, national origin, creed, and socioeconomic status. Also, as part of the shift from making the punishment fit the criminal (rehabilitation model) to making the punishment fit the crime (the "just deserts" model), Congress directed the Commission to downplay "individualizing" factors such as ties to family and community, occupation, and education.

Scholars (including feminists) differ in how they frame questions of gender equity in sentencing policy. The debate is not over whether gender differences exist; the general consensus is that they do. There also tends to be agreement that gender differences should be accounted for in sentencing. Instead, scholars disagree on how much emphasis should be placed on "the presumption of formal, legal neutrality, and…the circumstances under which the law should recognize gender differences to foster more equitable treatment of women" (emphasis in original, Nagel and Johnson, 1994: 195, fn. 78). Nagel and Johnson (1994) characterize the debate as "special treatment" vs. "equal treatment."[16] Generally speaking, advocates of "special treatment" seek "justice," which in some instances may require women and men to be handled differently because of their special circumstances. The content of the Guidelines suggests that "equal treatment" — formal, legal equal treatment — has won out. The current Guidelines "explicitly mandate[s] that sex is not relevant in the determination of a sentence" (Raeder, 1993: 906). Although the Guidelines does not specifically address single parenthood, "the prevailing view in the appellate courts is that single parenthood is not *itself* an adequate basis for a downward departure" (Nagel and Johnson, 1994: 291). Nagel and Johnson (1994) defend the Guidelines against some of the criticisms that have been leveled against it.[17] Their arguments reflect the authors' assumption that the treatment of men offenders is the "neutral" standard or norm against which women's treatment is to be measured.

Nagel and Johnson acknowledge that incarceration may result in more serious collateral harm for single mothers, given that they potentially face losing custody of their children. However, they point out a variety of other situations that also could be used to justify a shorter sentence, such as offenders who risk losing their businesses, marriages, or residence in the United States. Attempting to make such intersubjective comparisons (and adjusting punishment accordingly) increases the likelihood of the very disparity and discrimination in sentencing that the Guidelines seek to overcome.

Less convincing is the authors' response to criticisms on the grounds that the incarceration of single mothers needlessly disrupts children's lives. Here Nagel and Johnson express concern that permitting women's primary child care responsibilities to be used to justify a reduced sentence may unintentionally reinforce gender stereotypes.

> Such a policy would effectively use the criminal law to reward women for their status as mothers (or, alternatively, to punish women for not having children). It would say in effect, `you have violated the criminal law, but we'll overlook that so you can do what you are supposed to do — care for your children' (emphasis added, Nagel and Johnson 1994: 208).

Taking primary parenting responsibilities into account is a problem only if the consideration is extended just to women primary parents. Instead of defining the source of the problem as our unwillingness to incarcerate mothers, as the authors of the Guidelines have done, perhaps consideration should be given to the relative ease with which fathers (particularly black fathers) are incarcerated and the impact this has had on black families.[18]

In her objection to the Guidelines, Raeder (1993) observes that adopting a model of women's de-incarceration for sentencing men may be more humane for both men and women. Instead, the reverse has occurred; the result has been described as "equality with a vengeance" (1993: 925). Raeder proposes that sentencing policy distinguish between single parenting and primary parenting responsibilities. While both should be considered as mitigating circumstances which justify giving a lower sentence than the guidelines recommend (a downward departure), single parenting downward departures should become the norm rather than the exception.[19] In this way, gender-linked roles such as care provider to children can be considered fairly in sentencing both women and men.

Raeder (1993) cautions against equating equality (represented by longer or more severe sentences for women) with justice. She argues that "gender-neutral"/"equal treatment" approach to sentencing has harmed women, since the current sentencing model is not neutral at all, but actually is based on the punishment of violent male offenders and major drug dealers. Moreover, gender bias in sentencing cannot be eliminated simply by legislating gender neutrality because society is not gender-neutral. Offense type and severity, prior record, and indicators of stability such as family and employment all reflect gendered patterns. The effect of downplaying or ignoring the influence of family ties (in order to avoid disadvantaging poor black males) has been to sentence women more severely than previously. If women have disproportionately and justifiably benefitted from being sentenced less severely because of their family responsibilities, then they are disproportionately harmed when the considerations are withdrawn. The result is anything but neutral.

Where Can a Critical Feminist Perspective Take Us?

The form of the Guidelines is disappointing, but unsurprising. The Guidelines simply comprise the top row of a brick wall constructed of non-feminist, noncritical thought. There are signs, however, that the wall is crumbling. Since the eighties, chivalry- and paternalism-based explanations of gender differences gradually have been replaced by attempts to examine the social locations attendant to gender that may account for differences in the way men and women are sentenced. For example, a growing literature has emerged to explore the relationship among gender, parenthood, and sentencing (c.f., Bickle and Peterson, 1991; Daly 1987a; 1987b; 1989a; 1989b; Kruttschnitt, 1984; 1982, 1980-81; Kruttschnitt and Green, 1984). Most of these studies did not conduct separate analyses by race, therefore it is not possible to determine whether the findings regarding children/dependents hold true for all women and men.

Herein lies the challenge of the fourth and fifth stages in the feminist transformation of criminology (Daly, 1995). In these stages, women and minority men are at the center of knowledge, instead of being studied as "problems" or "anomalies." By focusing on women and minority men, the researcher is compelled to consider aspects of their lives that otherwise might be ignored. Black (or multi-ethnic) feminist theory offers significant promise of advancing the field in this regard. As used here, black feminist criminology refers to a theoretical-political identity, rather than the racial identity of the theorist or the phenomenon being examined. It involves applying a racialized gender conscious-ness to the subject of criminological inquiry (Daly and Stephens, 1995). Black feminism highlights the role of race in shaping women and men's experiences in the criminal justice system by assuming multiple and interwoven sites of inequality. Hill Collins (1991) and others also encourage scholars to adopt the standpoint of the subordinated group. A standpoint approach calls attention to characteristics of minority women and men's lives that have been misrepresented in the literature — if not ignored outright. Further, it facilitates the identification of racist and sexist effects of ostensibly race- and gender-neutral sentencing policy and practices (Daly and Stephens, 1995; Rice, 1990).[20]

In criminology, standpoint feminism has been featured most often in spe-cific areas such as rape, sexual assault and domestic violence (Smart 1990). Although the utility of a black feminist approach to the study of sentencing has yet to be fully explored, evidence exists of its promise. For example, I recently conducted a study involving an all-black sample of men and women convicted of drug offenses (Flavin, 1995). Previous research had indicated that as many as one-quarter of black women prisoners and over one-half of black men prisoners did not live with their children prior to being incarcerated (Bureau of Justice Statistics, 1994). This knowledge prompted the consideration of offenders who are parents but do not live with their children — something that the existing literature has ignored entirely. Thus, in addition to incorporating a wide array of legal and quasi-legal characteristics (such as prior convictions, type of of-fense, number of plea bargains, drug use history, number of current convictions), variables indicating whether or not the offender had children and whether or not he/she lived with these children were also included.[21]

The findings challenge the widely accepted notion that women with children consistently benefit from having their status as mothers taken into account. Living with children resulted in less severe sentences for black women but generally not for black men. On the face, this finding supports the widespread assumption that women are accorded preferential treatment: They benefit from having their child care responsibilities taken into account in a way that men offenders do not. However, the consideration of child care responsibilities was not extended to women who do not live with their children; these women were sentenced more severely than both women who live with children and women who do not have any children.[22] These findings suggest that, while the law may acknowledge (with less severe sentences) that familied black women are subjected to greater social control, black women who do not live with their children may be punished more severely because they are perceived as failing to meet this obligation. Thus, for black women who do not live with their children, the cultural ideology of "woman as mother" may be a double-edged sword.[23]

As these findings demonstrate, standpoint perspectives offer criminologists the opportunity not only to challenge what is "known" but also to produce new knowledge about historically marginalized groups. It offers an alternative to treating women as "others" compared to a male "norm," and promotes acknowledgment of the wide range of differences present in every group.

For the most part, the response of mainstream sentencing researchers to the complex intersections of class, race and ethnicity, and gender has been to overgeneralize and over-simplify (e.g., "Women are sentenced less severely than men" or "Blacks are sentenced more severely than whites"). Other researchers, including some postmodernists and feminists, respond to the same issues by resorting to analyses which border on the incomprehensible (DeKeseredy and Schwartz, 1996). Standpoint feminism, in contrast, offers a means of grasping some of the complexities while avoiding the extremes of over-simplification and obfuscation.

Conclusion

In recent years, more scholars are examining the "wall" of criminological theory and finding it flawed. Feminist criminology, by boring a hole in the wall, permits us to see what lies on the other side while weakening the wall itself. The same is true of other critical theories that provide alternatives to traditional criminology — most notably left realism, peacemaking and postmodernism. Feminism, however, offers the field a more developed set of unifying propositions than either postmodern or peacemaking criminology while giving more attention to patriarchy and gendered dimensions of the law than does left realism (DeKeseredy and Schwartz, 1996; Edwards, 1990).

As stated at the beginning of this chapter, feminism is not a monolithic enterprise. Yet a consensus exists among feminists that in mainstream approaches women and minority men do not figure centrally in the production of knowledge. Thus, to date, the fifth and final stage of feminist transformation exists only in the minds of those who can envision a discipline where "[a]ll men and women, rich and poor, of diverse racial and ethnic backgrounds, and of different sexualities, are socially located in relations of class, race, and gender...[where we] see that all members of U.S. society are at the intersection of these relations" (Daly, 1995: 449-450). In sum, it is not possible to state definitively what structure will replace the wall that feminists are razing. But given the growing recognition of the contributions of standpoint feminism and other critical feminist theories, the creation of a new structure promises to be a more inclusive and democratic endeavor than those preceding it.

Notes

1. Alternatively, one could advocate "raising" the wall. To raise a wall implies either adding to the existing structure or building another one. In fact, this is what scholars of women offenders traditionally have done. They either have tried to extend existing theories to explain women's experience with the criminal justice system, or offered new theories that were based on sexist assumptions. The problem with walls in general is that one must stand on top of them in order to see the rest of the world. To do so distorts one's vision. Moreover, a position atop a wall is precarious and can be safely occupied only by a few people at a time. People perched on walls have a vested interest in keeping others off in order to preserve their privileged position.

2. Obviously, feminist approaches are not the only critical perspectives that can be used to evaluate sentencing. However, feminism's historic interest in the ways in which women experience subordination on the basis of their sex and the means of eliminating that subordination permits perhaps the richest insight into the problem of sexism in sentencing.

3. The basic tenets of the major feminist theories have been summarized elsewhere (Daly and Chesney-Lind, 1988; Tong, 1989). One important distinction should be made, however, between liberal feminists and critical brands of feminism. Marxist, socialist, radical, and black feminists differ in the emphasis they place on economic, biological, racial, and sexual sources of oppression (or some combination thereof). Unlike liberal feminists, none of these groups have illusions of reforming the existing system. Rather they aim to fundamentally restructure private and public life and to recast relations between women and men in political terms. Critical feminists object to liberal approaches not only for failing to question the existing system, but also for wanting equality in it. As Colette Price framed the issue nearly twenty years ago, "'Do we really want equality with men in this nasty competitive capitalist system?' 'Do we want to be equally exploited with men?' 'Do we want a piece of the pie or a whole different pie?'" (1978:94).

4. This chapter refers to "black men and women" rather than "African-American men and women" because the former term acknowledges other origins such as Dominica, Jamaica, or Haiti. The problem with this choice is that it disregards the heterogeneity in histories and experiences among blacks of different ethnicities (Rice 1992).

5. As Tonry (1994) points out that comparing blacks' proportion of the general population to their presence in prisons and jails suggests a disproportion favoring whites of three or four to one. Comparing black and white incarceration rates per 100,000 population of the racial group suggests a disproportion of six to seven times to one.

6. "Double bind" is something of a misnomer given that the relations of race and gender are not additive, but multiplicative or interactive. "[I]t is not just or simply that black women are subject to 'more' disadvantage than white women. Their oppression is of a qualitatively different kind" (Rice, 1990:64).

7. The term "sexist" is broadly used here to refer to the ways in which our intellectual universe has been shaped by one sex (male) rather than by two.

8. The exception, of course, is those instances where the laws themselves have referenced social characteristics. For example, up until a few years ago, some states did not recognize marital rape as a prosecutable offense. Even today, although all fifty states have marital rape laws, twenty-nine carry exceptions (Hall, 1993).

9. Paternalism refers to a view that women need protection and are not fully responsible for their actions. Chivalry refers to a reluctance to inflict harm on a woman

accompanied by an unwillingness to believe that a woman could really be criminal (Moulds, 1980: 280). Moulds makes a case for distinguishing between chivalry and paternalism. However, because the effects of the concepts are difficult to separate empirically, I will refer to the two phenomena jointly.

10. Steffensmeier (1995:94) defines masculine crimes as those offenses "involving physical strength, elements of coercion and confrontation with the victim, and/or specialized skills."

11. Some support for this notion does exist. Moyer (1992) reports studies showing that historically, several states had laws requiring women to receive longer sentences than men when convicted of certain crimes. Another study found that women charged with abducting and fondling children receive harsher judicial outcomes than men (Wilbanks 1986).

12. There are fundamental differences in the way the two theories view the etiology of female criminality (see Simon and Landis [1991] for a summary of some of these differences). However, because the implications of the two theories for judicial outcome are similar, they will be discussed together.

13. This chapter distinguishes between "sex" and "gender." As used here, "sex" refers to the physically defined categories of female and male, whereas "gender" refers to the system of meaning associated with the sexes through social arrangements (Kramer 1991).

14. See Daly and Bordt's (1995) analysis of the statistical literature on sex effects and sentencing. The authors' assessment of the quality of studies is based in part on controls for prior record and type of offense.

15. The idea for a structural approach is not new. Over a decade ago, Hagan and Bumiller (1983) suggested it as an alternative to the individual-processual approach that conceptualizes race or gender as an exogenous variable exercising its influence through an extended causal chain of judicial processing. However, the individual-processual approach continues to dominate the thinking in sentencing research (Odubekun 1992).

16. As the authors themselves acknowledge (see fn. 78), these terms are inapt since both camps aspire for more equitable treatment of women.

17. In addition to family responsibilities, Nagel and Johnson's discussion also addresses pregnancy, and coercion, duress and abuse. Due to space constraints, only the debate surrounding the consideration of family responsibilities is presented here.

18. Over ninety percent of black women who have children live with them, compared to only fifty-one percent of black men (U.S. Census, 1993). Statistics suggest that among black offenders, the proportion living with their children is lower. A study of black women prisoners found that the majority of black women prisoners lived with their children before entering prison (Bureau of Justice Statistics 1994). However, around one-quarter did not. The statistics on male inmates were not broken down by race. However, the same study found that only slightly more than half of the men lived with their children prior to incarceration. Given that black men are less likely to live with their children than white men (Hatchett et al., 1991), the percent of black offenders who lived with their children prior to entering prison is probably less than fifty percent.

19. Raeder's thoughtful discussion of gender and the federal sentencing guidelines is far more comprehensive than can be summarized here. Interested readers are encouraged to consult her work.

20. Readers are directed to Cain's (1990) discussion in support of standpoint feminism as well as Smart's (1993) critique of it.

21. Other features of many black families (i.e., the role of extended family members and the matrifocal family structure) were also incorporated into the model using indicators of whether or not the offender lived with other family members, had family members living in the surrounding area, and the number of these family members who were women.

22. Because black men were not accorded consideration of their parenting responsibilities to begin with, they are not sentenced more punitively when this consideration is withdrawn.

23. Daly (1987a, 1987b, 1989a, 1989b) also suggests the attention to women's family responsibilities may reflect judges' practical concern with obtaining replacement for child care. Daly's notion of "familial paternalism" or "family-based justice" is based on the idea that the state finds it easier to replace any economic support provided by a male breadwinner than the childcare provided by a mother. Arrangements for child care presumably are already in place for those women who do not live with children, enabling the judges to sentence these women without regard for securing child care. If Daly's assertions held true in the study under discussion, one would expect women who do not live with children and those who do not have children to be sentenced identically. The finding that women who do not live with children are sentenced most severely of all women suggests that other forces are operating.

12

A Geometry of Its Own: Restorative Justice, Relationships and Community in Democracy

Liz Elliott

Really, universally, relations stop nowhere, and the
exquisite problem of the artist is eternally but to
draw, by a geometry of his own, the circle
within which they shall happily appear to do so.[1]

Henry James was referring above to the problem of the novelist in curtailing unnecessary developments in a work of fiction, but the metaphor of the "geometry of his own" can be used to appreciate an important dimension of restorative justice and its vulnerability to co-optation. Although usually recognized in its more limited variation as a criminal justice diversion or alternative measures program for young, non-violent first-time offenders, restorative justice (RJ) holds deeper meanings about building peaceful communities. Communities are constituted by the relationships between individuals and groups; RJ responds to harm-doing, criminal or otherwise, through attention to the health of these relationships.

Current Western criminal justice systems operate through the actions of individuals who occupy different roles within them – victims, offenders, police officers, lawyers, correctional personnel, to name a few. The geometry of James's "artist" in criminal justice is a circle drawn tightly around the culpable individual, in reference to individual responsibility. The salient questions for the state adversarial system are: "Was a crime committed?" "Who did it?" and ""What do they deserve?" The perpetrator of the crime himself becomes the cause of crime; therefore the solution to crime is found in the response to the offender, usually through punishment and/or "treatment." This is sometimes incarceration, a practice that damages or frequently severs any relationships the individual might have had. Where crime is understood as the problem of the "criminal" alone, crime prevention strategies tend to focus on the punishment and liberty of the convicted. The culpable individual morphs into the punishable individual. The "crime and punishment" perspective further extends beyond the individual to social systems. Seen through this perspective, the criminalization of social problems lends itself to the pursuit of "solutions" to these problems that are often punitive and completely within the appropriate ambit of the state.

On this basis, it seems that RJ and retributive justice[2] are incompatible in both "theory" and practice. The familiar system pits a contest between the "offender"[3] and the state, displacing the actual victim into the status of "witness" (if s/he is still alive) and channeling attention to a determination of the offender's consequences for the act(s) already committed. RJ, conversely, facilitates a dialogue with the offender, victim and other stakeholders with the goal of sharing perspectives on what happened, how what happened affected each person, and generating mutually agreed upon responses to harm done that intend to address future implications in a wider community context. Both process and product in the two approaches differ fundamentally, and where RJ has been deployed within the current system–or where community-based RJ programs are significantly controlled by the state–RJ is in danger of being co-opted by the criminal justice status quo. More importantly for the purposes of the discussion to follow, the role of "community," which is conceptually essential to RJ, takes on a diminished and subservient role in co-opted programs which are directed by the state.

In this chapter I hope to make the case that the focus on relationships in RJ is a critical feature of the paradigm that holds important implications for the expressions of RJ in the context of modern western criminal justice systems and, more broadly, the *practice* of democracy itself. The potential of RJ for improving the integrity of the democratic ideal and its lived realities is crippled in criminal justice literature, which generally entertains the possibilities of RJ only when they do not challenge the status quo of existing legal systems of criminal justice. This is where co-optation is rife, as RJ becomes yet another "program" that is "owned and operated" by a government institution. A case example of a municipal government hostile takeover of a community-driven RJ program is offered to demonstrate the nuances of state cooptation, in which the drive towards case-processing trumped community development.

In the following pages the issue of these limits, the differing objectives of community and state and the specter of co-optation speak to the dilemma raised by Henry James in the "exquisite problem of the artist," that is, how to draw the circle within which all of the relationships affected by harm are included. The question of *who* determines these limits and which objectives are privileged when they come into conflict is explored. In this new casting, the implications of RJ for participatory democracy in grassroots communities are supported by critical criminology.

Restorative Justice and Relationships

The task of defining restorative justice is not for the faint of heart. Many attempts over the years have been made (e.g., Bazemore and Schiff, 2001; Cragg, 1992; Johnstone, 2002; Van Ness and Strong, 2002; Zehr, 1990, to name but a few). There have been concerns with both words constituting the term "restorative justice" – "restorative" being problematic for some who challenge the implication that social justice is sidelined by restoring relationships to their previously unequal state (Llewellyn and Howse, 1999; Morris, 2000), and "justice" for those who are not comfortable with the tendency of democratic institutions to co-opt RJ as a criminal justice program on the basis of its "justice" implications (Elliott, 2004). More recently, Howard Zehr has articulated RJ in more general terms, to keep its potential more open-textured: "It is a kind of coherent value system that gives us a vision of the good, how we want to be together...they are values that seem to have some universality" (in Coben and Harley, 2004: 268). This focus on values, as the case study demonstrates, is a significant feature of RJ and should be a marker of program integrity.

A focus on relationships frames a different understanding of justice; as Zehr noted, "crime is a violation of people and relationships" (1990: 181). The pursuit of this vision of justice, then, is an attempt to right the relationships between people that were either created by the harm or pre-existed it. This includes the victim and the offender, as well as the affected community. The critical RJ questions that require responses are "Who has been hurt?" "What are their needs?" and "Whose obligations are these?" (Zehr, 2002: 21). In restorative approaches to justice the goal is to heal individuals and their relationships. The circle of attention is widened to include the significant relationships affected by the harm. In expanding the relational nexus of the crime/harm, attempts to find solutions to the problems raised by the harm are sought in a broader context of relationships.

The importance of relationships in understanding and responding to our social and natural environments has been highlighted in many cultures. Interconnection is a primary indigenous belief, so it follows that the restoration of balance to relationships is a significant feature of the response to crime. The centrality of connectedness in aboriginal cultures is key to the understanding of crime itself; in Navajo systems, for example, it is said that the wrongdoer "acts as if he has no relatives" (Yazzie and Zion, 1996: 162). Modern versions of RJ also have roots in Judeo-Christian cultures, which have traditionally emphasized social relationships in pursuing justice. Herman Bianchi's work (1994) on the idea of justice – "the most basic concept of law" (p. x) – is a fine example of revisiting of traditional systems for the wisdom at the roots of a *tsedaka*[4] model. Michael Hadley notes that RJ "requires all of us to come to grips with who we are, what we have done, and what we can become in the fullness of our humanity…it is concerned with restoring the moral bond of community" (Hadley, 2001: 9).

Relationships, Community and Social Capital

Criminal justice systems in western societies have become the one-stop shopping spot for social welfare. No longer do they merely process – in a system guided by policies, rules and laws – detected lawbreaking in society. Thanks to an enthusiasm in the late twentieth century to download mental health services from hospitals to the streets and an eagerness to generally criminalize other social problems, criminal justice systems have become an expanded dumping ground for people suffering from a wide range of human miseries such as trauma symptoms, substance addiction, mental disorders, lack of success in forming healthy relationships, family dysfunction, and so on. Community ownership of other problems was gradually transferred to institutional professionals and systems. Concerned about the diminishing state of "the community" and the rise of "professionals," McKnight observed that the criminal justice system compensates for the failings of economic, political, or social systems, which consequently deters the reform of these systems by removing people from open society who are its products (1995: 145).

The idea that a growing criminal justice system in a democratic society could be akin to a canary in a coalmine shifts the analysis and reframes the focus of study from the individual as a "deviant" (hence his/her incarceration) to social institutions as "unhealthy" (hence the need for critical analyses). The recent trend in western democracies to create particular problem-solving courts (drug court, mental health court, community courts and in Canada, Gladue courts[5]) is an acknowledgement *within* the criminal justice system that its traditional tools are insufficient for the challenges at hand. Its solution is to expand its functions and tools, but all the same the solutions are sought through a formal criminal justice system. In so doing, the impetus to examine the system in a wider context of other social institutions and informal networks is again de-centered, and a focus on issues of social justice derailed.

Our immediate interest here is with what appears to be a disenfranchising of informal social networks by the formal criminal justice system: the everyday relationships we have with various others in our lives that form the life and pulse of a community, long after the offices of formal institutions have closed for the day. They constitute what has been described as "social capital" – "that intangible 'something' that exists between individuals and organizations within a community. Most people can recognize social capital as being the connections and trusting contacts that people make while going about their daily business" (Kay, 2006: 163). By definition, social capital can be seen as something *outside* of the appropriate purview of governing institutions. It may be found in community groups such as bowling leagues or reading clubs, or in the connections between residents of a well-integrated neighborhood.

Robert Putnam's research on social capital (2000) demonstrated what has been understood for a long time: relationships matter for the health of individuals and society. The impact of social bonds for the individual is a staple in criminological theory, but as Putnam notes, the positive effects extend beyond the simple calculation of specific individuals' relationships: "[A] well-connected individual in a poorly connected society is not as productive as a well-connected individual in a well-connected society. And even a poorly connected individual may derive some of the spillover benefits from living in a well-connected community" (2000: 20). Thus the contribution of a generalized good will into the network of one's relationships accrues benefits somewhere along the line, even for those in the collective whose contributions are minimal. The significance of social capital, then, for crime prevention and reintegration of both harm-doers and the harmed is notable, and is a key component of RJ. If crime is a violation of people and relationships, as asserted in RJ, then a key task within its practice is the healing of individuals and relationships. Restorative justice must be engaged in the development of community in order to attend to the needs of people affected by harm, and it must do so in ways that are guided by core values.

As will be demonstrated in the case study to follow, this is not what RJ programs always do in practice. First, however, it will be necessary to address the thorny topic of "community" in Western democracies, and then to note its importance to the reintegration aspect of conflict and crime. In bureaucratic discourses, "community" tends to be a catch-all term that essentially means anything that is not a state institution. The re-assertion of community in RJ has generated ample discourse on the meanings of the term. Arguing that "community is not a place," McCold and Wachtel (1998) suggest that community is a "perception of connectedness" to others and to a group which may or may not be tied to a specific geographical setting such as a neighborhood. Clear and Karp (1999) wrestle with the concept in the context of "community justice," asserting that "community" is "an entirely practical concept.... For each of us, community is the complex interlocking of human relationships upon which we rely to live daily life" (p. 60). Outside of the specific realm of restorative justice, advocates of building community in the workplace (Manning, Curtis, and McMillen, 1996) note:

> To require that a community agree on everything would be unrealistic and would reduce the richness that comes from diversity. But a community must agree on something. There has to be a core of shared values. Of all the ingredients of community, this is most important.
>
> Values define the character of a community. What people say is important, what they do is more important, but what they value is most important (p. 38).

In combination, then, a working definition of community would include the ideas of connectedness, relationships and values. We may not have the precise language to express it concretely, but we know it when we feel it. Community, then, may also be found in *affect*, the biological aspect of emotion. In the context of restorative processes, Nathanson asserts: "Everything we're doing is to build the sense of connection, and connection is *always* an affective experience."[6]

This idea of community is a flashpoint for critical analyses of RJ. In large measure, this is because the "idea" of community is often confused with the "ideal" of community. This is especially the case in government rhetoric about RJ and the role of "community." Given the limits of expression by government in policies, rules and laws, "community" is stripped of its affective meaning. "The community" becomes an amorphous ideal that has no concrete meaning. In government discourse, as Mowbray notes in the Australian context, "'Community'…is often used because of its aptitude for creating positive regard for the organizations, policies or programmes to which it is applied – and their underlying motives. If the term community is attached to something, the direct implication is that it is wholesome – and its proponents caring, responsive and progressive" (2005: 257). Pavlich goes further, suggesting that community is also an image created by "restorative justice governmentalities" in efforts to discern its differences from state criminal justice "by appealing to visions of community that are closely aligned with – if not largely created by – state agencies" (2005: 84).

Can a person have a relationship with a state agency? Individuals may well develop relationships with other individuals employed by state agencies, but state institutions are run by people functioning in specific *roles* and people in these roles can and do change often over the course of any specific shared project. The people in these roles, further, are public servants compelled to follow the reigning government's mandate whether or not they personally believe in it. In this sense, a "relationship" holds a very different connotation, one perhaps of a strategic alliance or a limited business partnership rather than an affective interpersonal connection. In any event, the state is *not* a person and it is difficult to conceive how a state could force or impose genuine relationships between people in a community, except perhaps unintentionally by their common unity of opposition to state practices that infringe on their individual autonomy. Indeed, as Pavlich has noted that in the context of criminal justice, "strong communities are…residual by-products of active individual participants who voluntarily take charge of restoring themselves and righting relationships distorted by criminal events" (2005: 89) rather than being the product of governments. Weak interpersonal relationships produce weak communities, which in turn embody weak social capital. Societies with weak social capital are more dependent on state institutions for governance, as individual capacities to handle civil life are atrophied. The implications of this are illustrated in the following case study.

Case Study

In a small community of about 33,000 people located outside of Vancouver, British Columbia, an informal gathering of local folks interested in learning about RJ philosophy met monthly for about a year. The group was created in 2001 as a result of a report generated by independent contractors hired to meet with community groups and assess the community's needs for crime prevention through social development,[7] under the direction of an appointed advisory committee to the local municipal government. Among its handful of recommendations, the report highlighted the need for a grassroots restorative justice group. A couple of local citizens, including the author, initiated the meetings through public service announcements, which eventually resulted in the creation of the restorative justice coalition consisting of about fifteen members. The monthly meetings were informal and intended to be informative, with films, guest speakers, and mainly circle gatherings[8] where members talked about concerns they had with ongoing and emerging community problems and the unsatisfying responses to these by formal systems. The group eventually came to the position that solutions to these problems would require significant shifts in the ways that both individuals and institutions framed and responded to social issues. A small grant was secured, and the coalition organized a three-day peacemaking circle training to introduce RJ values and processes to targeted change agents in the community, a group that included local judges, police officers, teachers, probation officers, former prisoners, ministers and other community members at large.

At the same time, the municipality-appointed advisory committee had created a sub-committee to look at developing an RJ program. Eventually the coalition was invited to engage with this committee to work towards developing a tangible program to which criminal justice cases could be referred. The committee included a local police representative and elected member of the municipal council (a retired police officer), who wanted to have a program in place in anticipation of the then-impending Youth Criminal Justice Act (YCJA)[9] which included many provisions for extra-judicial measures accommodated by RJ processes. A gathering of the coalition to discuss this possible merger with the more formal committee resulted in disparate positions and a lack of consensus. Some members from the coalition argued that RJ was first about building relationships, and that that included relationships with representatives of the institutions with which the coalition was ultimately to engage. Others believed that institutions were incapable of changing to accommodate full citizen participation and that the coalition should remain separate to avoid co-optation.

Three coalition members[10] joined the formal committee to work on the project of establishing an inclusive RJ program that was to include institutional stakeholders and community members. A sub-committee (referred to as a "Select Committee") was struck and included the three coalition members, two other community members from the municipal advisory committee, and four institutional representatives from the same committee (police, school district, provincial social services and the district municipal council); this select committee then met monthly for about two years. The issue of securing funding was a major topic of discussion, as was the overall purpose of a RJ program. Generally, the institutional members were concerned about a program to process cases generated by the new YCJA as well as neighborhood disputes, relieving institutions of more minor nuisances; the community members articulated a broader vision of RJ as community development, whereby cases were opportunities to unpack and respond to deeper local problems. Community members also expressed the need to work with institutions to help them to understand and incorporate RJ values within their own practices, through memoranda of understanding (MOUs) that outlined reciprocity of restorative values between the institutions and the community.

The funding issue was first addressed when the local municipal government agreed to subsidize a part time position for an RJ coordinator, with in-kind donations from other institutions. A coordinator was hired by the select committee to build the program with an administrative structure. Training money for the first wave of recruited volunteers was furnished by the now-defunct coalition, which had managed to build a very modest fund from small provincial grants. Relationships with institutional partners were created and MOUs were drafted. In the eyes of the community members, the first stage of an all-partner community RJ program was almost complete, but there were other community development stages to develop and deliver that would use specific conflicts as opportunities to determine and respond to the wider community problems that precipitated the conflicts. Given the larger community development strategy at stake[11] the select committee's community members articulated a longer term project that would necessitate the services of a fulltime conflict resolution coordinator as well as a fulltime aftercare/community coordinator.

Problems soon unfolded with questions around the accountability and reporting responsibilities of the new coordinator. The municipal government administrators expected to oversee the contract deliverables, but had no experience with the sub-committee or with the field of RJ. The select committee worked closely with the coordinator and most of its members had expected that reporting and accountability was more properly a matter of its concern. As the workload increased and the coordinator requested full time employment, the municipal government finally agreed in 2006 to fund such a position with administrative support including office space. The select committee was invited to celebrate this development at a dinner, and then its members were subsequently notified that the municipal government had decided to disband the select committee because it had been determined by the council representative on the committee that its work was done. In its stead the municipal government, represented by the now fulltime coordinator, would meet a couple of times a year with the other institutional representatives from the select committee but was no longer interested in grassroots community input. "Community representation," it was explained was more properly met by the involvement of locally elected politicians who were perceived to be the "true" representatives of the community.

As crisply explained by the coordinator in a final meeting of the select committee, "This program is *owned and operated* by the District." Requests in the meeting for a decision on the fate of the select committee and the program's direction to be made by the committee's established practice of consensus were dismissed by the municipal administrator in attendance, as was a subsequent final request to have the decision made by the more familiar and established process of democratic vote. And so a governing community engagement with RJ died with a resort to authoritarian and autocratic rule.

In the aftermath of these events, a representative from the now-excluded five community members attended a district council meeting in late 2006 and requested a restorative process (dialogue circle) with the elected municipal politicians, responsible municipal employees and all members of the now defunct select committee to process the harm that was created as a result of the decision. The deposed community members argued that the District decision and how it was rendered were at odds with the RJ program's stated vision ("aspires to be a community-based service that supports, promotes and practices holistic processes and values intended to establish community connectivity, understanding and safety"[12]) and values ("Inclusive, Ethical, Safe, Respectful, Humility"[13] [sic]) as conceived by the whole select committee. The District elected council agreed to the dialogue circle in the public meeting, but a few weeks later the individual community members received letters from a municipal hall employee informing us that the dialogue circle process agreed to was cancelled. The co-optation – of community governance, of values and of process – was then complete, and relationships between former committee members, divided along the line between community volunteers and paid government representatives, were destroyed.

Discussion: Case Processing or Community Development?

The case study raises a number of interesting points regarding restorative justice and its co-optation by government agencies. In particular, a focus on relationships and community is especially revealing. The District administration, working with "a geometry of its own," circumscribed the place of relationships and community in restorative justice as totally within its direction and control. The program is currently governed by the District through its employees, who recruit, train and supervise volunteers according to the policies and mandate of the District. The volunteers (community) work for their program coordinators who work for the local (District) government; the coordinators do not work for the volunteers as they would for a non-profit community-based organization. Responses to challenges about the real community content of the program resort to the notion that the trained volunteer facilitators "represent" the community, although they have no decision-making power within the program to guide its direction or mandate or even, surprisingly, to hold the program and its sponsors accountable to its own vision and values. Essentially, the only governance capacity of the community in this example is found in the same mechanism of any other government service – at the voting booth, every three years.

The long term vision of building community, relationship by relationship, guided by shared core values was also negated in this case study. Since the structure of the program is hierarchical and accountability is not mutually shared between district employees, volunteers, elected council members or community members at large, the articulated values of the program stand more as hollow statements than as animated practices. Indeed, the program's "Guiding Principles"[14] resemble a shopping list of "playing the opposites"[15]: being community driven vs. institutionally based; developing and maintaining relationships with all stakeholders in our community and operating as a collaborative interagency model; promoting the resolution of conflict and/or incidents of harm through dialogue and in a manner which is consistent with the principles of restorative justice; and so on. Since its operation, the dispute between the deposed community members and the District, as well as at least one dispute between a citizen and the local police agency, have not lead to RJ processes at all, since the institutions that were allegedly signatories to the agreements are not held accountable to the values and vision of the program to which they have signed on as partners. As a result, relationships among former colleagues have been harmed and dissolved; one outside observer of this whole event noted, "There seems to be a lot of conflict in this restorative justice!"

There are many RJ programs operating in various places in western democracies under the aegis, blatantly or by arm's length, of government direction and control. In this case, the municipal government used taxpayers' money to absorb the volunteer community efforts as its own, and appropriated RJ language and terms while continuing to operate on the basis of "business as usual." The outcome is reminiscent of the hopeful 1980s drive for alternatives to incarceration that ultimately served to widen the criminal justice net (McMahon, 1992). There is, however, a difference between the two movements. Alternatives to incarceration efforts had largely been acts of resistance to the status quo in criminal justice, whereas RJ operates from its own paradigm of thought and practice based on other foci such as relationships, values, and peacemaking processes. This difference signifies the importance of RJ as a stand-alone program responding to conflict and harm according to the principles and values of its own paradigm, rather than resisting existing criminal justice policies and practices or, as the case demonstrates, becoming co-opted by them.

There is a promise of RJ, despite the case study, that is found in the deeper meanings of what it is to build relationships guided by values, and why this is important for building and sustaining vibrant democracies. Two issues need to be discussed in order to develop this thought. First is the idea of RJ as driven by either the primary goal of case-processing, signified by the reference point of "the file," – or community development, signified by its dominant focus on interpersonal relationships. Second, is a consideration of how restorative justice values and processes, if guiding community development, enable a building of grassroots capacity for living together more peacefully and the competency to handle more conflicts without state intervention. Relationships are key to both of these.

The dominant expressions of RJ are found in the realm of criminal justice, and to another degree in education, where the paradigm of conflict resolution is generally adversarial, retributive and administrative. Many community-based organizations are able to function within these systems while maintaining their integrity of values and principles, albeit with the expected ongoing tensions. And organizations using well-trained volunteers may contribute to community development by affording selected citizens the opportunity to gain and practice conflict resolution skills outside of formal institutions. The limitation of these programs and organizations, however, is that the primary goal is case-processing rather than community development. Community organizations in these positions seek case files from state institutions, where the goal is to process and, ultimately, "close the file"; furthermore, they are often evaluated, for the purposes of financial sustainability by state agencies, on the basis of numbers of cases or files handled and completed.

There is another concern with a hierarchical "partnership" between community groups and state agencies. Notions of community-based RJ that rely heavily on government support will always be vulnerable to the shifting winds of political priorities. The example of the abandonment of RJ support in 2002 by the Royal Canadian Mounted Police (RCMP), Canada's national police force, in its shift of focus from community policing to "public safety interoperability"[16] highlights a basic problem with this reliance of community RJ on state institutions for referrals and even in-kind support. More concerning, however, is the idea that the community justice forum model adopted by the RCMP and still operating in many community organizations with RCMP involvement can be used for purposes other than community problem-solving, but rather intelligence gathering for investigation purposes (Deukmedjian, 2008). Thus, in its most sinister rendering, RJ programs that are in some way beholden to police agencies may unwittingly play the role of informant facilitation.[17] It would then be necessary for community-based agencies to monitor implications of their own practices against their values and to have the capacity to disengage from partnerships that might compromise the integrity of the agency's purpose. This highlights implications related to the governance of RJ programs, and whether those directed by state agencies, be they municipal governments or criminal justice system sectors, will guide their decisions by RJ values or state priorities when the two goals conflict.

When RJ practices over-identify with the objectives of formal institutions the focus is driven by case-processing expectations, and tensions arise when the objectives of RJ (to determine who was hurt, what their needs are, and who has obligations to repair harms) conflict with those of the existing systems (to determine if a crime was committed or a rule broken, who did it, and what they deserve for doing so). Meeting the needs of the parties in conflict may not occur in a time frame that coincides with the schedules and deadlines of the criminal justice system. Handling a few cases very well over a perhaps protracted time period may well be more valuable to the long-term interests of the community than handling a large number of cases quickly, but state-driven evaluation criteria do not usually account for this. Some conflicts may not make restorative processes at all, having been deemed by state representatives alone as being too serious for anything but the conventional institutional response. The mandates and jurisdictions of the institutions may overrule the ability of the RJ organization to deliver on its own promises or potential. Community may be drawn in as volunteer mentors or conflict process facilitators, but the value to its development will rest primarily in the relationships built specifically between those affected by harm and the community volunteers and within the boundaries determined by institutions.

A community development focused RJ program or organization is less concerned with meeting the needs of institutions than it is with meeting the needs of the people involved in, and affected by, conflicts. The focus is to build the community, relationship by relationship. Conflicts are thus seen as opportunities to learn about what is not working in the community, to offer opportunities for dialogue and problem-solving for individuals and the wider community. The geometry of restorative justice then becomes a widening circle of relationships. The circle extends as far as it needs to in order to end the cycle of dysfunction, including violence, in sets of relationships.[18] Sustainability and integrity of these relationships come in the ongoing efforts to think and act in ways that reflect shared values, where people and processes "walk the talk." Employees and volunteers of the program are called to act in the ways we expect of the conflict process participants, indeed, if anything to *model* shared democratic values. The needs of the people and the health of their relationships, in the broader context of community capacity-building and the development of social capital, are the central objective of the program or organization.

If the promise of RJ is to be realized to its fuller potential, it seems clear that it must stand apart from government institutions, with the autonomy of community-based status. This status at least offers the greater possibility of reflexive responses to the needs of the people than the entrenched demands of bureaucratic government institutions. Community-based organizations may well work with institutions on various levels, where the benefits of encounter are mutually responsive to their respective interests; they may also choose not to work with these institutions in specific situations if doing so compromises the integrity of the RJ mandate. As a "bottom-up" approach, RJ needs to be nested in its roots rather than pushed from the top down. The significance of a "grassroots" approach of RJ, aside from the needs of specific people in certain conflicts, can be explained with a return to the concepts of community and democracy.

Restorative Justice as Community Development and
Practices of Democracy

Democracy, like community, is another word that implies something whole-some. North Americans use the word "democracy" as if it was a self-evident virtue of modern society. Democracy implies equality and freedom. Its etymo-logical root – "the people rule" – suggests a vision of active citizenship. Our recent ancestors and contemporaries have died in wars defending or ostensibly promoting it. Yet, the concept seems distant in practice in modern democracies, where the only tangible vestige of "the people rule" is a trip to the ballot box every few years, at least if one is not legally disenfranchised from that process and has the requisite motivation to show up as an informed voter. Citizens in democracies, where the only expectation of them is to vote, have become disengaged from the processes that govern them. As Braithwaite notes, "In the historical period when representative democracy is sweeping away one dictatorship after another, democracy is becoming more shallow in its meaning for human lives. The lived experience of modern democracy is alienation. The feeling is that elites run things, that we do not have a say in any meaningful sense" (1999: 1). This intimates a largely ignored or understated possibility for RJ processes.

The *idea* of democracy has become a potent rationale for foreign policy of western states, but how well is it realized as a substantive *experience* or daily *practice* of its citizens? Braithwaite describes the problem:

> ...how can citizens hack a path to the heartland of the democracy if the democracy has no strategy for teaching them how to be democratic citizens? Circles and con-ferences about matters that ordinary people care about in their lived experience can teach them. If all students experience and witness serious acts of bullying at school and care about this, then before they reach adulthood all can have the experience of participation in circle solving of a difficult problem on which there are multiple perspectives.

And democracy is something that must be taught. We are not born democratic. We are born demanding and inconsiderate, disgruntled whiners, rather than born listeners. We must learn to listen, to be free and caring, through deliberation that sculpts responsible citizenship from common clay [Barber, 1992].

Punitive criminal justice, like the accountability mechanisms of the contem-porary state more generally, teach us not to be democratic, not to be citizens (1999: 2).

Skill development and practice in living democratic ideals is difficult when processes of conflict resolution have been taken over by governments. Christie, in an early seminal work in RJ literature (1977), distilled this concern in the idea of "conflicts as property," where disputes between people/groups were "stolen" by professionals, thereby stripping citizens of the potential dynamic education of democratic life. How else does a community discuss and clarify community norms and values, except through the vestiges of letters to editors of local newspapers or radio call-in shows? And while these examples may offer venues for the selective presentation of strong opinions, in what ways do they offer possibilities for dialogue on smaller conflicts and issues that may impact more immediately on the lives of individual citizens?

The focus of a community development approach to RJ would cultivate opportunities for citizens to engage in values-based processes to address interpersonal or inter-group conflicts on terms that meet the needs of the individuals and community over those of state institutional policies and mandates. This would not be constrained to criminal justice conflicts, but ideally would begin with child rearing and educational practices. Kohn's argument against behaviorism and control of children through punishments and rewards crystallizes the problem of growing good values from the inside out (1999: 161): He explains (p. 172-3):

> Indeed, if an auditorium were filled with bank robbers, wife batterers, and other assorted felons, we would likely find that virtually all of them were punished as children. Whether the punishments were called "consequences" is irrelevant: what matters is that these people were trained to focus not on what they were doing and whether it was right, but on what would happen to them if someone more powerful didn't like what they did. Thus, if it is argued that punishments and rewards are appropriate for children because adults act in response to these inducements, our answer is yes, some do. But are they the sort of adults we want our children to become?

Kohn's critique of conventional approaches to teaching children how to be good people and citizens is reminiscent of Miller's indictment of "poisonous pedagogy" (1983) in her examination of the roots of violence. Bloom (1997) extends Miller's idea in her work on creating sanctuaries where emotional safety is a paramount requirement, with a lean towards the development of vibrant democracies. She suggests, "Children need to learn the process of practicing democracy from the moment they set foot in a school. The classroom needs to be children's first experience in learning how to do group process while preserving individual integrity" (p. 233). Restorative processes offer this possibility, when they are grounded in shared core values. A democratic society works best if its citizens' individual conduct adheres to core democratic values. The goal is to cultivate citizens whose conduct is driven by internal inducements (personal integrity) than external ones (avoidance of negative consequences to oneself).

The concept of a circle – apart from being a useful group process alluded to by both Braithwaite and Bloom, and to demonstrate expanding concentricity of engagement in conflict resolution processes – is an apt tool for exploring the values of democracy, specifically, those of equality, inclusion, respect and justice. In a circle, every participant is required to listen more than they talk; everyone is equal, without the caveats of hierarchical processes; everyone who feels a need to participate is theoretically included; all concerns are respected in the dialogue; and decision-making processes embody core values.[19] Further, the circle is also a symbolic and practical container of the emotional outputs generated in the dialogue by the participants most affected. Conflicts that are emotionally charged are particularly suitable for restorative responses. Well trained and skilled restorative process facilitators can assist participants, as individuals and a group, to manage shame and create the conditions in which empathy becomes the mutative force in the conflict resolution circle.[20] This is the substance of community development, where the real work of reweaving the broken fabric of the community, relationship by relationship, occurs. This is where the possibilities for a lived democracy may be practiced and experienced.

For critical criminology, it is fitting that the focus of RJ be rooted in the objectives of grassroots community development above the case-processing demands of state institutions. State institutions were created to meet the needs of the people in democracies – that the needs of the state could come to overrule the needs of the people is a practical and political perversion. Community development strategies of RJ programs, at least, offer the hope of real community engagement with current problems that forecast potential harms and crimes. As Quinney asserts (2000: 21):

> What is important in the study of crime is everything that happens before crime occurs. The question of what precedes crime is far more significant to our understanding than the act of crime itself. Crime is the reflection of something larger and deeper.
>
> As a critical criminologist, I find it ever more difficult to witness crime or to think about crime. Instead, I envision a world without crime, and that vision comes from imagining a world that would not produce crime. To be critical, to be a critical criminologist, is to imagine what might be possible in this human existence.
>
> ...The struggle is to create a humane existence, and such an existence comes only as we act peacefully toward ourselves and one another.

Restorative justice offers possibilities of response towards the realization of Quinney's critical vision – at least in the variation of restorative justice as that which is focused on individual relationship building and healing; community development as driven by the real needs of process participants over the needs of state institutions; and building individual skills, through values-based processes, helpful for living peacefully in a democracy with minimal state intervention.

Notes

1. From the "Preface to the New York Edition" of *Roderick Hudson* (1986, orig. 1875) by Henry James.
2. Llewellyn and Howse (1999) define retributive justice in comparison to restorative justice in their Law Commission of Canada publication, *Restorative Justice – A Conceptual Framework*: "Retributive and restorative justice share a common conceptual ground in their commitment to establishing/re-establishing *social* equality between the wrongdoer and the sufferer of wrong. Retributive justice is, at its root, concerned with restoration of equality in relationship.... Retributive theory identifies the achievement of social equality with a particular set of historical practices

(typical of a wide range of societies) often known as punishment. In other words, retributive justice names punishment as the necessary mechanism through which such equality is to be achieved; it identifies the very idea of restoration with punishment. It attempts to restore social equality through retribution against the wrongdoer exercised through isolating punishment. By contrast, restorative justice problematizes the issue of what set of practices can or should, in a given context, achieve the goal of restoring social equality" (pp. 30-31). The Law Commission of Canada was eliminated in 2006 by the newly incumbent federal Conservative Party.

3. The terms "offender" and "victim" are laden with the assumptions of the retributive adversarial criminal justice system. In fact, most people are both victims and offenders at different times in their lives. Traditionally understood "victims" can break laws and not be apprehended; "offenders", particularly those with lengthy criminal records, are often adults or youth with childhood victimization experiences that were never responded to by the criminal justice system. A further problem with the term "offender" in the specific context of incarceration has been noted by Ross and Richards (2003): "We also avoid the term 'offender,' because a person may be convicted of a criminal offense but may not be an offender. The term also suggests that the person so identified is in some way offensive (as in 'offensive odor') (p. 13).

4. The *tsedaka* model of justice is described in the first chapter of Bianchi's *Justice as Sanctuary: Toward a New System of Crime Control* (1994). Bianchi suggests that original meanings and practices of "justice" in western histories have been lost in "translation" errors of anachronism. Older meanings of justice were eunomic (integrative) rather than anomic (alienating).

5. There are three Gladue (Aboriginal Persons) Courts in Toronto, at the Old City Hall Courts, at the 1000 Finch Courts and at College Park. The courts derive their name from the 1999 decision of the Supreme Court of Canada—R v. Gladue—that set out the parameters of section 718.2(e) of the Criminal Code regarding the sentencing of offenders, and in particular, Aboriginal offenders. Information at: http://www.aboriginallegal.ca/gladue.php

6. Donald Nathanson in the DVD production, *A Healing River: An Invitation to Explore Restorative Justice Values & Principles* (Douglas & Moore, 2004).

7. The idea of "crime prevention through social development" refers to practices of crime prevention that relate to social practices and services that are generated *outside* of the criminal justice system. For example, a key social development strategy to reduce crime would be to offer meaningful assistance and supports to traumatized (physically and emotionally) children who, if uncared for, have a greater likelihood of harming others as they become older.

8. A common restorative justice practice is to meet in a circle. The term "gathering" is used to avoid the connotations of the term "meeting," with its chairperson and governance by conventional means such as Robert's Rules of Order. A circle gathering will be governed instead by the use of a "talking piece," which is an object passed from person to person in the circle; the only person who is authorized to speak is the one holding the talking piece. Everyone has the right to pass if they choose not to speak. This egalitarian process ensures that all people have the structured opportunity to speak if they wish.

9. The *YCJA* was implemented on April 1, 2003.

10. Including the author.

11. The community development strategy was a much discussed and integral aspect of the sub-committee's discussions over two years. Since the original community

RJ coalition was borne of the municipal advisory committee's "crime prevention through social development" document, the bigger project of building social capital and addressing larger social problems was a key focus.

12. Retrieved from http://www.mission.ca/Asset2127.aspx?method=1 on October 1, 2007.

13. See footnote 8.

14. See footnote 8.

15. Victor Hassine, an author serving a life sentence in Pennsylvania, described the practice of "playing the opposites" in his book *Life Without Parole: Living in Prison Today* 2nd edition (1999). His editors note: "Inmates who play the opposites routinely lie to staff members when asked to express a desire or a preference. This game assumes that prison officials inevitably use their immense authority against the best interests of prisoners; misleading staff members is the only way for inmates to get what they want" (p. 29).

16. Deukmedjian (2008) reviews the history of the RCMP engagement with restorative justice as related to larger organizational priorities and shifting strategies of national governance. The new focus on public safety interoperability refers to a practice of information gathering, rather than community consultation.

17. A similar problem has been raised in the context of RJ processes that hold potential implications for insurance companies. See Ouellette (2005), for example.

18. An excellent example of a program which seeks to end cycle of sexual abuse in families based on restorative values and principles (albeit inexplicitly) is the Yellowhead Family Sexual Assault Treatment Program in Hinton, Alberta, Canada. In this program, the circle of intervention is as large as it needs to be, is inclusive of multi-generations of family members, and takes place initially over 16-24 months and then by five years of follow-up. More information at: http://www.members.shaw.ca/tonymartens/index.htm

19. The universal or core values of restorative justice generally include the following: respect, honesty, trust, humility, sharing, inclusivity, empathy, courage, forgiveness, and love (Pranis, Stuart and Wedge, 2003, pp. 34-45).

20. Donald L. Nathanson (1997) argued communities need to express their emotions. In his view, "a community is a public group of people linked by scripts for systems of affect modulation. It is formed and maintained by the following rules: 1) Mutualization of and group action to enhance or maximize positive affect. 2) Mutualization of and group action to diminish or minimize negative affect. 3) Communities thrive best when all affect is expressed so these first two goals may be accomplished. 4) Mechanisms that increase the power to accomplish these goals favor the maintenance of community, mechanisms that decrease the power to express and modulate affect threaten the community." Arguing against the idea that shame was the significant factor in reconciliation, Nathanson states that "The mutative force is empathy, not shame."

References

Adams, Kenneth and Charles R. Cutshall. 1987. "Refusing to Prosecute Minor Offenses: The Relative Influence of Legal and Extralegal Factors." *Justice Quarterly*, 4: 595-609.

Adler, Freda. 1975. *Sisters in Crime*. New York: McGraw-Hill.

Agirre, Xabier. 2007. Personal Communication. 14 April 2007.

Alaska Judicial Council. 2007. "Offender Recidivism Figures." *Alaska Justice Forum*, 23(4, 5-6. Available http://justice.uaa.alaska.edu/forum/23/4winter2007/c_recidivism.html

Albanese, Jay S. 1993. *Dealing With Delinquency: The Future of Juvenile Justice*. Chicago, IL: Nelson-Hall.

Amadiume, Ifi and An-Na'im, Abdullahi (Eds.) 2000. *The Politics of Memory: Truth, Healing and Social Justice* London: Zed Books.

Anderson, Kevin. 1991. "Radical Criminology and the Overcoming of Alienation: Perspectives from Marxian and Gandhian Humanism." In H. E. Pepinsky and Richard Quinney (Eds.), Criminology *as Peacemaking*, Bloomington, IN: Indiana University Press, 14-29.

Anderson, Margaret. 1988. "Moving our Minds: Studying Women and Reconstructing Sociology." *Teaching Sociology*, 16, 23-132.

Arrigo, Bruce. 2003. "Postmodern Justice and Critical Criminology: Positional, Relational, and Provisional Science." In M. D. Schwartz and S. E. Hatty (Eds.), *Controversies in Critical Criminology*. Cincinnati, OH: Anderson Publishing Co., 43-56.

Alvelos, H., 2004. "The desert of imagination in the city of signs" in Ferrell, J., et al. (Eds.) *Cultural Criminology Unleashed*, London: GlassHouse.

Auletta, Ken. 1982. *The Underclass*. New York: Random House.

Austin, James, Marino A. Bruce, Leo Carroll, Patricia L. McCall, and Stephen C. Richards. 2001. "The Use of Incarceration in the United States." *Critical Criminology*, 10, 1, 17-41.

Austin, James. 2003. "What's Wrong with Corrections? In Jeffrey Ian Ross and Stephen C. Richards (Eds.) *Convict Criminology*. Belmont, CA: Wadsworth, 15-36.

Austin, James and Barry Krisberg. 1982. "Wider and Stronger Nets:" The Dialectics of Criminal Justice Reform." *Journal of Research in Crime and Delinquency*, 18, 1, 65-96.

Bailey, David. 1985. *Patterns of Policing: A Comparative International Analysis*. New Brunswick, NJ: Rutgers University Press.

Balbus, I. 1971. "The Concept of Interest in Pluralist and Marxian Analysis." *Politics and Society*, 1, 51-77.

Bannister, S. and D. Milovanovic. 1990. "The Necessity Defense: Substantive Justice and Oppositional Linguistic Praxis." *International Journal of the Sociology of Law*, 18, 2, 79-198.

Banton, Michael. 1964. *The Police in the Community*. New York: Basic Books.

Barak, Gregg L. 1982. "Punishment and Corrections." *Crime and Social Justice*, 18, 08-117.

Barak, Gregg. 1988. "Newsmaking Criminology: Reflections on the Media, Intellectuals, and Crime." *Justice Quarterly*, 5: 565-587.

Barak, Gregg. 1994. "Mediated Crime and the ACJS." *ACJS Today*, *13*, 3, November/December.

Barak, Gregg. (Ed.). 1995. *Media, Process, and the Social Construction of Crime: Studies in Newsmaking Criminology*. New York: Garland.

Barak, Gregg. 1998. "Time for an Integrated Critical Criminology." In J. Ross (Ed.), *Cutting the Edge: Current Perspectives in Radical/Critical Criminology and Criminal Justice*. Westport, CT: Praeger, 34-39.

Barak, Gregg 2007 "Doing Newsmaking Criminology from within the Academy." *Theoretical Criminology*, 11:191-207.

Barber, Benjamin R. 1992. *An Aristocracy of Everyone: The Politics of Education and Future of America*. New York: Oxford University Press.

Bassiouni, M. Cherif. 2006. *Crimes of War: The Book*. Retrieved from http://www.crimesofwar.org/thebook/crimes-against-humanity.html.

Bauman, Zygmunt. 1990. *Thinking Sociologically*. Oxford: Blackwell.

Bazemore, Gordon and Mara Schiff (Eds.). 2001. *Restorative Community Justice: Repairing Harm and Transforming Communities*. Cincinnati, OH: Anderson Publishing Company.

Bazemore, G. and M. Schiff 2005. *Juvenile Justice Reform and Restorative Justice: Building Theory and Policy from Practice*. Portland, OR: Wilan.

Beck, Allen J. and D. Gilliard. 1995. *Prisoners in 1995*. Washington, DC: Bureau of Justice Statistics, U.S. Department of Justice. NCJ 151654.

Beck, Allen J. and P. Harrison. 2001. *Prisoners in 2000*. Washington, DC: Bureau of Justice Statistics, U.S. Department of Justice. NCJ 18207.

Beck, Allen J. and J.C. Karlberg. 2001. *Prison and Jail Inmates*. Washington, DC: Bureau of Justice Statistics.

Beck, Allen J. and B.E. Shipley. 1989. *Recidivism of Prisoners Released in 1983*. Washington, DC: Bureau of Justice Statistics, U.S. Department of Justice.

Becker, Howard S. 1963. *Outsiders: Studies in the Sociology of Deviance*. New York: Free Press.

Bennett, W. J., DiIulio, J., and J. Walters 1996. *Body Count: Moral Poverty and How to Win America's War Against Crime and Drugs*. New York: Simon and Schuster.

Berg, Bruce. 1992. *Law Enforcement: An Introduction to Police in Society*. Needham Heights, MA: Allyn and Bacon.

Berger, Bennett, M. 1995. *An Essay on Culture. Symbolic Structure and Social Structure*. Berkeley: University of California Press.

Berger, P. and Luckmann T. 1966. *The Social Construction of Reality*. Harmondsworth: Penguin.

Berk, Richard, Alec Campbell, Ruth Klap, and Bruce Western. 1992. "The Deterrent Effect of Arrest in Incidents of Domestic Violence: A Bayesian Analysis of Four Field Experiments." *American Sociological Review*. 57: 698-708.

Bernard, Thomas. 1992. *The Cycle of Juvenile Justice*. New York: Oxford University Press.

Bianchi, Herman. 1994. *Justice as Sanctuary: Toward a New System of Crime Control*. Bloomington: Indiana University Press.

Bianchi, Herman, and Rene van Swaaningen. (Eds.) 1986. *Abolitionism: Towards a Non-repressive Approach to Crime*. Amsterdam: Free University Press.

Bickle, Gayle S. and Ruth D. Peterson. 1991. "The Impact of Gender-Based Family Roles on Criminal Sentencing." *Social Problems*, 38: 372-394.

Bilchik, Shay. 2007. "The Importance of Universal School-Based Programs in Preventing Violent and Aggressive Behavior." *American Journal of Preventive Medicine*, 33, 2, 101-103.

Bijleveld, Catrien. 2007. "So Many Missing Pieces: Some Thoughts on the Methodology of the Empirical Study of Gross Human Rights Violations." Paper presented at the Expert Meeting at Maastricht University. 13-14 April.

Binder, Arnold and Gilbert Geis. 1984. "Ad Populum Argumentation in Criminology: Juvenile Justice as Rhetoric." *Crime and Delinquency*, 30, 4: 624-647.

Bishop, Donna M., Charles E Frazier., Lanza-Kaduce, L., and L. Winner 1996. "The Transfer of Juveniles to Criminal Court: Does It Make a Difference?" *Crime and Delinquency*, 422, 171-191.

Bishop, Donna M. and Charles E. Frazier. 1984. "The Effects of Gender in Charge Reduction." *Sociological Quarterly*, 25: 385-396.

Bittner, Egon. 1970. *The Functions of Police in Modern Society*. Rockville, MD: National Institute of Mental Health.

Bittner, Egon. 1974. "Florence Nightingale in Pursuit of Willie Sutton: A Theory of Police." In Herbert Jacob (Ed.), *The Potential for Reform in Criminal Justice*. Beverly Hills, CA: Sage, 17-44.

Black, Donald. 1980. *The Manners and Customs of the Police*. New York: Academic.

Blad, John R., Hans van Mastrigt, and Niels A. Uldriks. (Eds.) 1987. *The Criminal Justice System as a Social Problem: An Abolitionist Perspective*. Rotterdam, Netherlands: Erasmus University.

Blomberg, Thomas G. 1977. "Diversion and Accelerated Social Control." *Journal of Criminal Law and Criminology*, 68, 2: 274-282.

Blomberg, Thomas G. 1995. "Beyond Metaphors: Penal Reform as Net-Widening." In Thomas G. Blomberg and Stanley Cohen (Eds.), *Punishment and Social Control*. New York: Aldine de Gruyter, 2-14

Blomberg, Thomas G.and Stanley Cohen (Eds.), 1995. *Punishment and Social Control*. New York: Aldine de Gruyter, 2-14

Bloom, Sandra. 1997. *Creating Sanctuary: Toward the Evolution of Sane Societies*. New York: Rutledge.

Blumstein, Alfred, Jacqueline Cohen, Susan E. Martin, and Michael H. Tonry (Eds.), 1983. *Research on Sentencing: The Search for Reform, Volumes I and II*. Washington, D.C.: National Academy Press.

Boekhout van Solinge, T. 2008. "Eco-Crime: the Tropical Timber Trade." In D. Siegel and H. Nelen, *Organized Crime*, Dordrecht: Springer

Bonczar, Thomas P. 2003. *Prevalence of Imprisonment in the U.S. Population, 1974-2001*. Washington, DC: Bureau of Justice Statistics, U.S. Department of Justice. NCJ 197976.

Bondeson, Ulla V. 1994. *Alternatives to Imprisonment: Intentions and Reality*. Boulder, CO: Westview Press.

Books Not Bars 2008. See website at http://ellabakercenter.org/page.php? pageid=2 about the ongoing campaign to reform California's youth prisons.

Boritch, Helen. 1992. "Gender and Criminal Court Outcomes: An Historical Analysis." *Criminology*, 30, 3: 293-325.

Boritch, Helen and John Hagan. 1987. "Crime and Changing Forms of Class Control: Policing Public Order in 'Toronto the Good' 1859-1955." *Social Forces*, 66, 307-335.

Bovenkerk, F., D. Siegel and F. van Gemert 2009) *Culturele Criminologie in Nederland*, Hague: Boom Publisher.

Bowker, Lee H. 1978. *Women, Crime and the Criminal Justice System*. Lexington, MA: Heath.

Bowker, L. 1980. "A Theory of Educational Needs of Law Enforcement Officers." *Journal of Contemporary Criminal Justice*, 1, No. 1, 17-24.

Box, Steven, and Chris Hale. 1982. "Economic Crisis and the Rising Prisoner Population in England and Wales." *Crime and Social Justice*, 17: 20-35.

Bradley, Rebekah and Katrina Davino. 2002. "Women's Perception of the Prison Environment: When Prison is 'The Safest Place I've Ever Been.'" *Psychology of Women Quarterly*, *26*, 4: 351-359.

Braithwaite, John. 1989/1994. *Crime, Shame, and Reintegration*. Cambridge: Cambridge University Press.

Braithwaite, John. 1993. "Shame and Modernity." *British Journal of Criminology*, 33, 1-18.

Braithwaite, John. 1999. "Democracy, community and problem solving." Paper presented at the Building Strong Partnerships for Restorative Practices conference, Burlington, Vermont, August 5-7. Downloaded from iirp.org/library/vt/vt_brai.html on April 24, 2007.

Braithwaite, John. 2002. *Restorative Justice and Responsive Regulation*. New York: Oxford University Press.

Braithwaite, John. 2003. ("What's wrong with the sociology of punishment," *Theoretical Criminology*, Vol. 7, No 1, pp 5-28)

Braithwaite, John. 2004. ("Methods of Power for Development: Weapons of the weak, weapons of the strong," *Michigan Journal of International Law*, Vol. 27 pp.297-)

Braithwaite, John. 2007. "Encourage Restorative Justice." *Criminology and Public Policy*, *6*, 4: 689-696.

Braswell, Michael. 1990. "Peacemaking: A Missing Link in Criminology." *Criminologist*, 15: 3-5.

Brown, Michael K. 1988. *Working the Street: Police Discretion and the Dilemmas of Reform*. New York: Russell Sage Foundation.

Burnett, D. 1993. "Shame and Modernity." *British Journal of Criminology*, 33,-18.

Burnett, D. M., Noblin, C. D., and V. Prosser 2004. "Adjudicative Competency in a Juvenile Population." *Criminal Justice and Behavior*," 31, 438-462.

Burns, Ronald G. and Michael J. Lynch 2004 *Environmental Crime: A Sourcebook*. New York: LFB Scholarly Publishing.

Bureau of Justice Statistics. 1992. *Drugs, Crime, and the Justice System*. Washington, DC: Government Printing Office.

Bureau of Justice Statistics. 1994. *Women in Prison, Special Report*. Washington, DC: U.S. Department of Justice.

Burroughs, Williams. 1959. *Naked Lunch*. London: Calder.

Bursik, Robert. J. Jr. and Harold. G. Grasmick. 1993. *Neighborhoods and Crime: Effective Dimensions of Effective Community Control*. New York: Lexington Books.

Bushnell, J 1990. *Moscow Graffiti*. Boston: Unwin Hyman.

Byrne, James. 1986. "The Control Controversy: A Preliminary Examination of Intensive Probation Supervision in the United States." *Federal Probation*, 2: 4-16.

Cain, Maureen. 1990. "Realist Philosophy and Standpoint Epistemologies or Feminist Criminology as a Successor Science." In Loraine Gelsthorpe and Allison Morris (Eds.), *Feminist Perspectives in Criminology*. Buckingham: Open University Press, 124-140.

Caldwell, M. F., Vitacco, M., and G. J. Van Rybroek 2006. "Are Violent Delinquents Worth Treating? A Cost Benefit Analysis." *Journal of Research in Crime and Delinquency*, *43*, 148-168.

Campbell, Anne. 1981. *Girl Delinquents*. Oxford: Basil Blackwell.

Carney, P 2009. "The Critical Thrust of Cultural Criminology." In Shoham, S. et al. (Eds.) *The International Review of Criminology*. New York: Taylor and Francis.

Casburn, Maggie. 1979. *Girls Will Be Girls*. London: Women's Research and Resources Centre.

Casey, Pamela, David B. Rottman, and Chantal G. Bromage. 2007. Problem-Solving Justice Toolkit. Washington, DC: National Center for State Courts. Available: http://www.ncsconline.org/D_Research/Documents/ProbSolvJustTool.pdf

Cassesse, Antonio. 2002. *The Rome Statute of the International Criminal Court: A Commentary*. Vol. I. New York: Oxford Press

Center for Court Innovation. ND. Available online: http://www.courtinnovation.org/

Center for the Research of Criminal Justice (CRCJ). 1977/1982. *The Iron Fist and the Velvet Glove: An Analysis of the US Police*. Berkeley: CA: Center for Research on Criminal Justice.

Chamblin, Mitchell. 1989. "Conflict Theory and Police Killings." *Deviant Behavior*, 10, 353-368.

Chambliss, William. J. (and Harry King) 1984. *Harry King*. New York: Macmillan.

Chambliss, William. 1994. "Policing the Ghetto Underclass: The Politics of Law and Law Enforcement." *Social Problems*, 41, 77-194.

Chambliss, William and R. Seidman. 1971. *Law, Order, and Power*. Reading, MA: Addison- Wesley.

Christie, Nils. 1977. "Conflicts as Property." *British Journal of Criminology*, 17, 1, 1-11.

Christie, Nils 1981. *Limits to Pain*. New York: Columbia University Press.

Christie, Nils. 1984. Crime, Pain and Death," Issue No. 1 of New Perspectives on Crime and Justice: Occasional Papers. Akron, PA Mennonite Central Committee.

Christie, Nils. 1993. *Crime Control as Industry*. London: Routledge.

Cicourel, A. 1968. *The Social Organization of Juvenile Justice*. New York: Wiley.

Clarke, Michael. 1990. *Business Crime: Its Nature and Control*. Cambridge: Polity.

Clear, Todd R. 1994. *Harm in American Penology: Offenders, Victims, and Their Communities*. Albany: State University of New York Press.

Clear, Todd R. and David R. Karp. 1999. *The Community Justice Ideal: Preventing Crime and Achieving Justice*. Boulder, CO: Westview Press.

Clemmer, Donald. 1940. *The Prison Community*. New York: Holt, Rinehart, and Winston.

Clinard, Marshall B. and Richard Quinney. 1967/1973. *Criminal Behavior Systems: A Typology*, 2nd edition. New York: Holt, Rinehart and Winston.

Cobban, Helena. 2007. *Amnesty After Atrocity: Healing Nations After Genocide and War Crimes*. Boulder, London: Paradigm Publishers.

Coben, James and Penelope Harley. 2004. "Intentional Conversations About Restorative Justice, Mediation and the Practice of Law." *Hamline Journal of Public Law and Policy*, 25, 2, 237-334.

Cohen, Phil. 1979. "Policing the Working-Class City." In B. Fine et al. (Eds.) *Capitalism and the Rule of Law*. London: Hutchinson, 118-136.

Cohen, Stanley. 1972. *Folk Devils and Moral Panics*. London: Macgibbon and Kee.

Cohen, Stanley. 1979. "The Punitive City: Notes on the Dispersal of Social Control." *Contemporary Crises*, 3: 339-363.

Cohen, Stanley.1980. *Folk Devils and Moral Panics: The Creation of the Mods and Rockers*. New York: St. Martin's Press.

Cohen, 1985. *Visions of Social Control*. Oxford: Polity Press.

Cohen, Stanley 1988/1992. *Against Criminology*. New Brunswick: Transaction Publishers.

Collins, Patricia Hill. 1991. *Black Feminist Thought*. New York: Routledge.

Collins, R. 1988. *Theoretical Sociology*. New York: Harcourt Brace Jovanovich.

CNN.com. 2006. "U.S. Population Now 300 million and Growing." October 17. Retrieved April 1, 2008, from http://www.cnn.com/2006/US/10/17/300.million. over/index.html.

Connecticut Statistical Analysis Center. 2007. *State of Connecticut Recidivism Study: Annual Report* (March 1, 2007). Office of Policy and Management, Criminal Justice Policy and Planning.

Corbette, Ronald and Gary T. Marx. 1991. "Critique: No Soul in the New Machine: Technofallacies in the Electronic Monitoring Movement," *Justice Quarterly*, 8, 399-414.

Committee on the Status of Women in Sociology. 1986. *The Treatment of Gender in Research*. Pamphlet. Washington, DC.: American Sociological Association.

Cordella, Peter. 1996. "A Communitarian Theory of Social Order." In Peter Cordella and Larry Siegel (Eds.) *Readings in Contemporary Criminological Theory*. Boston: Northeastern University Press, 379-392.

Cosgrove, Stuart. 1984. "The Zoot-Suit and Style Warfare." *Radical America*, 18: 38-51.

Cragg, Wesley. 1992. *The Practice of Punishment: Towards a Theory of Restorative Justice*. New York: Routledge.

Crew, B. Keith. 1991. "Sex Differences in Criminal Sentencing: Chivalry or Patriarchy." *Justice Quarterly*, 8:59-83.

Crews, Angela. 2008. "Arab Americans." In R. Toth, G. Crews and C. Burton (Eds.), *In the Margins: Special Populations and American Justice*, 83-100. Upper Saddle River, NJ: Prentice-Hall.

Cullen, Francis and Karen E. Gilbert. 1982. *Reaffirming Rehabilitation*. Cincinnati, OH: Anderson.

Cunneen, C and J. Stubbs .2004. "Cultural Criminology and Engagement with Race, Gender and Post-Colonial Identities." In Jeff Ferrell et al. (Eds.), *Cultural Criminology Unleashed*, London: GlassHouse Press.

Cummins, Eric. 1994. *The Rise and Fall of California's Radical Prison Movement*. Stanford, CA: Stanford University Press.

Curran, Debra A. 1983. "Judicial Discretion and Defendant's Sex." *Criminology*, 21: 41-58.

Currie, Dawn. 1993. "Unhiding the Hidden: Race, Class, and Gender in the Construction of Knowledge." *Humanity and Society*, 17, 1: 3-27.

Currie, Elliot. 1985. *Reckoning: Drugs, the Cities, and the American Future*. New York: Hill and Wang.

Currie, E. 1985. *Confronting Crime: An American Challenge*. New York: Pantheon.

Daly, Kathleen. 1987a. "Discrimination in the Criminal Courts: Family, Gender, and the Problem of Equal Treatment." *Social Forces*, 66, 52-75.

Daly, Kathleen.1987b. "Structure and Practice of Familial-Based Justice in a Criminal Court." *Law and Society Review*, 21: 267-290.

Daly, Kathleen. 1989a. "Neither Conflict Nor Labeling Nor Paternalism will Suffice: Intersections of Race, Ethnicity, Gender, and Family in Criminal Court Decisions." *Crime and Delinquency*, 35, 36-68.

Daly, Kathleen. 1989b. "Re-thinking Judicial Paternalism: Gender, Work-Family Relations, and Sentencing." *Gender and Society*, 3: 9-36.

Daly, Kathleen. 1989c. "Gender and Varieties of White-Collar Crime." *Criminology*, 27: 769-793.

Daly, Kathleen. 1994. *Gender, Crime and Punishment*. New Haven, CT: Yale University Press.

Daly, Kathleen. 1995. "Looking Back, Looking Forward: The Promise of Feminist Transformation." In Barbara Raffel Price and Natalie J. Sokoloff (Eds.), *The Criminal Justice System and Women*, 2nd edition, New York: McGraw-Hill, Inc.

Daly, Kathleen and Meda Chesney-Lind. 1988. "Feminism and Criminology." *Justice Quarterly*, 5: 497-538.

Daly, Kathleen and Rebecca L. Bordt. 1995. "Sex Effects and Sentencing: An Analysis of the Statistical Literature." *Justice Quarterly*, 12, 1, 41-173.

Daly, Kathleen and Deborah Stephens. 1995. "The 'Dark Figure' of Criminology." In Nicole Hahn Rafter and Frances Heidensohn (Eds.), *International Feminist Perspectives in Criminology*. Buckingham: Open University Press, 189-215.

Das, Dilip. 1983. "Conflict Views on Policing: An Evaluation." *American Journal of Police*, 3, 1, 51-83.

Davis, Angela. 2003. *Are Prisons Obsolete?* New York: Seven Stories Press.

Davis, Nanette J. and Karlene Faith. 1987. "Women and the State: Changing Models of Social Control." In John Lowman, Robert J. Menzies, and T. S. Palys (Eds.), *Transcarceration: Essays in the Sociology of Social Control*. Aldershot, UK: Gower, 170-187.

Dean-Myrda, Mark C. and Francis T. Cullen. 1985. "The Panacea Pendulum: An Account of Community as a Response to Crime." In Lawrence F. Travis (Ed.) *Probation, Parole, and Community Corrections*. Prospect Heights, IL: Waveland Press, 9-29.

DeKeseredy, Walter. 2003. "Left Realism on Inner City Violence." In M. D. Schwartz and S. Hatty (Eds.), *Controversies in Critical Criminology*. Cincinnati, OH: Anderson Publishing Co., 29-42.

DeKeseredy, Walter and Martin D. Schwartz. 1996. *Contemporary Criminology*. Belmont, CA: ITP/Wadsworth Publishing Co.

DeKeseredy, Walter and Ron Hinch. 1991. *Women Abuse: Sociological Perspectives*. Toronto: Thompson Educational Publishing.

Denzin, Norman. 1990. "Reading 'Wall Street': Postmodern Contradictions in the American Social Structure." In Byran S. Turner (Ed.) *Theories of Modernity and Postmodernity*. London: Sage, 31-44.

Deukmedjian, John Edward. 2008. "The Rise and Fall of RCMP Community Justice Forums: Restorative Justice and Public Safety Interoperability in Canada." *Canadian Journal of Criminology and Criminal Justice* (forthcoming).

Dew-Becker, I. and R.J. Gordon. 2005. "Where Did the Productivity Growth Go? Inflation Dynamics and the Distribution of Income." *Brookings Papers on Economic Activity*, 2, 67-127.

Dodge, Mary. 2007. "From Pink to White with Various Shades of Embezzlement: Women Who Commit White-Collar Crimes." In H. N. Pontell and G. Geis (Eds.) *International Handbook of White-Collar and Corporate Crime*. New York: Springer, 379-404.

Douglas, Cathie and Larry Moore. 2004. *A Healing River: An Invitation to Explore Restorative Justice Values and Principles* [Motion Picture]. Kaslo, BC: Heartspeak Productions.

Duncan, Martha G. 1988. "'Cradled on the Sea:' Positive Images of Prison and Theories of Punishment." *California Law Review*, 76, 6, 201-1247.

Dunham, Roger G and Geoffrey Alpert. (Eds.) 1997. *Critical Issues in Policing: Contemporary Readings* 3rd edition. Prospect Heights, IL: Waveland Press.

Durkheim, Émile. 1952. *Suicide*. New York: Free Press.

Durkheim, Émile. 1893/1960. *The Division of Labour in Society*. Glencoe, IL: Free Press.

Durose, Matthew R. and Patrick Langan. 2007. *Felony Sentences in State Courts, 2004*. Washington, DC: Bureau of Justice Statistics. NCJ215646.

Edwards, Richard. 1979. *Contested Terrain: The Transformation of the Workplace in the Twentieth Century*. New York: Basic Books.

Edwards, Susan. 1990. "Violence against Women: Feminism and the Law." In Loraine Gelsthorpe and Allison Morris (Eds.), *Feminist Perspectives in Criminology*, Buckingham, UK: Open University Press, 145-159.

Eggen, Dan and R. Jeffrey Smith. 2004. "FBI Agents Allege Abuse of Detainees at Guantanamo Bay." *Washington Post.* December 21, 2004. Available: www.washingtonpost.com/wp-dyn/articles/A14936-2004Dec20.html.

Eichler, Margrit. 1988. *Nonsexist Research Methods: A Practical Guide.* Winchester, MA: Allen and Unwin, Inc.

Eldefonso, Edward and Walter Hartinger. 1976. *Control, Treatment, and Rehabilitation of Juvenile Offenders.* Beverly Hills, CA: Glencoe Press.

Elias, Robert. 1991. "Crime Control as Human Rights Enforcement." In Harold E. Pepinsky and Richard Quinney (Eds.), *Criminology as Peacemaking.* Bloomington: Indiana University Press.

Elliott, Liz. 2004. "Restorative Justice in Canadian Approaches to Youth Crime: Origins, Practices, and Retributive Frameworks." In *Understanding Youth Justice in Canada,* Kathryn Campbell (Ed.). Toronto: Pearson.

Eldefonso E. and W. Hartinger 1976. *Control, Treatment, and Rehabilitation of Juvenile Offenders.* Beverly Hills, CA: Glencoe Press.

Elrod, Preston 1998. Similarities in conservative and liberal juvenile justice policies: Is there a critical alternative? In J. I. Ross (Ed.). *Cutting the Edge: Current Perspectives in Radical/Critical Criminology and Criminal Justice.* Westport, CT: Praeger, 165-180.

Elrod, Preston and D. Kelley 1995. "The Ideological Context of Changing Juvenile Justice." *Journal of Sociology and Social Welfare,* 22, 57-75.

Elrod, Preston and R. S. Ryder 2005. *Juvenile Justice: A Social Historical and Legal Perspective.* Sudbury, MA: Jones and Bartlett.

Empey, L. T., Stafford, M.C., and C. H. Hay 1999. *American Delinquency: Its Meaning and construction,* 4th edition. Belmont, CA: Wadsworth.

Eribon, Didier. 1991. *Michel Foucault.* Cambridge, MA: Harvard University Press.

Erickson, M. and J. Gibbs. 1980 "Punishment, Deterrence, and Juvenile Justice." In D. Shichor and D. Kelley (Eds.) *Critical Issues in Juvenille Justice.* Lexington, MA: Lexington Books, 193-202.

Ericson, Richard V. 1982. *Reproducing Order: A Study of Police Patrol Work,* Toronto: University of Toronto Press.

Ericson, Richard V. Patricia M. Baranek, and Janet B.L. Chan. 1989. *Negotiating Control.* Toronto: University of Toronto Press.

Ericson, Richard V. and Kevin Carriere 1994. "The Fragmentation of Criminology." In David Nelkin (Ed.) *The Futures of Criminology.* Thousand Oaks, CA: Sage, 89-109.

Fagan, J. A. 1995. "Separating the Men from the Boys: The Comparative Advantage of Juvenile Versus Criminal Court Sanctions on Recidivism among Adolescent Felony Offenders." In J. C. Howell, B. Krisberg, J. D. Hawkins, and J. J. Wilson (Eds.), *Serious, Violent, and Chronic Juvenile Offenders: A Sourcebook* (,238-260. Thousand Oaks, CA: Sage.

Faith, Karlene. 1993. *Unruly Women: The Politics of Confinement and Resistance.* Vancouver: Press Gang.

Featherstone, M. 1991. *Consumer Culture and Postmodernity,* London: Sage.

FBI. 2007. Crime in the United States, 2006. Retrieved March 10, 2008 at http://www.fbi.gov/research.htm.

Felson, Marcus. 1998. *Crime and Everyday Life,* 2nd edition. Thousand Oaks, CA: Pine Forge Press.

Ferdinand, T. N. 1989. "Juvenile Delinquency or Juvenile Justice: Which Came First?" *Criminology, 27,* 79-106.

Ferrell, Jeff. 1992. "Making Sense of Crime." *Social Justice,* 19(2) 110-123.

Ferrell, Jeff. 1993. "The World Politics of Wall Painting." *Social Justice,* 20, 88-202.

Ferrell, Jeff. 1994. "Confronting the Agenda of Authority: Critical Criminology, Anarchism, and Urban Graffiti." In Gregg Barak (Ed.), *Varieties of Criminology*. Westport, CT: Praeger, 161-178.

Ferrell, Jeff. 1995a. "Urban Graffiti: Crime, Control, and Resistance." *Youth and Society*, 27: 73-92.

Ferrell, Jeff. 1995b. "Style Matters: Criminal Identity and Social Control." In Jeff Ferrell and Clinton R. Sanders (Eds.), *Cultural Criminology*. Boston: Northeastern University Press, 169-189.

Ferrell, Jeff.1996a. *Crimes of Style: Urban Graffiti and the Politics of Criminality*. Boston: Northeastern University Press..

Ferrell, Jeff. 1996b. "Slash and Frame." In Gregg Barak (Ed.), *Representing O.J.: Murder, Criminal Justice, and Mass Culture*. Guilderland, NY: Harrow and Heston, 46-50.

Ferrell, Jeff. 1997. "Against the Law: Anarchist Criminology." In Brian MacLean and Dragan Milovanovic (Eds.), *Thinking Critically About Crime*. Vancouver: Collective Press, 146-154.

Ferrell, Jeff. 1998. "Criminalizing Popular Culture." In Donna Hale and Frankie Bailey (Eds.), *Popular Culture, Crime, and Justice*. Belmont, CA: Wadsworth, 71-83.

Ferrell, Jeff. 1999. "Cultural Criminology." *Annual Review of Sociology*, 25, 395-418

Ferrell, Jeff. 2001/2002. *Tearing Down the Streets*. New York: St Martins/Palgrave.

Ferrell, Jeff. 2003. "Cultural Criminology." In M. D. Schwartz and S. Hatty (Eds.) *Controversies in Critical Criminology*. Cincinnati, OH: Anderson Publishing Co., 71-84.

Ferrell, Jeff 2004a. "Boredom, Crime, and Criminology." *Theoretical Criminology* 8(3) 287-302.

Ferrell, Jeff, 2004b. "Speed Kills." In Ferrell, J. et al. (Eds), *Cultural Criminology Unleashed*, London: GlassHouse.

Ferrell, Jeff. 2006. *Empire of Scrounge*. New York: NYU Press.

Ferrell, Jeff. 2007. "For a Ruthless Cultural Criticism of Everything Existing." *Crime, Media, Culture* 3(1): 91-100.

Ferrell, Jeff and Clinton R. Sanders (Eds.) 1995. *Cultural Criminology*. Boston: Northeastern University Press.

Ferrell, Jeff, Keith J. Hayward, Morrison, M., and Prsedee, M. (Eds.) 2004. *Cultural Criminology Unleashed*, London: Glasshouse/Rutledge.

Ferrell, Jeff, Keith J. Hayward, and Jock Young. 2008. *Cultural Criminology: An Invitation*, London: Sage.

Finckenauer, J. O. 1982. *Scared Straight! And the Panacea Problem*. Englewood Cliffs, NJ: Prentice-Hall.

Findlay, M and U. Zvekic (Eds.). 1993. *Alternative Policing Styles: Cross Cultural Perspectives*. Deventer, Netherlands: Kluwer.

Flavin, Jeanne M. 1995. "Of Punishment and Parenthood: The Role of Family-Based Social Control in Explaining Gender Differences in Sentencing." Doctoral dissertation. American University, Washington, DC.

Foucault, Michel. 1977a. *Power/Knowledge*. New York: Pantheon.

Foucault, Michel. 1977b. *Discipline and Punish: The Birth of the Prison*. London: Allen Lane.

Frazier, Charles E. and Donna M. Bishop. 1990. "Jailing Juveniles in Florida: The Dynamics of Compliance with a Sluggish Federal Reform Initiative." *Crime and Delinquency*, 36(4): 427-442.

Friedrichs, David. 1980. "Radical Criminology in the United States: An Interpretive Understanding." In James A. Inciardi (Ed.), *Radical Criminology: The Coming Crisis*, Beverly Hills, CA: Sage, 35-60.

Friedrichs, David. 1983. "Victimology: A Consideration of the Radical Critique." *Crime and Delinquency*, 29: 283-294.

Friedrichs, David. 1996a. *Trusted Criminals: White Collar Crime in Contemporary Society.* Belmont, CA: ITP/Wadsworth Publishing Co.

Friedrichs, David. 1996b. "Peacemaking Criminology and the Punitive Conundrum: A New Foundation for Social Control in the Twenty-First Century?" In Christine Sistare (Ed.), *Punishment: Social Control and Coercion.* New York: Peter Lang Co., 29-54.

Friedrichs, David. 1996c. "Critical Criminology and Progressive Pluralism: Strength in Diversity for These Times." *Critical Criminology,* 7, 21-128.

Friedrichs, David O. 2004. "Enron et al.: Paradigmatic White Collar Crime Cases for the New Century." *Critical Criminology,* 12: 113-132.

Friedrichs, David O. 2007a. *Trusted Criminals: White Collar Crime in Contemporary Society,* 3rd edition. Belmont, CA: Thomson/Wadsworth Publishing Co.

Friedrichs, David O. 2007b. "White-Collar Crime in a Postmodern, Globalized World." In Henry N. Pontell and Gill Geis (Eds.) *International Handbook of White-Collar and Corporate Crime.* New York: Springer, 163-186.

Friedrichs, David O. and Jessica Friedrichs. 2002. "The World Bank and Crimes of Globalization: A Case Study." *Social Justice,* 29: 13-36.

Free the Jena 6 2007. Fight for justice in Jena, Louisiana. Retrieved March 21, 2008 at http://www.freethejena6.org.

Fuller, John. 2003. "Peacemaking Criminology." In M. D. Schwartz and S. E. Hatty (Eds.). *Controversies in Critical Criminology.* Cincinnati, OH: Anderson Publishing Co., 85-96.

Garfinkel, H. 1956. "Conditions of Successful Degradation Ceremonies." *American Journal of Sociology,* 61, 420-424.

Garland, David. 1990. *Punishment in Modern Society: A Study in Social Theory.* Chicago: University of Chicago Press.

Geis, Gilbert, and Colin Goff. 1992. "Lifting the Cover from Undercover Operations: J. Edgar Hoover and Some Other Criminologists." *Crime, Law and Social Change,* 18: 91-104.

Gelsthorpe, Loraine and Allison Morris (Eds.), 1990. *Feminist Perspectives in Criminology.* Buckingham: Open University Press, 124-140.

Gendreau, P. and Bob Ross. 1979. "Effective Correctional Treatment: Bibliotherapy for Cynics." *Crime and Delinquency,* 25: 463-489.

Gendreau, P. and C. Goggin 2000. Correctional Treatment: Accomplishments and Realities. In P. Van Voorhis, M. Braswell, and D. Lester (Eds.), *Correctional counseling and rehabilitation,* 4th edition., 289-298. Cincinnati, OH: Anderson.

Gerber, Jurg, and Susan L. Weeks. 1992. "Women as Victims of Corporate Crime: A Call for Research on a Neglected Topic." *Deviant Behavior,* 13: 325-347.

Giddens, Anthony. 1984. *The Constitution of Society: Outline of the Theory of Structuration.* Oxford: Polity Press.

Giddens, Anthony. 1990. *The Consequences of Modernity.* Stanford, CA: Stanford University Press.

Giddens, Anthony.1991a. *Introduction to Sociology.* New York: W. W. Norton.

Giddens, Anthony. 1991b. *Modernity and Self-Identity.* Stanford, CA: Stanford University Press.

Gilbert, J. 1986. *A Cycle of Outrage: America's Reaction to the Juvenile Delinquency in the 1950s.* New York: Oxford University Press.

Glaser, Bill. 2003. "Therapeutic Jurisprudence: An Ethical Paradigm for Therapists in Sex Offender Treatment Programs." *Western Criminology Review,* 42, 143-154.

Glaze, Lauren E. and Thomas P. Bonczar. 2007. *Probation and Parole in the United States,2006.* Washington, DC: Bureau of Justice Statistics, U.S. Department of Justice. NCJ220218.

Ginzburg, Carlo. 2000. *Rapporti di forza. Storia, retorica, prova*. Milan: Feltrinelli.

Goffman, Erving. 1963. *Stigma: Notes on the Management of Spoiled Identity*. New York: Simon and Shuster.

Goldstein, Herman. 1977. *Policing a Free Society*. Cambridge, MA: Ballinger.

Goldstein, Herman. 1979. "Improving Policing: A Problem-Oriented Approach." *Crime and Delinquency*, 252, 236-258.

Golins, Gerald L. 1980. "Utilizing Adventure Education to Rehabilitate Juvenile Delinquents." Educational Resources Information Center (ERIC), Las Cruces: New Mexico State University.

Goodstein, Lynne. 1992. "Feminist Perspectives and the Criminal Justice Curriculum." *Journal of Criminal Justice Education*, 2, 65-181.

Gordon, Diana. 1991. *The Justice Juggernaut: Fighting Street Crime, Controlling Citizens*. New Brunswick, NJ: Rutgers University Press.

Gottschalk, Marie. 2006. *The Prison and the Gallows: The Politics of Mass Incarceration in America*. New York: Cambridge University Press.

Gould, Eric, Bruce Weinberg, and David Mustard. 2002. "Crime Rates and Local Labor Market Opportunities in the United States, 1977-1997." *Review of Economics and Statistics*, 84, 1: 45-61.

Green, Penny and Tony Ward. 2004. *State Crime*. London: Pluto Press.

Greenberg, David F. 1977a. "Delinquency and the Age Structure of Society." *Contemporary Crises*, 1, 89-223.

Greenberg, David F. 1977b. "The Dynamics of Oscillatory Punishment Process." *Journal of Criminal Law and Criminology*, 68: 643-651.

Griffin, P. 2003. *Trying and Sentencing Juveniles as Adults: An Analysis of State Blended Sentencing and Sentencing Laws*. Pittsburgh, PA: National Center for Juvenile Justice.

Grisso, T., et al. 2003. "Juveniles' Competence to Stand Trial: A Comparison of Adolescents' and Adults' Capacities as Trial Defendants." *Law and Human Behavior*, 27, 333-363.

Grunfeld, Fred. 2007. "The Role of Bystanders in Rwanda and Srebrenica." Paper presented at the Expert Meetings at Maastricht University. 13-14 April.

Haan, Willem de. 1991. "Abolitionism and Crime Control: A Contradiction in Terms." In K. Stenson and P. Colwell (Eds.), *The Politics of Crime Control*. London: Sage, 203-217.

Hadley, Michael L. (Ed.). 2001. *The Spiritual Roots of Restorative Justice*. Albany: State University of New York Press.

Hagan, John. 1989. "Why Is There So Little Criminal Justice Theory? Neglected Macro and Micro-Level links between Organizations and Power." *Journal of Research in Crime and Delinquency*, 26, 16-135.

Hagan, John and Kristin Bumiller. 1983. "Making Sense of Sentencing Research: A Review and Critique of Sentencing Research." In A. Blumstein, J. Cohen, S. Martin and M. Tonry (Eds.), *Research on Sentencing: The Search For Reform, Volume II*, Washington, DC: National Academy Press.

Hall, Mimi. 1993. "Marital Rape Laws Examined." *USA Today*, November 9, A3: 6.

Hall, Stuart and Tony Jefferson. (Eds.), 1976. *Resistance through Rituals*. London: Hutchinson.

Hall, S and Winlow, S 2007. "Cultural Criminology and Primitive Accumulation." *Crime, Media, Culture*, 3(1) 82-90.

Hamm, Mark S.1997. *Apocalypse in Oklahoma*. Boston: Northeastern University Press.

Hamm, Mark S. 2002. *In Bad Company*. Boston: Northeastern University Press.

Hamm, Mark S. 2004. "The USA Patriot Act and the Politics of Fear." In Jeff Ferrell et al. (Eds.) *Cultural Criminology Unleashed*. London: GlassHouse.

Hamm, Mark S. 2007. "High Crimes and Misdemeanours: George W. Bush and the Sins of Abu Ghraib." *Crime, Media, Culture*, 3, 3, 259-284.

Haney, Craig, W. C. Banks and Philip Zimbardo. 1973. "Interpersonal Dynamics in a Simulated Prison." *International Journal of Criminology and Penology*, *1*, 69-97.

Harding, Sandra. 1987. *Feminism and Methodology*. Bloomington: Indiana University Press.

Harring, Sidney L. 1976. "The Development of the Police Institution in the United States." *Crime and Social Justice*, Vol. ? Spring-Summer, 54-59.

Harring, Sidney. 1978. "Police Suppression of Tramps in Buffalo in the Depression of 1893-94." *Law and Society Review*, 18.

Harring, Sidney. 1981a. "Policing a Class Society: The Expansion of the Urban Police in the Late Nineteenth and Early Twentieth Century." In David Greenberg (Ed.) *Crime and Class: Essays in Modern Marxism*. Palo Alto, CA: Goodyear, 292-313.

Harring, Sidney. 1981b. "The Taylorization of Police Work: Prospects for the 1980s." *Insurgent Sociologist*, 11, 1, 25-31.

Harring, Sidney. 1982. "The Police Institution as a Class Question: Milwaukee Socialists and Police: 1900-1915." *Science and Society*, 46, 97-221.

Harring, Sidney. 1983. *Policing a Class Society*. New Brunswick, NJ: Rutgers University Press.

Harring, Sidney and Lorraine McMullin. 1975. "The Buffalo Police 1872-1900: Labor Unrest, Political Power and the Creation of the Police Institution." *Crime and Social Justice*, 4, Winter: 5-14.

Harris, M. Kay. 1983. "Strategies, Values, and the Emerging Generation of Alternatives to Incarceration." *New York University Review of Law and Social Change*, 12, 1, 141-170.

Harvey, D .1990. *The Condition of Postmodernity,* Cambridge, MA: Blackwell.

Hassine, Victor. 1996/1999. *Life Without Parole: Living in Prison Today,* 2nd edition. Edited by Thomas J. Bernard, Richard McCleary and Richard A. Wright, with a foreword by John Irwin. Los Angeles, CA: Roxbury Publishing Company.

Hatchett, Shirley J. Donna L. Cochran, and James S. Jackson. 1991. "Family Life." In James S. Jackson (Ed.), *Life in Black America*. Newbury Park, CA: Sage, 46-83.

Hayward, Keith 2001. "Crime, Consumerism and the Urban Experience." PhD Thesis, University of East London.

Hayward, Keith 2004. *City Limits: Crime, Consumer Culture and the Urban Experience.* London: GlassHouse.

Hayward, Keith and Hobbs, D. 2007. "Beyond the Binge in Booze Britain: Market-Led Liminalization and the Spectacle of Binge Drinking." *British Journal of Sociology* 58: 3 437-456.

Hayward, Keith and Presdee, M. 2009. *Framing Crime: Cultural Criminology and the Image*. London: Routledge/GlassHouse.

Hayward, Keith and Yar, M. 2006. "The 'Chav' Phenomenon: Consumption, Media and the Construction of a New Underclass." *Crime, Media, Culture*, 2: 1, 9-28.

Hayward, Keith and Jock Young. 2004. "Cultural Criminology: Some Notes on the Script." *Theoretical Criminology*, 8: 3, 259-273.

Hayward, Keith and Jock Young. 2007. "Cultural Criminology." In Maguire, M., Morgan, R., and Reiner (Eds.) *The Oxford Handbook of Criminology*, 4th edition, Oxford: Oxford University Press

Hemmens, Craig. 2008. "A Righteous Stand: ACJS and Criminal Justice Policy." *ACJS Today*, 33, 1, 13-15.

Henry, Stuart. 1991. "The Post-Modern Perspective in Criminology." In Brian MacLean and Dragan Milovanovic (Eds.), *New Directions in Critical Criminology*. Vancouver: Collective Press, 71-78.

Henry, Stuart and Dragan Milovanovic. 2003. "Constitutive Criminology." In M. D. Schwartz and S. E. Hatty (Eds.) *Controversies in Critical Criminology*. Cincinnati, OH: Anderson Publishing Co., 57-70.

Hersh, Seymour M. "Torture at Abu Ghraib." *New Yorker*, May 10, 2004. Available: www.newyorker.com/fact/content/?040510fa_fact.

Hillyard, Paddy, Christina Pantazis, Steve Tombs, and Dave Gordon 2004. *Beyond Criminology: Taking Harm Seriously*. London: Pluto Press.

Hinch, Ronald, and Walter DeKeseredy. 1992. "Corporate Violence and Women's Health at Home and in the Workplace." In B. Bolaria and H. Dickinson (Eds.), *The Sociology of Health Care in Canada*, 2nd edition. Toronto: Harcourt Brace Jovanovich.

Hirschi, Travis, and Michael Gottfredson. 1987. "Causes of White-Collar Crime." *Criminology*, 25, 949-974.

Hirshorn, Michael. 1988. "The Doctorate Dilemma." *New Republic*, 198, 23, 24-27.

Hirst, Paul Q. 1975a. "Marx and Engels on Law, Crime, and Morality." In I. Taylor, P. Walton, and J. Young (Eds.) Critical *Criminology*, London: Routledge and Kegan Paul, 203-232.

Hirst, Paul Q. 1975b. "Radical Deviancy Theory and Marxism: A Reply to Taylor and Walton." In Ian Taylor, P. Walton, and J. Young (Eds.), *Critical Criminology*. Boston: Routledge and Kegan Paul.

Holmes, Steven A. 1994. "The Boom in Jails is Locking Up Lots of Loot." *New York Times*, November 6: E-3.

Horton, John. 1981. "The Rise of the Right: A Global View." *Crime and Social Justice*, 15: 7-17.

Howe, A. 2003. "Managing Men's Violence in the Criminological Arena." In Sumner, C (Ed.), *The Blackwell Companion to Criminology*, Oxford: Blackwell.

Huddleston, C. West, K. Freeman-Wilson, D.B. Marlowe, and A. Roussell. 2005. "Painting the Current Picture: A National Report Card on Drug Courts and Other Problem Solving Court Programs in the United States," Vol. 1, No. 2. Washington, DC: National Drug Court Institute.

Hudson, Barbara. 1997. "Punishment or Redress? Current Themes in European Abolitionist Criminology." In Brian D. MacLean and Dragan Milovanovic (Eds.), *Thinking Critically about Crime*. Vancouver: Collective Press, 131-138.

Hughes, Kristen. 2006. Justice Expenditure and Employment in the United States, 2003. Washington, DC: Bureau of Justice Statistics, U.S. Department of Justice. NCJ212260.

Hulsman, Louk. 1974. "Criminal Justice in the Netherlands." *Delta: A Review of Arts, Life and Thoughts in the Netherlands*, 7-19.

Hunt, Alan. 1990a. "Post-Modernism and Critical Criminology." *The Critical Criminologist*, 2, 5-6, 17.

Hunt, Alan. 1990b. "The Big Fear: Law Confronts Postmodernism." *McGill Law Journal*, 35: 508-540.

Hunt, Alan. 1991. "Postmodernism and Critical Criminology." In Brian D. MacLean and Dragan Milovanovic (Eds.), *New Directions in Critical Criminology*, Vancouver, BC: The Collective Press, 799-86.

Hunt, Jennnifer. 1990. "The Logic of Sexism Among Police." *Women and Criminal Justice*, 1, 2: 3-30.

Hurtado, Aida. 1989. "Relating to Privilege: Seduction and Rejection in the Subordination of White Women and Women of Color." *Signs*, 144: 833-855.

Huizinga, D., et al. (2007). *Disproportionate Minority Contact in the Juvenile Justice System: A Study of Differential Minority Arrest/Referral to Court in Three Cities*. Unpublished report submitted to the Office of Juvenile Justice and Delinquency prevention. Retrieved March 1, 2008, from http://www.ncjrs.gov/pdffiles1/ojjdp/grants/219743.pdf.

Inciardi, James A., (Ed.), 1980. *Radical Criminology: The Coming Crises*. Beverly Hills, CA: Sage.

International Court of Justice. 2005. "The Court." Online. <www.icj-cij.org/court/index.php?p1=1andPHPSESSID=7b883991ec91e9ad2e7e822d149a87ff>.

International Monetary Fund.

Irwin, John. 1970. *The Felon*. Englewood Cliffs, NJ: Prentice-Hall.

Irwin, John. 1985. *The Jail: Managing the Underclass in American Society*. Berkeley: University of California Press.

Irwin, John. 2007. *The Warehouse Prison: Disposal of the New Dangerous Class*. New York: Oxford University Press.

Irwin, John and James Austin. 1997. *It's About Time*. Belmont, CA: Wadsworth.

Jackson, Pamela Irving and Leo Carroll. 1981. "Race and the War on Crime: The Sociopolitical Determinants of Municipal Police Expenditures in 90 Non-Southern Cities." *American Sociological Review*, 46, 290-305.

Jacobs, David. 1979. "Inequality and Police Strength: Conflict Theory and Coercive Control in Metropolitan Areas." *American Sociological Review*, 44, 4, 913-925.

Jacobs, David and David Britt. 1979. "Inequality and the Use of Deadly Force: An Ecological Test of the Conflict Model." *Social Problems*, 26: 403-412.

Jacobs, David and Ronald E. Helms. 1977. "Testing Coercive Explanations for Order." *Social Forces*. 75, 4: 1361-1392.

Jacobs, David and Robert M. O'Brien. 1998. "The Determinant of Deadly Force: A Structural Analysis of Police Violence." *American Journal of Sociology*, 103, 4: 837-862.

Jacobs, M. D. 1990. *Screwing the System and Making It Work: Juvenile Justice in the No-Fault Society*. Chicago: University of Chicago Press.

James, Henry. 1986/1875. *Roderick Hudson*. Markham, ON: Penguin Books Canada.

Jameson, F. 1977. "Imaginary and Symbolic in Lacan: Marxism, Psychoanalytic Criticism, and the Problem of the Subject." *Yale French Studies*, 55/56: 338-395.

Jameson, F .1991. *Postmodernism or the Cultural Logic of Late Capitalism*, London: Verso.

Jamieson, Katherine M. and Anita Neuberger Blowers. 1993. "A Structural Examination of Misdemeanor Court Disposition Patterns." *Criminology*, 3, 2: 243-262.

Jankowski, Louis W. 1992. *Correctional Populations in the United States, 1990*. Washington, DC: U.S. Department of Justice, Bureau of Justice Statistics.

Jefferson, Tony. 1987. "Beyond Paramilitarism." *British Journal of Criminology*, 27, 47-53.

Jefferson, Tony. 1990. *The Case Against Paramilitary Policing*. Philadelphia, PA: Milton Keynes.

Jencks, Charles. 1977. *The Language of Post-Modern Architecture*. New York: Rizzoli.

Jenkins, P 1999. "Fighting Terrorism as if Women Mattered." In Jeff Ferrell and N. Websdale (Eds.), *Making Trouble*. New York: Aldine.

Johnson, Robert and Hans Toch. 1982. *The Pains of Imprisonment*. Prospect Heights, IL: Waveland Press.

Johnstone, Gerry. 2002. *Restorative Justice: Ideas, Values, Debates*. Portland OR: Willan Publishing.

Kahn, Robert S. 1996. *Other People's Blood: U.S. Immigration Prison in the Regan Decade*. Boulder, CO. Westview Press.

Kappeler, Victor. (Ed.)1995. *The Police and Society*. Prospect Heights, IL: Waveland Press.

Katz, J. 1988. *Seductions of Crime*. New York: Basic Books.

Kauzlarich David and Ronald Kramer. 1998. *Crimes of the American Nuclear State: At Home and Abroad*. Boston: Northeastern University Press.

Kay, Alan. 2006. "Social Capital, the Social Economy and Community Development." *Community Development Journal*, 41, 2, 160-173.

Kelling, George L. and Mark H. Moore 1988. "The Evolving Strategy of Policing." *Perspectives on Policing*. Washington, DC: National Institute of Justice.

Kirchhoff, S. 2006. Fed's Yellen: Income Gap Poses Risk. *USA Today*. November 7. Retrieved March 3, 2008 from http://www.usatoday.com/money/economy/fed/2006-11-07-incomeusat_x.htm.

Klein, Dorie. 1973. "The Etiology of Female Crime: A Review of the Literature." *Issues in Criminology*, 8: 3-30.

Kline, Sue. 1992. "A Profile of Female Offenders." *Federal Prisons Journal*, 3, 1: 33-35.

Klockars, Carl B. 1979. "The Contemporary Crisis of Marxist Criminology." *Criminology*, 16, 477-515.

Klockars, Carl B. 1985. *The Idea of the Police* Beverly Hills, CA: Sage.

Klockars, Carl B. 1993. "The Legacy of Conservative Ideology and Police." *Police Forum* 3, 1, 1-6.

Klockars, Carl B. and Stephen D. Mastrofski (Eds.). *Thinking About Police*. New York: McGraw Hill.

Knopp, Fay Honey et al. 1976. *Instead of Prisons: A Handbook for Abolitionists*. Orwell, VT: Safer Society Press.

Knopp, Fay Honey. 1991. "Community Solutions to Sexual Violence: Feminist/Abolitionist Perspectives." In Harold E. Pepinsky and Richard Quinney (Eds.), *Criminology as Peacemaking*. Bloomington: Indiana University Press, 181-193.

Kohn, Alfie. 1991. *Punished by Rewards: The Trouble with Gold Stars, Incentive Plans, A's, Praise, and Other Bribes*. Boston: Houghton Mifflin Company.

Kornbluh, J 1998. *Rebel Voices: An IWW Anthology*. Chicago: Charles Kerr.

Kramer, Laura. 1991. *The Sociology of Gender: A Text-Reader*. New York: St. Martins Press.

Kramer, Ronald C. 1985. "Humanistic Perspectives in Criminology." *Journal of Sociology and Social Welfare*, 12: 469-87.

Kramer, Ronald C. 1989. "Criminologists and the Social Movement Against Corporate Crime." *Social Justice*, 16: 146-164.

Kramer, Ronald. 1990. "Toward an Integrated Theory of State-corporate Crime." Presented at the American Society of Criminology. Baltimore, MD.

Kramer, Ronald C. and Raymond Michalowski. 2005. "War, Aggression, and State Crime: A Criminological Analysis of the Invasion and Occupation of Iraq." *British Journal of Criminology* 45 (4): 446-469.

Kraska, Peter. 1996. "Enjoying Militarism: Political/Personal Dilemmas in Studying U.S. Police Paramilitary Units." *Justice Quarterly*, 13, 3, 405-429.

Kraska, Peter. 1997. "Militarizing American Police: The Rise and Normalization of Paramilitary Units." *Social Problems* 44, 1, 1-18.

Kraska, Peter and Victor Kappeler. 1995. "To Serve and Pursue: Exploring Police Sexual Violence against Women." *Justice Quarterly*, 12: 85-111.

Krisberg, Barry. 2005. *Juvenile Justice: Redeeming Our Children*. Thousand Oaks, CA: Sage.

Krisberg, Barry, Ira M. Schwartz, Paul Litsky, and James Austin 1986. "The Watershed of Juvenile Justice Reform." *Crime and Delinquency, 32*, 5-38.

Krohn, Marvin D., James P. Curry, and Shirley Nelson-Kilger. 1983. "Is Chivalry Dead?" *Criminology*, 21, 3: 417-437.

Kruttschnitt, Candace. 1980-1981. "Social Status and the Sentences of Female Offenders." *Law and Society Review*, 15, 2: 247-265.

Kruttschnitt, Candace 1982. "Women, Crime and Dependency: An Application of the Theory of Law." *Criminology*, 19: 495-513.

Kruttschnitt, Candace. 1984. "Sex and Criminal Court Dispositions: The Unresolved Controversy." *Journal of Research in Crime and Delinquency,* 21: 213-32.

Kruttschnitt, Candace and Donald E. Green. 1984. "The Sex-Sanctioning Issue: Is it History?" *American Sociological Review*, 49: 541-555.

Langan, Patrick and D. Levin. 2002. *Recidivism of Prisoners Released in 1994*. Washington, DC: Bureau of Justice Statistics, U.S. Department of Justice. NCJ193427.

Lanza-Kaduce, L. 1982. "Formality, Neutrality and Goal Rationality: The Legacy of Weber in Analyzing Legal Thought." *Journal of Criminal Law and Criminology*, 73: 533-60.

Laub, John H. 1983. *Criminology in the Making*. Boston: Northeastern University Press.

Lemert, Edwin. 1993. "Visions of Social Control: Probation Considered," *Crime and Delinquency*, 39, 4: 447-461.

Lemkin, Raphael. 1944. *Axis Rule in Occupied Europe*. Washington, DC: Carnegie Endowment for International Peace.

Leonard, K. K., Pope, C. E., and W. H. Feyerherm (Eds.). 1995. *Minorities in Juvenile Justice*. Thousand Oaks, CA: Sage.

Leo, Richard. 1996. ""Police Scholarship for the Future: Resisting the Pull of the Policy Audience." *Law and Society Review*, 30, 865-879.

Lerman, Paul. 1977."Delinquency and Social Policy." *Crime and Delinquency*, 23, 4, 383-393.

Levi, Michael. 1987. *Regulating Fraud. White-Collar Crime and the Criminal Process*. London: Tavistock.

Levitt, Steven D. 1996. "The Effect of Prison Population Size on Crime Rates: Evidence from Prison Overcrowding Litigation." *Quarterly Journal of Economics*, 111, 2: 319-351.

Levitt, Steven D. 1997. "Using Electoral Cycles in Police Hiring to Estimate the Effect of Police on Crime." *American Economic Review*, 87, 3:270–290.

Llewellyn, Jennifer J. and Robert Howse. 1999. *Restorative Justice: A Conceptual Framework*. Ottawa, ONT: Law Commission of Canada.

Liedka, R., A. Piehl, B. Useem. 2006. "The Crime-Control Effect of Incarceration: Does Scale Matter?" *Criminology and Public Policy*, 5, 2:245-276.

Lilly, Robert J. and Paul Knepper. 1993. "The Commercial Corrections Complex." *Crime and Delinquency*, 39, 2: 150-166.

Lilly, Robert J., Richard A. Ball, G. David Curry, and John McMullen. 1993. "Electronic Monitoring of the Drunk Driver: A Seven Year Study of the Home Confinement Alternative, *Crime and Delinquency*, 39, 4: 462-484.

Lilly, Robert J., Richard Ball, and Ronald Huff. 1988. *House Arrest and Correctional Policy: Doing Time at Home*. Newbury Park, CA: Sage.

Lilly, J. Robert, Francis T. Cullen, and Richard A. Ball. 2007. *Criminological Theory: Context and Consequences*. Thousand Oaks, CA: Sage.

Lincoln, Abraham. 1858. "A House Divided Against Itself Cannot Stand." Speech delivered at the Republican State Convention in Springfield, Illinois, June 16. Available online: http://www.nationalcenter.org/HouseDivided.html.

Lindner, C. and M. R. Savarese 1984. "The Evolution of Probation." *Federal Probation,* 48, 3-10.

Lipton, Douglas, Robert Martinson, and Judith Wilks. 1975. *The Effectiveness of Correctional Treatment*. New York: Praeger.

Llewellyn, Jennifer J. and Robert Howse. 1999. *Restorative Justice: A Conceptual Framework*. Ottawa, ONT: Law Commission of Canada.

Lochner, Lance and Enrico Moretti. 2004. "The Effect of Education on Crime: Evidence From Prison Inmates, Arrests, and Self-Reports." *American Economic Review*, *94*, 1: 155-189.

Lotke, Eric and Jason Ziedenberg. 2005. *Tipping Point: Maryland's Overuse of Incarceration and the Impact on Community Safety*. Baltimore, MD: Justice Policy Institute.

Lombroso, Cesare and William Ferrero. 1895. *The Female Offender*. London, England: T. Fisher Unwin.

Lowman, John, Robert J. Menzies, and T. S. Palys (Eds.), *Transcarceration: Essays in the Sociology of Social Control*. Aldershot, UK: Gower,

Lowe, W. J. 1984. "The Lancashire Constabulary, 1845-1870: The Social and Occupational Function of a Victorian Police Force." *Criminal Justice History*, 4: 41-62.

Lundman, Richard J. 1993. *Prevention and Control of Juvenile Delinquency*. New York: Oxford University Press.

Lury, C. 1996. *Consumer Culture*. Cambridge: Polity.

Lynch, Michael. 1987. "Quantitative Analysis and Marxist Criminology: Some Old Answers to a Dilemma." *Crime and Social Justice*, 29: 110-27.

Lynch, Michael. 1989b. "Radical Criminology, Radical Policy?" A paper presented at the Annual Meeting of the Criminal Justice Sciences, Washington, DC.

Lynch, Michael. 1996. "Assessing the State of Radical Criminology." In Peter Cordella and Larry Siegel (Eds.), *Readings in Contemporary Criminological Theory*. Boston: Northeastern University Press, 294-304.

Lynch, Michael and W. Byron Groves. 1986/1989a. *A Primer in Radical Criminology* (2nd Edition). Albany, NY: Harrow and Heston.

Lynch, J. P. and William Sabol. 2004. "Assessing the Effects of Mass Incarceration on Informal Social Control in Communities." *Criminology and Public Policy*, *3*, 267-294.

Lynch, Michael J. and Raymond J. Michalowski. 2006. *A Primer in Radical Criminology: Critical Perspectives on Crime, Power and Identity*. Monsey, NJ: Criminal Justice Press.

Lyng, S 1990. 'Edgework." *American Journal of Sociology* 95(4) 851-886.

Lyng, S. and M. Bracey 1995) "Squaring the One Percent: Biker Style and the Selling of Cultural Resistance." In Jeff Ferrell and Clinton Sanders (eds), *Cultural Criminology*. Boston: Northeastern University Press

MacLean, Brian D., and Dragan Milovanovic. 1989. *New Directions in Critical Criminology*. Vancouver, BC: The Collective Press.

_____. and Harold E. Pepinsky (Eds.), 1993. *We Who Would Take No Prisoners*. Vancouver: Collective Press.

MacKinnon, Catharine A. 1989. *Toward a Feminist Theory of the State*. Cambridge, MA: Harvard University Press.

Maguire, Kathleen and Ann L. Pastore. (Eds.), 1994. *Sourcebook of Criminal Justice Statistics—1993*. Washington, DC: U.S. Department of Justice, Bureau of Justice Statistics.

_____ (Eds.). 1995. *Sourcebook of Criminal Justice Statistics 1994*. U.S. Department of Justice, Bureau of Justice Statistics. Washington, DC: USGPO.

_____. (Eds.). 1996. *Sourcebook of Criminal Justice Statistics 1995*. U.S. Department of Justice, Bureau of Justice Statistics. Washington, DC: USGPO.

Manning, George; Kent Curtis; and Steve McMillen. 1996. *Building Community: The Human Side of Work*. Cincinnati, OH: Thomson Executive Press.

Manning, Peter. 1974. "Dramatic Aspects of Policing." *Sociology and Social Research*, 59, 21-29.

_____ 1978. "The Police: Mandate, Strategies and Appearances." In Manning, Peter and John Van Maanen (Eds.), *Policing: A View from the Streets*. Santa Monica, CA: Goodyear Publishing.

_____. 1979a. "Metaphors of the Field: Varieties of Organizational Discourse." *Administrative Science Quarterly*, 24: 660-671.

_____. 1979b. *Police Work: The Social Organization of Policing*. Cambridge, MA: MIT Press.

_____. 1988. *Symbolic Communication: Signifying Calls and the Police Response*. Cambridge, MA: MIT Press.

Marenin, Otwin. 1982. "Parking Tickets and Class Repression: The Concept of Policing in Critical Theories of Criminal Justice." *Contemporary Crisis*, 6, 241-266.

Marlowe, D. 2004. "Drug Court Efficiency Versus Effectiveness. Join Together." Available: http://www.jointogether.org/news/yourturn/commentary/2004/drug-court-efficacy-vs.html.

Maruna, Shadd and Thomas P. LeBel. 2003. "Welcome Home? Examining the 'Reentry Court' Concept from a Strengths-Based Perspective." *Western Criminology Review*, 4, 2:91-107.

"Maryland Treatment Not Jail Bill Signed Into Law." *Drug War Chronicle*, May 14, 2004. Retrieved July 31, 2008, from http://stopthedrugwar.org/chronicle-old/337/md.shtml.

Marquis, Gregory. 1987. "Working Men in Uniform: The Early Twentieth Century Toronto Police." *Histoire Sociale/Social History*, 20, 259-277.

Marshall, Tony F. 1985. *Alternatives to Criminal Courts: The Potential for Non-Judicial Dispute Settlement*. Brookfield, VT: Gower.

Martin, Randy, Robert J. Mutchnick, and Timothy W. Austin. 1990. *Criminological Thought—Pioneers Past and Present*. New York: Macmillan Publishing Company.

Martindale, D. 1960. *The Nature and Types of Sociological Theory*. Boston: Houghton Mifflin.

Martinson, Robert. 1974. "What works?-Questions and Answers about Prison Reform." *Public Interest*, (Spring): 22-54.

Marx, Gary T. 1980. "The New Police Undercover Work." *Urban Life*, 8, 4, 399-446.

Marx, Gary. 1981. "Ironies of Social Control: Authorities as Contributors to Deviance Through Escalation, Non-Enforcement, and Covert Facilitation." *Social Problems*, 28, 3, 221-246.

Marx, Karl. 1844. *The Economic and Philosophic Manuscripts of 1844*. New York: International Library.

Marx, Karl. 1859. *Critique of Political Economy*. New York: International Library.

Marx, Karl. 1964. *Early Writings*. Translated and edited by T. B. Bottomore. New York: McGraw-Hill.

Marx, Karl. 1967. *Capital*. New York: International Publishing House.

_____. 1970. *Contribution to the Critique of Political Economy*. New York: International Publishing House.

Marx, Karl, and Friedrich Engels. 1992. *Communist Manifesto*. New York: Bantam.

_____. 1972/1984. *The Eighteenth Brumaire of Louis Bonaparte*. Toronto: Norman Bethune Institute.

_____. 1972. "For a Ruthless Criticism of Everything Existing." In Robert C. Tucker (Ed.), *The Marx-Engels Reader*. New York: W. W. Norton, 7-10.

_____. 1975. *Wages, Price and Profit*. Peking: Foreign Languages.

Mathiesen, Thomas. 1965. *The Defense of the Weak: A Sociological Study of a Norwegian Correctional Institution*. London: Tavistock.

Mathiesen, Thomas. 1974. *The Politics of Abolition*. New York: John Wiley and Sons.

Mathiesen, Thomas. 1985. "The Arguments against Building More Prisons." In N. Bishop (Ed.), *Scandinavian Criminal Policy and Criminology 1980-1985*. Copenhagen: Scandinavian Research Council for Criminology, 89-98.

Mathieson, Thomas. 1990. *Prison on Trial*. London. Sage.

Matthews, Roger and Jock Young. 1992. *Issues in Realist Criminology*. London: Sage.

Matza, David. 1974. *Becoming Deviant*. Englewood Cliffs, NJ: Prentice-Hall.

Mauer, Marc, and Tracy Huling. 1995. *Young Black Americans and the Criminal Justice System: Five Years Later*. Washington, DC: The Sentencing Project.

May, Todd. 1989. "Is Post-Structuralist Political Theory Anarchist?" *Philosophy and Social Criticism*, 15: 167-182.

McCold, Paul and Benjamin Wachtel. 1998. "Community is Not a Place: A New Look at Community Justice Initiatives." *Contemporary Justice Review*, 1, No. 1, 71-85.

McDermott, J. 1994. "Criminology as Peacemaking, Feminist Ethics and the Victimization of Women." *Women and Criminal Justice*, 5: 21-44.

McIntosh, Peggy. 1984. "Interactive Phrases of Curricular Revision." In Bonnie Spanier, Alexander Bloom, and Darlene Borovick (Eds.) *Toward a Balanced Curriculum*. Cambridge, MA: Schenkman, 25-34.

McKnight. 1995. *The Careless Society: Community and its Counterfeits*. New York: Basic Books.

McMahon, Maeve W. 1992. *The Persistent Prison? Rethinking Decarceration and Penal Reform*. Toronto: University of Toronto Press.

McQueen, Rob. 1992. "Why Company Law is Important to Left Realists." In John Lowman and Brian D. MacLean, (Eds.) *Realist Criminology: Crime Control and Policing in the 1990s*. Toronto: University of Toronto Press, 177-202.

Melia, Mike. 2008. "Trial could bring US closer to closing Guantanamo." *USA Today*, August 5. Available online: http://abcnews.go.com/International/wireStory?id=5515723.

Melossi, Dario. 1985. "Overcoming the Crisis in Critical Criminology: Toward a Grounded Labeling Theory." *Criminology*, 23: 193-208.

Menzies, Ken. 1995. "State Crime by the Police and Its Control." in Jeffrey Ian Ross (Ed.), *Controlling State Crime*. New York: Garland Publishing, 141-162.

Merton, Robert. 1968. *Social Theory and Social Structure*. New York: Free Press.

Michalowski, Raymond. 1996. "Critical Criminology and the Critique of Domination: The Story of an Intellectual Movement." *Critical Criminology: An International Journal*, 7: 9-16.

Michalowski, Raymond J. and Ronald R. Kramer. 2006. (Eds.) 2006 *State-Corporate Crime: Wrongdoing at The Intersection of Business and Government*. New Brunswick, NJ: Rutgers University Press.

Miles, S. 1998. *Consumerism as a Way of Life*. London: Sage.

Miller, J. G. 1979. "The Revolution in Juvenile Justice: From Rhetoric to Rhetoric." In L. Empey (Ed.), *The Future of Childhood and Juvenile Justice*. Charlottesville: University Press of Virginia, 66-111.

Miller, J. G. 1991/1998. *Last One Over the Wall: The Massachusetts Experiment in Closing Reform Schools*, 3rd edition. Columbus, OH: Ohio State University Press.

Miller, Jerome G. 1979. "The Revolution in Juvenile Justice: From Rhetoric to Rhetoric." In L. Empey (Ed.), *The Future of Childhood and Juvenile Justice*. Charlottesville: University Press of Virginia.

Miller, Elanor. 1986. *Street Women*. Philadelphia: Temple University Press.

Miller, Walter B. 1958. "Lower Class Culture as a Generating Milieu of Gang Delinquency." *Journal of Social Issues*, 14: 5-9.

Miller, Walter B. 1973. "Ideology and Criminal Justice Policy." *Journal of Criminal Law and Criminology*, 642: 141-162.

Miller, 2003 (from Friedrichs)

Miller 1998 (from elrod)

Monkkonen, Eric. H. 1981. *Police in Urban America, 1860-1920*. Cambridge: Cambridge University Press.

Moore, Joan W. 1978. *Homeboys*. Philadelphia: Temple University Press.

Moore, Joan W. 1985. "Isolation and Stigmatization in the Development of the Underclass," *Social Problems*, 33: 1-12.

Moore, Mark and George Kelling. 1983. "To Serve and Protect: Learning From Police History." *Public Interest*, 7, Winter.

Morris, Allison. 1987. *Women, Crime and Criminal Justice*. Oxford: Basil Blackwell.

Morris, Norval and Michael Tonry 1990. *Between Probation and Parole*. New York: Oxford University Press.

Morris, Ruth. 2000. *Stories of Transformative Justice*. Toronto, ONT: Canadian Scholars' Press Inc.

Morrison, W., 1995. *Theoretical Criminology: From Modernity to Post Modernism*, London: Cavendish.

Moulds, Elizabeth F. 1980. "Chivalry and Paternalism: Disparities of Treatment in the Criminal Justice System." In Susan Datesman and Frank Scarpitti (Eds.), *Women, Crime, and Justice*. 277-299.

Mowbray, Martin. 2005. "Community Capacity Building or State Opportunism?" *Community Development Journal*, 40, 3, 255-264.

Moyer, Imogene L. (Ed.), 1992. *The Changing Roles of Women in the Criminal Justice System: Offenders, Victims, and Professionals*, 2nd edition. Prospect Heights, IL: Waveland Press.

MSNBC 2007. Rising Crime Blamed on Youth Violence, Gangs." Online. Available at http://www.msnbc.msn.com/id/18671013/.

Muir, W. 1977. *Police: Street Corner Politicians*. Chicago: University of Chicago Press.

Mullings, Leith. 1994. "Images, Ideology, and Women of Color." In Maxine Baca Zinn and Bonnie Thorton Dill (Eds.), Women *of Color in U.S. Society*. Philadelphia: Temple University Press, 265-289.

Mullins, Christopher W. and Dawn L. Rothe. 2007. "Darfur: The Forgotten Ones." *Critical Criminology*. 15, 2, 135-158.

Mullins, Christopher W and Dawn L Rothe. 2008. *Blood, Power and Bedlam*. New York: Peter Lang.

Musolino, Angela. 1988. "Judge's Attitudes toward Female Offenders." Unpublished manuscript cited in Rita Simon and Jean Landis *The Crimes Women Commit*, 1991. Lexington, MA: Lexington Books.

Muzzatti, Stephen. 2009. "Drive it Like you Stole It: Trangressive Pleasure and Automobiles in Television Advertisements." In Kevin Hayward and Michael Presdee. (Eds.) *Framing Crime: Cultural Criminology and the Image*, London: Routledge/GlassHouse.

Myers, Martha A. 1989. "Symbolic Policy and the Sentencing of Drug Offenders." *Law and Society Review*, 23, 2: 295-315.

_____. 1987. "Economic Inequality and Discrimination in Sentencing." *Social Forces*, 6, 3: 746-766.

_____ and Susette M. Talarico. 1986a. "The Social Contexts of Racial Discrimination in Sentencing." *Social Problems*, 33: 236-251.

_____. 1986b. "Urban Justice, Rural Injustice? Urbanization and its Effect on Sentencing." *Criminology*, 24: 367-391.

Nagel, Ilene and John Hagan. 1983. "Gender and Crime: Offense Patterns and Criminal Court Sanctions." In Michael Tonry and Norval Morris (Eds.), *Crime and Justice: An Annual Review of Research.* Chicago: University of Chicago Press, 4: 91-144.

_____ and Barry L. Johnson. 1994. "The Role of Gender in a Structured Sentencing System." *Journal of Criminal Law and Criminology,* 85, 1: 181-221.

Nalla, Mahesh K., Michael Lynch, and Michael J. Leiber. 1996. "Determinants of Police Growth, 1950-1988." *Justice Quarterly,* 14, 1, 115-143.

Nathanson, Donald L. 1997. "From Empathy to Community." In *The Annual of Psychoanalysis, Volume 25,* Jerome A. Winer (Ed.). Chicago: Chicago Institute for Psychoanalysis.

National Governor's Association. 2002. *NGA Prisoner Reentry Policy Academy.* Washington, DC: National Governor's Association.

Niederhoffer, Arthur. 1969. *Behind the Shield: The Police in Urban Society.* Garden City, NY: Anchor Books.

Nelken, David. 1994. "White-Collar Crime." In Maguire, Mike, Morgan, Rod and Reiner, Robert. (Eds.) *The Oxford Handbook of Criminology.* Oxford: Clarendon, 355-392.

New York Times. 1990. "States' Prisons Continue to Bulge, Overwhelming Efforts at Reform." May 20, pages A-1, 32.

_____. 1989. "Who Wants New Prisons? In New York, All of Upstate." June 9, pages B-1, 2.

_____ 1994. "Residents of Dying California Town See Future in a Prison." May 8: 28.

O'Brien, M 2005. "What Is *Cultural* About Cultural Criminology?" *British Journal of Criminology* 45: 599-612.

Odubekun, Lola. 1992. "A Structural Approach to Differential Gender Sentencing." *Criminal Justice Abstracts,* 29: 343-360.

Ohlin, Lloyd E. 1983. "The Future of Juvenile Justice Policy and Research." *Crime and Delinquency,* 29(3): 463-472.

Orland, Leonard. 1980. "Reflections on Corporate Crime: Law in Search of Theory and Scholarship." *American Criminal Law Review,* 17: 501-520.

Ouellette, Melissa. 2005. "The Involvement of Insurance Companies in Restorative Processes." In *New Directions in Restorative Justice: Issues, Practice, Evaluation,* Elizabeth Elliott and Robert M. Gordon (Eds.). Portland, OR: Willan Publishing, 228-241.

Orentlicher, Diane. 2006. *Crimes of War: The Book.* Retrieved from <www. crimesofwar. org/thebook/genocide.html.

Palmer, T. 1992. *The Re-Emergence of Correctional Intervention.* Newbury Park, CA: Sage.

Pareto, Vilfredo. 1980. *Compendium of General Sociology.* Minneapolis: University of Minnesota Press.

Parisi, Nicolette. 1982. "Are Females Treated Differently? A Review of The Theories and Evidence on Sentencing and Parole Decisions." In Nicole Rafter and Elizabeth Stanko (Eds.), *Judge, Lawyer, Victim, Thief.* Boston: Northeastern University Press, 205-220.

Park, Robert, Burgess, Ernest W.D. and McKenzie, Roderick D. 1925. *The City.* Chicago: University of Chicago Press.

Parlevliet, Michelle 1998. "Considering Truth. Dealing with a Legacy of Gross Human Rights Violations." *Netherlands Quarterly of Human Rights* 16, 141-174.

Parmentier, Stephan, Kris Vanspauwen, and Elmar Weitekamp 2001. "Restorative Justice for Victims of Mass Violence: Reconsidering the Building Blocks of Post-Conflict Justice." Paper presented at the Expert Meetings at Maastricht University. 13-14 April.

Paternoster, Raymond and Alex Piquero. 1995. "Reconceptualizing Deterrence: An Empirical Test of Personal and Vicarious Experiences." *Journal of Research in Crime and Delinquency*. 32(3): 251-287.

Paternoster, Raymond and Sally Simpson. 1996. "Sanction Threats and Appeal to Morality: Testing a Rational Choice Model of Corporate Crime." *Law and Society Review* 30: 549-583.

Patterson, C. 2006. *Resistance*, New York: Seven Stories Press.

Pavlich, George. 2005. *Governing Paradoxes of Restorative Justice*. Portland, OR: GlassHouse Press.

Pearce, Frank. 1992. "The Contribution of 'Left Realism' to the Study of Commercial Crime." In John Lowman and Brian D. MacLean (Eds.), *Realist Criminology: Crime Control and Policing in the 1990s*. Toronto: University of Toronto Press, 313-335.

Pearce, Frank. 2007. "An Age of Miracles?" In H. N. Pontell and G. Geis (Eds.) *International Handbook of White-Collar and Corporate Crime*. New York: Springer.

Pearce, Frank and Steve Tombs. 1992. "Realism and Corporate Crime." In Roger Matthews and Jock Young (Eds.), *Issues in Realist Criminology*. London: Sage, 70-101.

People v. Turner, 55 Ill. 280 1870.

Pepinsky, Harold E. 1974. "From White Collar Crime to Exploitation: Redefinition of a Field." *Journal of Criminal Law and Criminology*. 65: 225-233.

_____. 1976. *Crime and Conflict: A Study of Law and Society*. New York: Academic Press.

_____. 1978. "Communist anarchism as an alternative to the rule of criminal law." *Contemporary Crises*, 2: 315-327.

_____ and Paul Jesilow. 1984. *Myths that Cause Crime*. Cabin John, MD: Seven Locks Press.

_____. 1991a. "Peacemaking in Criminology." In Brian MacLean and Dragan Milovanovic (Eds.), *New Directions in Critical Criminology*. Vancouver: Collective Press, 107-110.

Pepinsky, Harold. 1999. "Abolishing Prisons." In B.W. Hancock and P.M. Sharp (Eds.). *Criminal Justice in America: Theory, Practice, and Policy*. New York: Prentice-Hall.

Pepinsky, Harold, and Richard Quinney. (Eds.). 1991. *Criminology as Peacemaking*. Bloomington: Indiana University Press.

Petersilia, Joan. 1985. *Probation and Felony Offenders*. Washington, DC: National Institute of Justice.

Petersilia, Joan. 1986. *Prison Versus Probation in California: Implications For Crime and Offender Recidivism*. Santa Monica, CA: Rand Corporation.

Petersilia, Joan. 2004. "What Works in Prisoner Reentry? Reviewing and Questioning the Evidence." *Federal Probation, 68, 2*: 4-8.

Pew Center on the States. 2008. *One in 100: Behind Bars in America 2008*. Public Safety Performance Project, Washington, DC: The Pew Charitable Trust Foundation.

Pfohl, Stephen and Avery Gordon. 1986. "Criminological Displacements: A Sociological Deconstruction." *Social Problems*, 33: 94-113.

Phillips, David. 1980. "A New Engine of Power and Authority: The Institution of Law Enforcement in England, 1780-1830." In V. A. C. Gatrell, Bruce Lenman and Geoffrey Parker (Eds.), *Crime and the Law: The Social History of Crime in Western Europe since 1500*. London: Europa Publications, 155-189.

Phillips, Dretha M. and Lois B. DeFleur. 1982. "Gender Ascription and the Stereotyping of Deviants." *Criminology*, 20, 431-448.

Piketty, T. and E. Saez. 2006, May 2. "The Evolution of Top Incomes: A Historical and International Perspective." *American Economic Review*, 96, 200-205.

Piquero, Nicole Leeper and Alex Piquero, Alex R. 2006. "Control Balance and Exploitative Corporate Crime." *Criminology*, 44, 2: 397-430.

Piquero, Alex and Raymond Paternoster. 1998. "An Application of Stafford and Warr's Reconceptualization of Deterrence to Drinking and Driving." *Journal of Research in Crime and Delinquency*. 35, 1, 3-39.

Piven, Frances Fox, and Richard A. Cloward. 1971. *Regulating the Poor: The Functions of Public Welfare*. New York: Vintage Books.

Platt, Anthony M. 1969/1977. *The Child Savers: The Invention of Delinquency*, 2nd edition. Chicago: The University of Chicago Press.

Platt, Anthony M. 1991. "The Child-Saving Movement and the Origins of the Juvenile Justice System." In R. Berger (Ed.), *The Sociology of Juvenile Delinquency*. Chicago: Nelson-Hall, 2-26.

Poe-Yamagata, E. and M. Jones 2000. *And justice for some*. New York: National Council on Crime and Delinquency.

Pogarsky, G., Kim, K., and R. Paternoster 2005. "Perceptual Change in the National Youth Survey: Lessons for Deterrence Theory and Offender Decision-Making." *Justice Quarterly, 22*, 1-29.

Pollack, Otto. 1950. *The Criminality of Women*. Philadelphia: University of Pennsylvania Press.

Pope, C. and W. Feyerherm 1990. "Minority Status and Juvenile Justice Processing." *Criminal Justice Abstracts, 22*, 327-336.

Poulantzas, N. 1973. *Political Power and Social Class*. Atlantic Fields, NJ: Humanities Press.

People v. Turner, 55 Illinois 280 1870.

President's Commission on Law Enforcement and Administration of Justice 1967. *The Challenge of Crime in a Free Society.* Washington, DC: U.S. Government Printing Office.

Pranis, Kay; Barry Stuart; and Mark Wedge. 2003. *Peacemaking Circles: From Crime to Community*. St. Paul, MN: Living Justice Press.

Prunier, Gerard. 2005. *Darfur: The Ambiguous Genocide*. Ithaca, NY: Cornell University Press.

Punch, Maurice. 1996. *Dirty Business*. London: Sage.

Putnam, Robert. 2000. *Bowling Alone: The Collapse and Revival of American Community*. Toronto: Simon and Schuster.

Puzzanchera, C. and W. Kang 2007. *Juvenile Court Statistics Databook*. Online. Available: http://ojjdp.ncjrs.gov/ojstatbb/jcsdb.

Quinney, Richard. 1962. «Retail Pharmacy as a Marginal Occupation: A Study of Prescription Violation.» Ph.D. Dissertation. University of Wisconsin.

Quinney, Richard. 1965. "A Conception of Man and Society for Criminology." *Sociological Quarterly*, 6: 119-27.

Quinney, Richard. 1970. *The Social Reality of Crime*. Boston: Little Brown.

Quinney, Richard. 1974. *Critique of Legal Order*. Boston: Little Brown.

Quinney, Richard. 1975. "Crime Control in Capitalist Society: A Critical Philosophy of Legal Order." In Ian Taylor, Paul Walton and Jock Young (Eds.), *Critical Criminology*. Boston: Routledge and Kegan Paul, 181-202.

Quinney, Richard. 1977/1980. *Class, State, and Crime*. New York: Longman.

Quinney, Richard. 2000. "Socialist Humanism and the Problem of Crime: Thinking about Erich Fromm in the Development of Critical/Peacemaking Criminology." In Kevin Anderson and Richard Quinney (Eds.). *Erich Fromm and Critical Criminology: Beyond the Punitive Society*, Chicago: University of Illinois Press.

Quinney, Robert. 1970. *The Problem of Crime*. New York: Dodd, Mead.

Raeder, Myrna S. 1993. "Gender and Sentencing: Single Moms, Battered Women, and Other Sex-based Anomalies in the Gender-Free world of the Federal Sentencing Guidelines." *Pepperdine Law Review*, 20: 905-990.

Rafter, Nicole Hahn. 1990. *Partial Justice: Women, Prisons and Social Control.* New Brunswick, NJ: Transaction Publishers.

Rafter, Nicole Hahn.1994. "Eugenics, Class, and the Professionalization of Social Control." In George Bridges and Martha Myers (Eds.), *Inequality, Crime, and Social Control.* Boulder, CO: Westview Press, 215-226.

Rafter, Nicole Hahn and Frances Heidensohn. 1995. "Introduction: The Development of Feminist Perspectives on Crime." In Nicole Hahn Rafter and Frances Heidensohn (Eds.), *International Feminist Perspectives in Criminology: Engendering a Discipline.* Buckingham: Open University Press, 1-14.

Raphael, Steven, and Rudolph Winter-Ebner. 2001. "Identifying the Effect of Unemployment on Crime." *Journal of Law and Economics*, 44, 1: 259–83.

Ratner, R.S., and John McMullen. 1983. "Social Control and the Rise of the 'Exceptional State' in Britain, the United States, and Canada." *Crime and Social Justice*, 19: 31-43.

Ray, G. 1978. "Class, Race and the Police: A Critique of the "Class Nature of the Urban Police During the Period of Black Municipal Power." *Crime and Social Justice*, 9, 63-69, 271-89.

Redhead, Steve. 1995. *Unpopular Cultures: The Birth of Law and Popular Culture.* Manchester, UK: Manchester University Press.

Regnery, Alfred S. 1985. "Getting Away With Murder." *Policy Review*, (Fall): 1-4.

Reiman, Jeffrey H. 1986/1995. *The Rich Get Richer and the Poor Get Prison: Ideology, Class, and Criminal Justice,* 4th edition. Boston: Allyn and Bacon.

Reiner, Robert. 1978a. "The Police in the Class Struggle." *British Journal of Law and Society*, 5, 166-184.

Reiner, Robert. 1978b. *The Blue Coated Worker: A Sociological Study of Police Unionism.* Cambridge: Cambridge University Press.

Reiner, Robert. 1986. *The Politics of Police.* Sussex: Wheatshaft Books.

Reno, Robert. 1993. "The Throwaway Employee." *Charlotte Observer*, September 16.

Rheinstein, M. 1954. *Max Weber on law in Economy and Society.* Cambridge, MA: Harvard University Press.

Rice, Marcia. 1990. "Challenging Orthodoxies in Feminist Theory: A Black Feminist Critique." In Loraine Gelsthorpe and Allison Morris (Eds.), *Feminist Perspectives in Criminology.* Milton Keynes: Open University Press, 577-669.

Rice, Marcia. 1992. "Challenging Orthodoxies in Feminist Theory: A Black Feminist Critique," In Lorraine Gelsthorpe and Allison Morris (Ed.) *Feminist Perspectives in Criminology.* Milton Keynes, England. Open University Press, 577-669.

Richards, Stephen C. 1990. "The Sociological Penetration of the American Gulag," *Wisconsin Sociologist*, 27, 4, Fall, 18-28.

Richards, Stephen. 1995. *The Structure of Prison Release.* New York: McGraw Hill.

Richards, Stephen C. 2003. "My Journey Through the Federal Bureau of Prisons." In Jeffrey Ian Ross and Stephen C. Richards (Eds.) *Convict Criminology.* Belmont, CA: Wadsworth, 120-149.

Richards, Stephen C. 2008. "USP Marion: The First Federal Super-Max," *The Prison Journal*, Vol. 88, No. 1, 6-22."

Richards, Stephen C. 2004a. "Penitentiary Dreams: Books Will Take You Anywhere You Want To Go." *Journal of Prisoners on Prisons.* 13: 60-73.

Richards, Stephen C. 2004b. "Born Illegal." In Ronald Berger and Richard Quinney (Eds.), *Storytelling Sociology: Narrative as Social Inquiry.* Boulder, CO: Lynne Rienner Publishers, 183-193.

Richards, Stephen and Richard S. Jones. 1997. "Perpetual Incarceration Machine: Structural Impediments to Post-Prison Success." *Journal of Contemporary Criminal Justice*, Vol. 13, No. 1: 4-22.

Richards, Stephen C., and Richard S. Jones. 2004. "Beating the Perpetual Incarceration Machine." In Shadd Maruna and Russ Immarigeon (Eds.), *After Crime and Punishment: Pathways to Offender Reintegration*. London: Willan, 201-232.

Richards, Stephen C. and Jeffrey Ian Ross. 2001. "The New School of Convict Criminology," *Social Justice*, 28, 1, 177-191.

Richey Mann, Coramae. 1989. "Minority and Female: A Criminal Justice Double Bind." *Social Justice*, 16, 4: 95-114.

Riley, Jason. 2008. "Inmate-Release Provision Sparks Concern." *Louisville Courier-Journal*, April 14. Retrieved April 23, 2008, from http://www.courier-journal.com/apps/pbcs.dll/article?AID=/20080414/NEWS0101/804140399/1008/NEWS01.

Riemer. Hans. 1937 "Socialization in the Prison Community." *Proceedings of the American Prison Association*, 151-155.

Roberg, Roy. R. and Jack Kuykendall. 1993. *Police and Society* Belmont, CA: Wadsworth Publishing Company.

Roberts, Albert R. 1998. "Treating Juveniles in Institutional and Open Settings." In A. R. Roberts (Ed.), *Juvenile Justice: Policies, Programs, Services*, 2nd edition. Chicago: Dorsey Press, 95-109.

Roberts, Albert R. 1989. *Juvenile Justice: Policies, Programs, and Services*. Chicago: Dorsey Press.

Robinson, Cyril D. 1978. "The Deradicalization of the Policeman: An Historical Analysis." *Crime and Delinquency*, 24, 129-151.

Robinson, Cyril. 1979. "Ideology as History: A Look at the Way Some English Police Historians Look at the Police." *Police Studies*, 2, 2, 35-49

Robinson, Cyril D. and Richard Scaglion. 1987. "The Origin and Evolution of the Police Function in Society: Notes Toward a Theory." *Law and Society Review*, 21, 1: 109-153.

Robinson, Cyril D., Richard Scaglion, and J. Michael Olivero. 1994. *Police in Contradiction: The Evolution of the Police Function in Society*. Westport, CT: Greenwood Publishing Group.

Roman, John, Wendy Townsend, Avinash Singh Bahti. 2003. *Recidivism Rates for Drug Court Graduates: Nationally Based Estimates, Final Report*. Washington, DC: The Urban Institute.

Rose, Dina and Todd Clear. 1998. "Incarceration, Social Capital, and Crime: Implications for Social Disorganization Theory." *Criminology*, 36, 441-479.

Rose, Dina. and Todd Clear. 2002. "Incarceration, Reentry, and Social Capital: Social Networks in the Balance." Paper prepared for the "From Prison to Home" conference, January 30-31, 2001. Washington, DC: The Urban Institute.

Rosencranz, John. 1986. "Probation, Supervision: Mission Impossible." *Federal Probation*, 1: 25-31.

Ross, Jeffrey Ian. 1995. "The Historical Treatment of Urban policing in Canada." *Urban History Review*, 24, 1: 36-52.

Ross, Jeffrey Ian. 1996. "The Current Status of Comparative Policing in the Curriculum." *Journal of Criminal Justice Education*, 7, 2, 263-273.

Ross, Jeffrey Ian 1998. *Cutting the Edge: Current Perspectives in Radical/Critical Criminology and Criminal Justice*. Westport, CT: Praeger.

Ross, Jeffrey Ian. and Stephen Richards (Eds.). 2003. *Convict Criminology*. Belmont, CA: Wadsworth.

Rothe, Dawn L. and David O. Friedrichs 2006 "The State of the Criminology of Crimes of the State." *Social Justice*, 33: 147-161.

Rothe, Dawn L. and Christopher W. Mullins. 2006a "'International Community': Legitimizing a Moral Collective Consciousness." *Humanity and Society.* 30(3):254-276.

Rothe, Dawn L. and Christopher W. Mullins. 2006b. "The International Criminal Court and United States Opposition." *Crime, Law and Social Change.* 45:201-226.

Rothe, Dawn L. and Christopher W. Mullins. 2006c. *The International Criminal Court: Symbolic Gestures and the Generation of Global Social Control.* Lanham, MD: Lexington Books.

Rothe, Dawn L. and Christopher W. Mullins. 2007 "Darfur and the International Legal Order: Genocide or Crime against Humanity?" *Humanity and Society.* 31(1):83-107.

Rothe, Dawn L, Christopher W. Mullins, and Kent Sandstrom. 2008. "The Rwandan Genocide: International Financial Policies and Human Rights." *Social Justice* (forthcoming).

Rothe, Dawn; Stephen Muzzatti; and Christopher W. Mullins. 2006. "Crime on the High Seas: Crimes of Globalization and the Sinking of the Senegalese Ferry Le Joola." *Critical Criminology.* 14:2: 159-180.

Rottman, David, and Pamela Casey. 1999. "Therapeutic Jurisprudence and the Emergence of Problem-Solving Courts." *National Institute of Justice Journal,* July, 12-19. Washington, DC: National Institute of Justice.

Rucker, Lila. 1991. "Peacemaking in Prisons: A Process." In Harold E. Pepinsky and Richard Quinney (Eds.) *Criminology as Peacemaking.* Bloomington: Indiana University Press, 172-179.

Ruggiero, Vincenzo 2005. Review: *City Limits: Crime, Consumer Culture and the Urban Experience, Theoretical Criminology,* 9: 4 497-499.

Ruggiero, Vincenzo. 2000. *Crime and Markets: Essays in Anti-Criminology.* Oxford: Oxford University Press.

Ruggiero, Vincenzo. 2005. "Dichotomies and Contemporary Social Movements." *City,* 9: 297-306.

Ruggiero, Vincenzo. 2007. "It's the Economy, Stupid: Classifying Power Crime." *International Journal of Sociology of Law* (forthcoming).

Ruggiero, Vincenzo and Nicola Montagna. 2008. *Social Movements: A Reader.* London: Routledge.

Russell, Ken and J. Robert Lilly, 1989. *The Electronic Monitoring of Offenders.* Leicester, UK. University of Leicester.

Rutherford, Andrew 1986. *Prisons and the Process of Justice: The Reductionist Challenge.* Oxford: Oxford University Press.

Ryan, Kevin and Jeff Ferrell. 1986. "Knowledge, Power, and the Process of Justice." *Crime and Social Justice*, 25: 178-195.

Ryerson, E. 1996. "Best-Laid Plans: The Ideal Juvenile Court." In R. Berger (Ed.), *The Sociology of Juvenile Delinquency,* 2nd edition. Chicago: Nelson-Hall, 11-25.

Sabol, William, H. Couture, and P. Harrision. 2007. *Prisoners in 2006.* Washington, DC: Bureau of Justice Statistics, U.S. Department of Justice. NCJ219416.

Sabol, William, T.D. Minton, and P.M. Harrison. 2007. *Prison and Jail Inmates at Midyear, 2006.* Washington, DC: Bureau of Justice Statistics, U.S. Department of Justice. NCJ217675.

Sadat, Leila Nadya and S. Richard Carden. 2000. "The New International Criminal Court: An Uneasy Revolution." *Georgetown Law Review.* 88: 381-474.

Sampson, R. J., Laub, J., and L. C. Allen 2001. "Explaining Crime over the Life Course." In R. Paternoster and R. Bachman (Eds.), *Explaining Criminals and Crime.* Los Angeles, CA: Roxbury, 97-112.

Sampson, R. J., Raudenbush, S. W., and F. Earls 1997. "Neighborhoods and Violent Crime: A Multilevel Study of Collective Efficacy." *Science,* 227, 918-924.

Sands, Phillip. 2005. *Lawless World: America and the Making and Breaking of Global Rules.* London: Allen Lane.

Santino, Umberto. 2000. *Storia del movimento antimafia.* Rome: Editori Riuniti.

Schlegel, Kip and David Weisburd. 1992. *White Collar Crime Reconsidered.* Boston: Northeastern University Press.

Schrager, Laura Shill and Short, James. 1977. "Toward a Sociology of Organizational Crime." *Social Problems*, 25: 407-19.

Schur, Edwin. 1973. *Radical Non-Intervention: Rethinking the Delinquency Problem.* Englewood Cliffs, NJ: Prentice-Hall.

Schultz, J. L. 1973. "The Cycle of Juvenile Court History." *Crime and Delinquency,* Vol. 19, No. 4. October, 457-476.

Schwartz, I. M. 1989. *(In)justice for Juveniles: Rethinking the Best Interests of the Child.* Lexington, MA: Lexington Books.

Schwartz, Martin D. 1989. "The Undercutting Edge of Criminology." *The Critical Criminologist,* 1: 1-2, 5.

_____. 1991. "The Future of Critical Criminology." In Brian D. MacLean and Dragan Milovanovic (Eds.), *New Directions in Critical Criminology*, Vancouver, BC: The Collective Press, 119-124.

Schwartz, Martin D. and Suzanne E. Hatty (Eds.) 2003. Controversies *in Critical Criminology.* Cincinnati, OH: Anderson Publishing Co.

Schwartz, Martin D. and David O. Friedrichs. 1994. "Postmodern Thought And Criminological Discontent: New Metaphors for Understanding Violence." *Criminology,* 32: 221-246.

Schwartz, Martin D. and Walter DeKeseredy. 1991. "Left Realist Criminology: Strengths, Weaknesses and the Feminist Critique." *Law, Crime and Social Change.* 15: 51-72.

Schwendinger, Herman and Julia Schwendinger. 1979. "Delinquency and Social Reform: A Radical Perspective." In L. Empey (Ed.), *Juvenile Justice: The Progressive Legacy and Current Reforms.* Charlottesville: University Press of Virginia.

Schwendinger, Herman and Julia Schwendinger.1983. *Rape and Inequality.* Beverly Hills, CA: Sage.

Schwendinger, Herman and Julia Schwendinger. 1991. "Introduction: Feminism, Criminology, and Complex Variables." In Brian D. MacLean and Dragan Milovanovic (Eds.), *New Directions in Critical Criminology.* Vancouver, BC: The Collective Press, 39-44.

Scott, James C. 1985. *Weapons of the Weak: Everyday Forms of Peasant Resistance.* New Haven, CT: Yale University Press.

Scott, James C.1990. *Domination and the Arts of Resistance.* New Haven, CT: Yale University Press.

"Sentencing: Maryland Governor Vetoes Bill to Give Two-Time Drug Sales Offenders Parole Eligibility." *Drug War Chronicle, 486,* May 18, 2007. Retrieved July 31, 2008, from http://stopthedrugwar.org/chronicle/486/maryland_governor_vetoes_sentencing_reform bill.

Sharpe, J. A. 1980. "Enforcing the Law in the Seventeenth-Century English Village." In V.A. C. Gatrell, Bruce Lenman, and Geoffrey Parker (Eds.), *Crime and the Law: The Social History of Crime in Western Europe since 1500.* London: Europa Publications, 97-119.

Shaw, C R. and H D. McKay. 1942. *Juvenile Delinquency and Urban Areas.* Chicago IL: University of Chicago Press.

Sherif, Carolyn Wood. 1987/1979. "Bias in Psychology." In Sandra Harding (Ed.), *Feminism and Methodology.* Bloomington: Indiana University Press, 37-56.

Siegel, L. and J. J. Senna 1997. *Juvenile Delinquency: Theory, Practice, and Law*. St. Paul, MN: West.

Silver, Allan. 1966. "The Demand for Order in Civil Society: A Review of Some Theses in the History of Urban Crime, Police and Riot." In David Bordua (Ed.), *The Police: Six Sociological Essays*. New York: Wiley, 1-24.

Simmel, G. 1900. *The Philosophy of Money*. London: Routledge and Kegan Paul.

_____.1906. "The Sociology of Secrecy and of Secret Societies." *American Journal of Sociology*, 11: 441-98.

_____.1908. *Conflict and the Web of Group Affiliations*. New York: Free Press.

Simmel, Georg. 1903/1971. *Individuality and Social Forms*. Chicago: University of Chicago Press.

Simon, David. R 1996/2006. *Elite Deviance*. Boston: Allyn and Bacon.

Simon, Jonathan. 1987. "The Emergence of a Risk Society: Insurance, Law, and the State," *Socialist Review*, 22: 772-800.

Simon, Rita. 1975. *Women and Crime*. Lexington, MA: Lexington Books.

Simon, Rita and Jean Landis. 1991. *The Crimes Women Commit, the Punishments They Receive*. Lexington, MA: Lexington Books.

Skolnick, Jerome. 1966. *Justice without Trial: Law Enforcement in a Democratic Society*. New York: Wiley.

Skriabine, P. 1989. *Clinique et Topologie*. (unpublished manuscript).

Slapper, Gary and Tombs, Steve. 1999. *Corporate Crime*. Harlow: Pearson Education.

Smart, Carol. 1990. "Feminist Approaches to Criminology or Postmodern Woman Meets Atavistic Man." In Loraine Gelsthorpe and Allison Morris (Eds.), *Feminist Perspectives in Criminology*. Milton Keynes, UK: Open University Press, 70-84.

_____. 1993. "Proscription, Prescription, Desire for Certainty? Feminist Theory in the Field of Law." *Law, Politics and Society*, 13: 37-54.

_____. 1976. *Women, Crime and Criminology: A Feminist Critique*. London: Routledge and Kegan Paul.

Smeulers, Alette. 2007. "Towards a Typology of Perpetrators of International Crimes And Other Gross Human Rights Violations." Paper presented at the Expert Meetings at Maastricht University. 13-14 April.

Smith, Pheny Z. 1993. *Felony Defendants in Large Urban Counties, 1990*. Washington, DC: U.S. Department of Justice, Bureau of Justice Statistics.

Snyder, Howard N. and Melissa Sickmund. 1995. *Juvenile Offenders and Victims: A Focus on Violence*. Statistics Summary. Washington, DC: OJJDP.

Soueif, A. 2003. "Genet's Palestinian Revolution." *Nation* (24 February), 25-29.

South, Nigel and Piers Beirne (Eds.) 2006. *Green Criminology*. Aldergate, UK: Ashgate.

Sparks, R.F. 1980. "A Critique of Marxist Criminology." In Norval Morris and Michael Tonry (Eds.), *Crime and Justice: An Annual Review of Research*. Chicago: University of Chicago Press.

Spelman, Willliam. 2000. "What Recent Studies Do (and Don't) Tell Us About Imprisonment and Crime." *Crime and Justice*, 27, 419-494.

Spelman, William. 2005. "Jobs or Jails? The Crime Drop in Texas." *Journal of Policy Analysis and Management*, 24: 133-165.

Spitzer, S. 1980. "Leftwing Criminology: An Infantile Disorder?" In James Inciardi (Ed.), *Radical Criminology*, Beverly Hills, CA: Sage, 169-190.

_____. 1993. "The Political Economy of Policing." in David F. Greenberg (ed.) *Crime and Punishment: Readings in Marxist Criminology*. Philadelphia: Temple University Press, 568-594.

Spohn, Cassia. 1994. "Crime and the Social Control of Blacks: Offender/Victim Race and the Sentencing of Violent Offenders." In George S. Bridges and Martha

Myers (Ed.), *Inequality, Crime and Social Control*. Boulder, CO: Westview Press, 249-268.

_____ and Jerry Cederbloom. 1991. "Race and Disparities in Sentencing: A Test of the Liberation Hypothesis." *Justice Quarterly*, 8: 305-327.

_____, John Gruhl, and Susan Welch. 1987. "The Impact of the Ethnicity and Gender of Defendants on the Decision to Reject or Dismiss Felony Charges." *Criminology*, 25: 175-191.

Spring, Joel H. 1972. *Education and the Rise of the Corporate State*. Boston: Beacon.

Stacey, Judith and Barrie Thorne. 1985. "The Missing Feminist Revolution in Sociology." *Social Problems*, 32, 301-316.

Stack, Carol B. 1974. *All Our Kin: Strategies for Survival in a Black Community*. New York: Harper Torchbooks.

Stafford, Mark and Mark Warr. 1993. "A Reconceptualization of General and Specific Deterrence." *Journal of Research in Crime and Delinquency*. 30(2): 123-35.

Steffensmeier, Darrell. 1995. "Trends in Female Crime: It's Still a Man's World." In Barbara Raffel Price and Natalie J. Solokoff (Eds.), *The Criminal Justice System and Women: Offenders, Victims, and Workers*. New York: McGraw-Hill, 89-104.

_____ and Miles D. Harer. 1991. "Did Crime Rise or Fall During the Reagan Presidency? The Effects of an 'Aging' U.S. Population on the Nation's Crime Rate." *Journal of Research in Crime and Delinquency*, 28 (August): 330-359.

_____, John Kramer and Cathy Streifel. 1993. "Gender and Imprisonment Decisions." *Criminology*, 31: 411-443.

Steiner, B., Hemmens, C., and V. Bell 2006. "Legislative Waiver Reconsidered: General Deterrent Effects of Statutory Exclusion Laws Enacted Post-1979." *Justice Quarterly*, 23, 34-59.

Steinhart, David and Barry Krisberg. 1987. "Children in Jail." *State Legislatures*, 13(3): 12-16.

Stemen, Don. 2007. *Reconsidering Incarceration: New Directions for Reducing Crime*. Center on Sentencing and Corrections, New York: Vera Institute of Justice.

Stretcher, Victor G. 1991. "Revising the Histories and Futures of Policing." *Police Forum*, 1, No. 1: 1-9.

Sullivan, Dennis and Larry Tifft. 2006. *Handbook of Restorative Justice*. London: Routledge.

Sullivan, Richard F. 1973. "The Economics of Crime: An Introduction to the Literature." *Crime and Delinquency*, 19, 2: 138-149.

Sutherland, Edwin H. 1948. "Crime of Corporations." In *On Analyzing Crime*. Chicago: University of Chicago Press, 788-96.

Sutherland, Edwin H. 1940. "White-Collar Criminality." *American Sociological Review*, 5: 1-12.

Sutherland, Edwin. H. 1983. *White-Collar Crime: The Uncut Version*. New Haven, CT: Yale University Press.

Sutherland, Edwin H. (ed.) (and Conwell, Chic) (pseudonym). 1937. *The Professional Thief: by a Professional Thief*. Annotated and Interpreted by Edwin H. Sutherland. Chicago: University of Chicago Press.

Sykes, Gresham. 1958. *The Society of Captives*. Princeton, NJ: Princeton University Press.

Sykes, Gresham M. 1974. "The Rise of Critical Criminology." *Journal of Criminal Law and Criminology*, 65, June: 206-213.

Swoboda, Frank. 1993. "Part-Time Workers Crowd Industrialized World, but Many being Shortchanged." *Charlotte Observer*, September 11, p. 6D.

Szockyj, Elizabeth and James G. Fox. (Eds.), 1996. *Corporate Victimization of Women*. Boston: Northeastern University Press.

Takagi, Paul. 1981. "The Walnut Street Jail: A Penal Reform to Centralize the Powers of the State." In David F. Greenberg (Ed.), *Crime and Capitalism: Readings in Marxist Criminology*. Palo Alto, CA: Mayfield, 279-292.

Tak, Peter J. 1994. "Community Service in the Netherlands." In Ugljesa Zvekic (Ed.) *Alternatives to Imprisonment in Comparative Perspective*. Chicago: Nelson-Hall.

Tannenbaum, Frank. 1936. *Crime and the Community*. Boston: Ginn.

Tappan, Paul. 1947. "Who Is the Criminal?" *American Sociological Review*. 12: 96-102.

Taylor, Ian, Paul Walton, and Jock Young. 1973/1974. *The New Criminology: For a Social Theory of Deviance*. London: Routledge and Kegan Paul.

_____, Paul Walton and Jock Young. 1975. *Critical Criminology*. Boston: Routledge and Kegan Paul.

The Second January Group. 1986. *After Truth: A Postmodern Manifesto*. London: Inventions Press.

Tift, Larry and Dennis Sullivan, 1980. *The Struggle to Be Human: Crime, Criminology and Anarchism*. Sanday, Orkney Islands: Cienfuegos Press.

Tittle, Charles. 1995. *Control Balance: Toward a General Theory of Deviance*. Boulder, CO: Westview Press.

Tombs, Steve. 2007 "'Violence", Safety Crimes and Criminology." *British Journal of Criminology* 27: 531-550.

Tombs, Steve and Dave Whyte. 2007. "Researching White-Collar and Corporate Crime in an Era of Neo-Liberalism." In Henry N. Pontell and Gill Geis (Eds.) International *Handbook of White-Collar and Corporate Crime*. New York: Springer, 125-147.

Tong, Rosemarie. 1989. *Feminist Thought: A Comprehensive Introduction*. Boulder, CO: Westview Press.

Tönnies, Ferdinand. 1887/1955. *Community and Association*. London: Routledge and Kegan Paul.

Tonry, Michael. 1995. *Malign Neglect: Race, Crime, and Punishment in America*. New York: Oxford University Press.

Truth and Reconciliation Commission of South Africa. 1998. *Truth and Reconciliation Commission of South Africa Report. Volume One*. Cape Town: Juta Publishers.

Tunnell, Kenneth D. 1995. "Silence of the Left: Reflections on Critical Criminology and Criminologists." *Social Justice*, 22, 89-101.

Umbreit, Mark. 1985. *Crime and Reconciliation: Creative Options for Victims and Offenders*. Nashville, TN: Abingdon Press.

United States. Bureau of the Census. 1993. *The Black Population in the United States: March 1992*. (Current Population Reports, Series P20-471. Washington, DC: U.S. Government Printing Office.

United States. Department of Justice, Federal Bureau of Investigation. 1998. *Uniform Crime Reports for the United States, 1997*. Retrieved April 1, 2008, from http://www.fbi.gov/ucr/Cius_97/97crime/97crime.pdf.

United States. 2007. *Crime in the United States, 2006*. Retrieved April 1, 2008, from http://www.fbi.gov/ucr/06cius.htm.United States Census Bureau. 2000. *Profile of General Demographic Characteristics, 2000*. Retrieved April 12, 2008, from http://censtats.census.gov/data/US/01000.pdf.

United States. 2007a. *Annual Estimates of the Population by Selected Age Group and Sex for the United States: April 1, 2000 to July 1, 2006*. Retrieved April 1, 2008, from http://www.census.gov/popest/national/asrh/NC-EST2006-sa.html.

United States. 2007b. *Monthly Population Estimates for the United States: April 1, 2000 to March 1,2008*. Retrieved April 12, 2008, from http://www.census.gov/popest/national/NA-EST2007-01.html.

United States Department of Labor. 2008. *President Bush's Prisoner Reentry Initiative: Protecting Communities by Helping Returning Inmates Find Work.* Available: http://www.dol.gov/cfbci/reentryfactsheet.htm

United States. Sentencing Commission. 1992. *Sentencing Commission Guidelines Manual.* Washington, DC: U.S. Sentencing Commission.

Unnever, James D. and Larry Hembroff. 1988. "The Prediction of Racial/Ethnic Sentencing Disparities: An Expectation States Approach." *Journal of Research on Crime and Delinquency,* 25, 1: 53-82.

Van den Haag, Ernest. 1982. "Could Successful Rehabilitation Reduce the Crime Rate?" *Journal of Criminal Law and Criminology,* 73, 3: 1022-1035.

Van Maanen, John. 1978. "The Asshole." In Peter Manning and John Van Maanen (Eds.) *Policing: A View from the Streets.* Santa Monica, CA: Goodyear.

Van Ness, Howard Zehr, and Kay Harris. 1989. "Justice: The Restorative Vision" Issue No. 7 of *New Perspectives on Crime and Justice: Occasional Papers.* Akron, PA: Mennonite Central Committee.

Van Ness, Daniel W. and Karen Heetderks Strong. 2002. *Restoring Justice,* 3rd edition.. Cincinnati, OH: Anderson Publishing.

Vaughn, Joseph B. 1989. "A Survey of Juvenile Electronic Monitoring and Home Confinement Programs." *Juvenile and Family Court Journal,* 40, 1-36.

Vito, Gennaro F. 1986. "Felony Probation and Recidivism: Replication and Response." *Federal Probation.* 4: 17-25.

Vollmer, August. 1936. *The Police and Modern Society* Berkeley, CA: Bureau of Public Administration, University of California.

Walker, J. L. 1990. "Sharing the Credit, Sharing the Blame: Managing Political Risks in Electronically Monitored House Arrest." *Federal Probation,* 54: 16-20.

Walker, Samuel. 1977. *A Critical History of Police Reform: The Emergence of Professionalism.* Lexington, MA: Lexington Books.

Walters, Suzanna Danuta. 1993. "Receptive Women: Consuming and Contesting TV Culture." *Contemporary Sociology,* 22: 735-737.

Weber, Max 1921/1968/1978. *Economy and Society,* Vols. 1 and 2. G. Roth and C. Wittich (Eds.). Los Angeles: University of California Press.

Weber, Max.. 1958. *The Protestant Ethic and the Spirit of Capitalism.* New York: Charles Scribner's Sons.

Weber, Max. 1925/1960. *The City.* London: Heinemann.

Weisheit, Ralph A. and Diane M. Alexander. 1988. "Juvenile Justice Philosophy and the Demise of Parens Patriae." *Federal Probation,* 521: 55-63.

Welch, Michael. 1994. "Jail Overcrowding: Social Sanitation and the Warehousing of the Urban Underclass." In Alan R. Roberts (Ed.), *Critical Issues in Crime and Justice,* Thousand Oaks, CA: Sage.

Welch, Michael. 1998. "Critical Criminology, Social Control, and an Alternative View of Corrections." In Jeffrey Ian Ross (Ed.). *Cutting the Edge: Current Perspective in Radical/Critical Criminology and Criminal Justice.* Westport, CT: Praeger, 107-121.

Welch, Susan, John Gruhl, and Cassia Spohn. 1984. "Sentencing: The Influence of Alternative Measures of Prior Record." *Criminology,* 22: 215-227.

Welch, Susan and Cassia Spohn. 1986. "Evaluating the Impact of Prior Record on Judges' Sentencing Decisions: A Seven-City Comparison." *Justice Quarterly,* 3: 389-407.

Wender, J 2001. "The Eye of the Painter and the Eye of the Police'" Paper presented at the 53rd Conference of the American Society of Criminology, Atlanta.

Wexler, David. 1993. "Therapeutic Jurisprudence and the Criminal Courts." *William and Mary Law Review, 35,* 279-299.

Wexler, David, and Bruce J. Winick. 1996. *Law in a Therapeutic Key: Developments in Therapeutic Jurisprudence.* Durham, NC: Carolina Academic Press.

Whiteacre, Kevin. 2004. *The Jury's Still Out on Drug Courts*. Join Together. Available: http://www.jointogether.org/news/yourturn/commentary/2004/the-jurys-still-out-on-drug.html.

Whyte, David. 2003. "Lethal Regulation: State-Corporate Crime and the United Kingdom Government's New Mercenaries." *Journal of Law and Society*, 30, 4, 575-600.

Wilbanks, William. 1986. "Are Female Felons Treated More Leniently by the Criminal Justice System*?*" *Justice Quarterly*, 3: 517-529.

Wiley, N. (Ed.), 1987. *The Marx-Weber debate*. Beverly Hills, CA: Sage.

Wilkins, Leslie T. 1991. *Punishment, Crime and Market Forces*. Brookfield, VT: Dartmouth.

Williams, Carol. 2008. "First Guantanamo War-Crimes Trial Set to Begin." *Los-Angeles Times*, July 18, 2008. Available: http://www.latimes.com/news/nationworld/nation/la-na-hamdan18-2008jul18,0,6575585.story

Williams, Frank P. III. 1984. "The Demise of the Criminological Imagination: A Critique of Recent Criminology." *Justice Quarterly*, 1: 91-106.

Williams, Hubert and P.V. Murphy. 1990."The Evolving Strategy of Police: A Minority View." *National Institute of Justice, Perspectives on Policing*, 13, January.

Wilson, James Q. 1963. "Police and their Problems: A Theory." *Public Policy*, Yearbook of the Harvard University School of Public Administration (Cambridge, MA), 12: 189-216.

Wilson, James Q. 1968. *Varieties of Police Behavior*. Cambridge, MA: Harvard University Press.

Wilson, James Q. 1975. *Thinking About Crime*. New York: Random House.

Wilson, James Q. and Richard J. Herrnstein. 1985. *Crime and Human Nature*. New York: Simon and Schuster.

Wilson, James Q. and George Kelling. 1982. "Broken Windows: Police and Neighborhood Safety." *Atlantic Monthly*, 249, March, 29-38.

Wilson, William Julius. 1978. *The Declining Significance of Race*. Chicago: University of Chicago Press.

Wilson, William Julius 1987. *The Truly Disadvantaged*. Chicago: University of Chicago Press.

Wilson, O. W. and Roy Clinton McLaren. 1977. *Police Administration*, 4th edition. New York: McGraw-Hill.

Winlow, S and Hall, S 2006. *Violent Night*, Oxford: Berg.

Winterdyk, J. and C. Griffiths 1984. "Wilderness Experience Programs: Reforming Delinquents or Beating around the Bush?" *Juvenile and Family Court Journal, 35*, 35-44.

Wolf, Robert V. 2007. *Principles of Problem Solving Justice*. New York: The Center for Court Innovation.

Worden, Rob. 1989. "Situational and Attitudinal Explanations of Police Behavior: A Theoretical Reappraisal and Empirical Assessment." *Law and Society Review*, 23, 4, 667-711.

_____ and Steve Brandl 1990. "Protocol Analysis of Police Decision-Making: Toward a Theory of Police Behavior." *American Journal of Criminal Justice*, 14, 2, 297-318.

Wright, Erik Olin. 1973. *The Politics of Punishment*. New York: Harper Colophon.

_____. 1978. *Class, Crisis, and the State*. New York: NLB.

Wright, Martin. 1988. "From Retribution to Restoration: A New Model for Criminal Justice. *New Life: The Prison Service Chaplaincy Review*, 5: 42-49.

Wright, Martin and Burt Galaway. (Eds.). 1989. *Mediation and Criminal Justice: Victims, Offenders and Community*. London: Sage.

Yar, M., 2005. "The Global "Epidemic" of Movie "Piracy": Crime-Wave or Social Construction?" *Media, Culture and Society*, 27(5): 677-96.

Yazzie, Robert and James W. Zion. 1996. "Navajo Restorative Justice: The Law of Equality and Justice." In Burt Galaway and Joe Hudson (Eds.) *Restorative Justice: International Perspectives*, Monsey, NY: Criminal Justice Press, 157-173.

Yellen, Janet L. 2006. Speech to the Center for the Study of Democracy, 2006-2007: Economics of Governance Lecture, November 6, University of California, Irvine. Available online: http://www.frbsf.org/news/speeches/2006/1106.html#f24

Young, Jock 2003. "Merton with Energy, Katz with Structure." *Theoretical Criminology* 7(3) 389-414.

Young, Jock, 2004. "Voodoo Criminology and the Numbers Game" in Jeff Ferrell et al. (Eds.) *Cultural Criminology Unleashed*. London: GlassHouse.

Young, Jock 2007. *The Vertigo of Late Modernity*, London: Sage.

Young, Jock, and Roger Matthews. 1992. *Rethinking Criminology: The Realist Debate*. London: Sage.

Young, P. 1992. "The Importance of Utopias in Criminological Thinking." *British Journal of Criminology*, 32: 423-37.

Young, T. R. 1983. "Social Justice vs. Criminal Justice: An Agenda for Critical Criminology." *Red Feather Institute: Transforming Sociology*, Series Special Packet 352.

Young, T. R. 1991. "The ABC of Crime: Nonlinear and Fractal Forms of Crime." *Critical Criminologist*, 3, 4: 13-14.

Young, T.R. 1992. "Chaos, Theory and Human Agency: Humanist Sociology in a Postmodern Age." *Humanity and Society*, 16, 4: 441-460.

Young, T. R. 1996. "Beyond Crime and Punishment: Part 1- Beginning with Pain and Imprisonment." *Critical Criminology*, 7, 1: 107-120.

Young, Vernetta D. 1986. "Gender Expectations and their Impact on Black Female Offenders and their Victims." *Justice Quarterly*, 3: 305-327.

Zappala, Salvatore. 2003. *Human Rights in International Criminal Proceedings*. New York: Oxford University Press.

Zehr, Howard. 1985. "Retributive Justice, Restorative Justice." Issue No. 4 of *New Perspectives on Crime and Justice: Occasional Papers*. Akron, PA: Mennonite Central Committee.

Zehr, Howard. 1990. *Changing Lenses*. Waterloo, ONT: Herald Press.

Zehr, Howard. 2002. *The Little Book of Restorative Justice*. Intercourse, PA: Good Books.

Zehr, Howard and Erle Sears. 1982. *Mediating the Victim-Offender Conflict*. Akron, PA: Mennonite Central Committee.

Zimbardo, Philip. 2007. *The Lucifer Effect: Understanding how Good People Turn Evil*. New York: Random House.

Zimring, Franklin E., and Gordon Hawkins. 1988. "The New Mathematics of Imprisonment." *Crime and Delinquency*, 34: 425-436.

About the Contributors

ANGELA WEST CREWS, Ph.D. is an associate professor of criminal justice at Marshall University in Huntington, West Virginia. She is active in the Academy of Criminal Justice Sciences as the chair of the Corrections Section, in the American Society of Criminology, and in the Southern Criminal Justice Association. Her interest in critical perspectives was sparked as a master's student at East Tennessee State University (ETSU) studying corporate crime and the tobacco industry, and was enhanced after her father was incarcerated at FMC-Lexington as a casualty of the Violent Crime Control Act of 1994. Her research interests are varied and involve all aspects of the criminal justice system, but share a policy analysis or program evaluation focus. Most recently, she has been interested in the measurement of concepts in law enforcement, in correctional policy analysis and program evaluation, and in policies related to prisoner release and reentry. Her areas of teaching include research methods and statistics, corrections, comparative justice systems, and criminological theory. She currently is working with her husband, Dr. Gordon Crews, writing two books on juvenile crime and violence.

ELIZABETH ELLIOTT. Ph.D is an associate professor and co-director of the Centre for Restorative Justice at the School of Criminology, Simon Fraser University in British Columbia, Canada. She has a history of activity in prisons and in restorative justice since 1981, first as a community-based social worker (1981-1986), then as a lecturer for the Prison Education Program in British Columbia federal prisons (1988-1991) and currently as a professor. Elliott lectures, presents and publishes in the areas of restorative justice, prisons and criminological theory. She is the co-editor of the recently published *New Directions in Restorative Justice* (Willan, 2005), has written several book chapters and journal articles on restorative justice or prison, is a founding editor (1988) of the *Journal of Prisoners on Prisons* (University of Ottawa Press), and is an editorial board member for the journal, Contemporary Justice Review (Routledge, Taylor and Francis Group). Elliott is currently a board member of the Canadian prisoner aid organization, the John Howard Society (B.C.) and the West Coast Prison Justice Society (Prisoners' Legal Services), and is a regular member of the restorative justice group FAVOUR, which meets weekly in Ferndale Institution (federal minimum security prison).

PRESTON ELROD, Ph.D. received his Ph.D. in sociology from Western Michigan University and currently serves as professor in the Department of Safety, Security, and Emergency Management at Eastern Kentucky University where he teaches courses on juvenile justice, crime prevention, and school safety. Among his published works are studies on citizens' attitudes toward the death penalty, juvenile justice policy development, public attitudes toward electronic monitoring, the effectiveness of interventions for juvenile probationers, and the experiences of adolescent jail inmates. He is the co-author of *Juvenile Justice: A Social, Historical and Legal Perspective*, second edition. Dr. Elrod is the former co-director of a model school-based delinquency reduction program and he has worked in juvenile justice as a court intake officer and as the supervisor of a juvenile probation department. He is also involved in community efforts to prevent delinquency and is past chair of the Madison County Delinquency Prevention Council. His present research focuses on school crime and victimization.

JEFF FERRELL, earned his PhD in sociology from the University of Texas at Austin, and is currently professor of sociology at Texas Christian University and visiting professor of criminology at the University of Kent, UK. He is the author of the books *Crimes of Style*, *Tearing Down the Streets*, *Empire of Scrounge*, and with Keith Hayward and Jock Young, *Cultural Criminology: An Invitation*. He is also the co-editor of the books *Cultural Criminology*, *Ethnography at the Edge*, *Making Trouble*, and *Cultural Criminology Unleashed*. Jeff Ferrell is the founding and current editor of the New York University Press book series *Alternative Criminology*, and one of the founding and current editors of the journal *Crime, Media, Culture*, winner of the 2006 Association of Learned and Professional Society Publishers' Charlesworth Award for Best New Journal. In 1998 he received the Critical Criminologist of the Year Award from the Division of Critical Criminology of the American Society of Criminology.

JEANNE FLAVIN. Ph.D. associate professor of sociology at Fordham University. She earned her Ph.D. in sociology from American University in 1995. Her scholarship examines the impact of the criminal justice system on women, and her papers have appeared in *Gender & Society*, *Justice Quarterly*, and the *Fordham University Urban Law Journal*. She co-authored the book, *Class, Race, Gender & Crime: Social Realities of Justice in America*, 2nd ed. (Rowman and Littlefield, 2007) and co-edited (with Mary Bosworth) *Race, Gender, and Punishment: From Colonialism to the War on Terror* (Rutgers, 2007). She has just published a new book, *Our Bodies, Our Crimes* (NYU, 2009) on the criminalization of women's reproduction. She proudly serves on the board of National Advocates for Pregnant Women and has received a Fulbright Award for 2008-2009 for research at the University of Cape Town, South Africa.

DAVID O. FRIEDRICHS, is professor of sociology/criminal justice and Distinguished University Fellow at the University of Scranton. He is the author of *Trusted Criminals: White Collar Crime in Contemporary Society* (ITP/Wadsworth, 1996; 2004; 2007) and *Law in Our Lives: An Introduction* (Oxford University Press, 2001; 2006) and editor of *State Crime: Volumes I and II* (Ashgate, UK, 1998). He has also published well over 100 journal articles, book chapters, encyclopedia entries, and essays. He served as editor of *Legal Studies Forum* (1985-1986) and president of the White Collar Crime Research Consortium (2002-2004). In November 2005 he received a Lifetime Achievement Award from the Division of Critical Criminology of the American Society of Criminology.

KEITH HAYWARD, PhD is a senior lecturer in criminology and sociology and director of studies for criminology at the School of Social Policy, Sociology and Social Research, University of Kent, UK. He has published widely in the areas of criminological theory (in particular the relationship between consumer culture and crime), cultural criminology, youth crime, popular culture, social theory, and terrorism and fanaticism. He is the author of *City Limits: Crime, Consumer Culture and the Urban Experience* (Routledge, 2004) the co-author of *Cultural Criminology: An Invitation* (Sage, 2008) and the co-editor of *Cultural Criminology Unleashed* (Routledge, 2004) *Framing Crime: Cultural Criminology and the Image* (Routledge, 2009), *Criminology* (Oxford University Press, second edition 2009) and *Fifty Key Criminological Thinkers* (Routledge, 2009). Dr. Hayward is also the founder of the International Cultural Criminology Conference series and runs the website: www.culturalcriminology.org.

CHRISTOPHER W. MULLINS, Ph.D. is an assistant professor in the Center for the Study of Crime, Delinquency and Corrections at Southern Illinois University Carbondale. His work focuses on violence of all types. He has published three books and numerous journal articles and book chapters on street violence, gender, and violations of international criminal law.

STEPHEN C. RICHARDS, earned his PhD from Iowa State University. He is an associate professor of criminal justice at the University of Wisconsin-Oshkosh. In 1983, he was convicted of conspiracy to distribute marijuana and sentenced to nine years. He served time in nine federal prisons, including United States Penitentiaries, Federal Correctional Institutions, and Federal Prison Camps. His work has appeared in numerous journals. Recent books include *Behind Bars: Surviving Prison* and *Convict Criminology* (with Jeffrey Ian Ross). Richards is a Soros Senior Justice Fellow and member of the American Society of Criminology National Policy Committee.

JEFFREY IAN ROSS, Ph.D. is an associate professor in the Division of Criminology, Criminal Justice and Forensic Studies, and a Fellow of the Center for International and Comparative Law at the University of Baltimore. He has researched, written, and lectured on national security, political violence, political crime, violent crime, corrections, and policing for over two decades. Ross' work has appeared in many academic journals and books, as well as popular outlets. He is the author, co-author, editor or co-editor of thirteen books including *Controlling State Crime*, and *Varieties of State Crime and its Control*. He is a respected and frequent source of scholarly and scientific information for local, regional, national and international news media including interviews with newspapers, magazines and radio and television stations. From 1995–1998, Ross was a social science analyst with the National Institute of Justice, a Division of the U.S. Department of Justice. In 2003, he was awarded the University of Baltimore's Distinguished Chair in Research Award. His website is www.jeffreyianross.com.

DAWN L. ROTHE obtained her PhD from Western Michigan University. Currently she is an assistant professor at Old Dominion University. Rothe is the author of over thirty articles appearing in *Social Justice, Humanity and Society, Crime, Law, and Social Change*, and *Journal of Critical Criminology* and book chapters as well as author of *Symbolic Gestures and the Generation of Global Social Control* (2006) published by Lexington (co-authored with Christopher W. Mullins) and co-author of *Power, Bedlam, and Bloodshed: State Crimes in Post-Colonial Africa* (2008) published by Peter Lang and sole author of *The Crime of All Crimes: An Introduction to State Criminality*. To be published by Lexington/Roman and Littlefield in 2009.

VINCENZO RUGGIERO is professor of sociology at Middlesex University in London (UK), where he is co-director of the Crime and Conflict Research Centre. He has conducted research on behalf of a number of international agencies, including the European Commission and the United Nations. He has worked on penal systems, illicit drug economies, organized and white-collar crime, social movements and political violence. In the year 2000 he was nominated for the award of Distinguished International Academic granted by the American Society of Criminology. His latest books are *Crime and Markets* (2000), *Movements in the City* (2001), *Crime in Literature: Deviance and Fiction* (2003), *Understanding Political Violence* (2006), and *Social Movements: A Reader* (2008).

Index

Printed in the United States
219709BV00002B/4/P